DREAMERS OF THE ABSOLUTE

Essays on Politics, Crime and Culture

Hans Magnus Enzensberger

translations by
Michael Roloff, Stuart Hood,
Richard Woolley and the author

RADIUS
An imprint of Century Hutchinson

An imprint of Century Hutchinson Ltd
62–65 Chandos Place, London WC2N 4NW

Century Hutchinson Australia Pty Ltd
PO Box 496, 16–22 Church Street, Hawthorn,
Victoria 3122, Australia

Century Hutchinson New Zealand Ltd
PO Box 40–086, Glenfield, Auckland 10
New Zealand

Century Hutchinson South Africa (Pty) Ltd
PO Box 337, Bergvlei 2012, South Africa

First published by Pluto Press
This edition published by Radius 1988

© Suhrkamp Verlag

The essays in this selection first appeared in German under the
following titles:

Bewußtseinsindustrie, © Suhrkamp Verlag, Frankfurt am Main 1962
*Zur Theorie des Verrats, Reflexionen vor einem Glaskasten, Rafael
Trujillo: Portrait eines Landesvaters, Die Träumer des Absoluten*, ©
Suhrkamp Verlag, Frankfurt am Main 1964
Bildnis einer Partei. Vorgeschichte, Struktur und Ideologie der PCC,
© Kursbuch Verlag, Berlin 1969
Baukasten zu einer Theorie der Medien, © Kursbuch Verlag, Berlin
1970
Revolutions-Tourismus, Zur Kritik der politischen Ökologie, ©
Kursbuch Verlag, Berlin 1973
All rights reserved

Set in 11/12pt Garamond Roman

Printed and bound in Great Britain by
Richard Clay Ltd, Bungay, Suffolk

British Library Cataloguing in Publication Data

Enzensberger, Hans Magnus
Dreamers of the absolute: essays on
ecology, media and power.
1. General essays in German
I. Title
083′.1

ISBN 0-09-173240-9

DREAMERS OF THE
ABSOLUTE

Contents

The Industrialization of the Mind

All of us, no matter how irresolute we are, like to think that we reign supreme in our own consciousness, that we are masters of what our minds accept or reject. Since the Soul is not much mentioned any more, except by priests, poets, and pop musicians, the last refuge a man can take from the catastrophic world at large seems to be his own mind. Where else can he expect to withstand the daily siege, if not within himself? Even under the conditions of totalitarian rule, where no one can fancy any more that his home is his castle, the mind of the individual is considered a kind of last citadel and hotly defended, though this imaginary fortress may have been long since taken over by an ingenious enemy.[1]

No illusion is more stubbornly upheld than the sovereignty of the mind. It is a good example of the impact of philosophy on people who ignore it; for the idea that men can "make up their minds" individually and by themselves is essentially derived from the tenets of bourgeois philosophy: secondhand Descartes, run-down Husserl, armchair idealism; and all it amounts to is a sort of metaphysical do-it-yourself.

We might do worse, I think, than dust off the admirably laconic statement which one of our classics made more than a century ago: "What is going on in our minds has always been, and will always be, a product of society."[2] This is a comparatively recent insight. Though it is valid for all human history ever since the division of labor came into being, it could not be formulated before the time of Karl Marx. In a society where communication was largely oral, the dependence of the pupil on the teacher, the disciple on the master, the flock on the priest was taken for granted. That the few thought and judged and decided for the many was a matter of course and not a matter for investigation. Medieval man was probably other-directed to an extent which our sociology would be at a loss to fathom. His mind was, to an enormous degree, fashioned and processed from "without." But the business of teaching and of indoctrination was perfectly straightforward and transparent—so transparent indeed that it became invisible as a problem. Only when the processes which shape our minds became opaque, enigmatic, inscrutable for the common man, only with the advent of industrialization, did the question of how our minds are shaped arise in earnest.

The mind-making industry is really a product of the last hundred years. It has developed at such a pace, and assumed such varied forms, that it has outgrown our understanding and our control. Our current discussion of the "media" seems to suffer from severe theoretical limitations. Newsprint, films, television, public relations tend to be evaluated separately, in terms of their specific technologies, conditions, and possibilities. Every new branch of the industry starts off a new crop of theories.[3] Hardly anyone seems to be aware of the phenomenon as a whole: the industrialization of the human mind. This is a process which cannot be understood by a mere examination of its machinery.

Equally inadequate is the term *cultural industry*, which has become common usage in Europe after World War II. It reflects, more than the scope of the phenomenon itself, the social status of those who have tried to analyze it: university professors and academic writers, people whom the power elite has relegated to the reservations of what passes as "cultural life" and who consequently have resigned themselves to bear the unfortunate name of cultural critics. In other words, they are certified as harmless; they are supposed to think in terms of *Kultur* and not in terms of power.

Yet the vague and insufficient name *cultural industry* serves to remind us of a paradox inherent in all media work. Consciousness, however false, can be induced and reproduced by industrial means, but it cannot be industrially produced. It is a "social product" made up by people: its origin is the dialogue. No industrial process can replace the persons who generate it. And it is precisely this truism of which the archaic term *culture* tries, however vainly, to remind us. The mind industry is monstrous and difficult to understand because it does not, strictly speaking, produce anything. It is an intermediary, engaged only in production's secondary and tertiary derivatives, in transmission and infiltration, in the fungible aspect of what it multiplies and delivers to the customer.

The mind industry can take on anything, digest it, reproduce it, and pour it out. Whatever our minds can conceive of is grist to its mill; nothing will leave it unadulterated: it is capable of turning any idea into a slogan and any work of the imagination into a hit. This is its overwhelming power, yet it is also its most vulnerable spot: it thrives on a stuff which it cannot manufacture by itself. It depends on the very substance it must fear most, and must suppress what it feeds on: the creative productivity of people. Hence the ambiguity of the term *cultural industry*, which takes at face value the claims of culture, in the ancient sense of the word, and the claims of an industrial process which has all but eaten it up. To insist on these claims would be naive; to criticize the industry from the vantage point of a "liberal education" and to raise comfortable outcries against its vulgarity will neither change it nor revive the dead souls of culture: it will merely help to fortify the ghettoes of educational programs and to fill the backward, highbrow section of the Sunday papers. At the same time, the indictment of the mind industry on purely esthetic grounds will tend to obscure its larger social and political meaning.

On the other extreme we find the ideological critics of the mind industry. Their attention is usually limited to its role as an instrument of straightforward or hidden political propaganda, and from the messages reproduced by it they try to distill the political content. More often than not, the underlying understanding of politics is extremely narrow, as if it were just a matter of taking sides in everyday contests of power. Just as in the case of the "cultural critic," this attitude cannot hope to catch up with the far-reaching effects of the industrialization of the mind, since it is a process which will abolish the distinction between private and public consciousness.

Thus, while radio, cinema, television, recording, advertising and public relations, new techniques of manipulation and propaganda, are being keenly discussed, each on its own terms, the mind industry, taken as a whole, is disregarded. Newsprint and publishing, its oldest and in many respects still its most interesting branch, hardly comes up for serious comment any longer, presumably because it lacks the appeal of technological novelty. Yet much of the analysis provided in Balzac's *Illusions Perdues* is as pertinent today as it was a hundred years ago, as any copywriter from Hollywood who happens to know the book will testify. Other, more recent branches of the industry still remain largely unexplored: fashion and industrial design, the propagation of established religions and of esoteric cults, opinion polls, simulation and, last but not least, tourism, which can be considered as a mass medium in its own right.

Above all, however, we are not sufficiently aware of the fact that the full deployment of the mind industry still lies ahead. Up to now it has not managed to seize control of its most essential sphere, which is education. The industrialization of instruction, on all levels, has barely begun. While we still indulge in controversies over curricula, school systems, college and university reforms, and shortages in the teaching professions, technological systems are being perfected which will make nonsense of all the adjustments we are now considering. The language laboratory and the closed-circuit TV are only the forerunners of a fully industrialized educational system which will make use of increasingly centralized programming and of recent advances in the study of learning. In that process, education will become a mass media, the most powerful of all, and a billion-dollar business.

Whether we realize it or not, the mind industry is growing faster than any other, not excluding armament. It has become the key industry of the twentieth century. Those who are concerned in the power game of today, political leaders, intelligence men, and revolutionaries, have very well grasped this crucial fact. Whenever an industrially developed country is occupied or liberated today, whenever there is a coup d'état, a revolution, or a counterrevolution, the crack police units, the paratroopers, the guerrilla fighters do not any longer descend on the main squares of the city or seize the centers of heavy industry, as in the nineteenth century, or symbolic sites like the royal palace; the new regime will instead take over, first of all, the radio and television stations, the telephone and telex exchanges, and the printing presses. And after having entrenched itself, it will, by and large, leave alone those who manage the public services and the manufacturing industries, at least in the beginning, while all the functionaries who run the mind industry will be immediately replaced. In such extreme situations the industry's key position becomes quite clear.

There are four conditions which are necessary to its existence; briefly, they are as follows:

1.) Enlightenment, in the broadest sense, is the philosophical prerequisite of the industrialization of the mind. It cannot get under way until the rule of theocracy, and with it people's faith in revelation and inspiration, in the Holy Book or the Holy Ghost as taught by the priesthood, is broken. The mind industry presupposes independent minds, even when it is out to deprive them of their independence; this is another of its paradoxes. The last theocracy to vanish has been Tibet; ever since, the philosophical condition is met with throughout the world.

2.) Politically, the industrialization of the mind presupposes the proclamation of human rights, of equality and liberty in particular. In Europe, this threshold has been passed by the French Revolution; in the Communist world, by the October Revolution; and in America, Asia, and Africa, by the wars of liberation from colonial rule. Obviously, the industry does not depend on the realization of these rights; for most people, they have never been more than a pretense, or at best, a distant promise. On the contrary, it is just the margin between fiction and reality which provides the mind industry with its theater of operations. Consciousness, both individual and social, has become a political issue only from the moment when the conviction arose in people's minds that everyone should have a say in his own destiny as well as in that of society at large. From the same moment any authority had to justify itself in the eyes of those it would govern; coercion alone would no longer do the trick; he who ruled must persuade, lay claim to people's minds and change them, in an industrial age, by every industrial means at hand.

3.) Economically, the mind industry cannot come of age unless a measure of primary accumulation has been achieved. A society which cannot provide the necessary surplus capital neither needs it nor can afford it. During the first half of the nineteenth century in Western Europe, and under similar conditions in other parts of the world, which prevailed until fairly recently, peasants and workers lived at a level of bare subsistence. During this stage of economic development the fiction that the working class is able to determine the conditions of its own existence is meaningless; the proletariat is subjected by physical constraint and undisguised force. Archaic methods of manipulation, as used by the school and by the church, the law and the army, together with old customs and conventions, are quite sufficient for the ruling minority to maintain its position during the earlier stages of industrial development. As soon as the basic industries have been firmly established and the mass production of consumer goods is beginning to reach out to the majority of the population, the ruling classes will face a dilemma. More sophisticated methods of production demand a constantly rising standard of education, not only for the privileged but also for the masses. The immediate compulsion which kept the working class "in their place" will slowly decrease. Working hours are reduced, and the standard of living rises. Inevitably, people will become aware of their own situation; they can now afford the luxury of having a mind of their own. For the first time, they become conscious of themselves in more than the most primitive and hazy sense of the word. In this process, enormous human energies are released, energies which inevitably threaten the established political and economic order. Today this revolutionary process can be seen at work in a great number of emergent nations, where it has long been artificially retarded by imperialist powers; in these countries the political, if not the economic conditions for the development of mind industries can be realized overnight.[4]

4.) Given a certain level of economic development, industrialization brings with it the last condition for the rise of a mind industry: the technology on which it depends. The first industrial uses of electricity were concerned with power and not with communications: the dynamo and the electrical motor preceded the amplifying valve and the film camera. There are economic reasons for this time lag: the foundations of radio, film, recording, television, and computing techniques could not be laid before the advent of the mass production of commodities and the general availability of electrical power.

In our time the technological conditions for the industrialization of the mind exist anywhere on the planet. The same cannot be said for the political and economic prerequisites; however, it is only a matter of time until they will be met. The process is irreversible. Therefore, all criticism of the mind industry which is abolitionist in its essence is inept and beside the point, since the idea of arresting and liquidating industrialization itself (which such criticism implies) is suicidal. There is a macabre irony to any such proposal, for it is indeed no longer a technical problem for our civilization to abolish itself. However, this is hardly what conservative critics have in mind when they complain about the loss of "values," the depravity of mass civilization and the degeneration of traditional culture by the media. The idea is, rather, to do away with all these nasty things, and to survive, as an elite of happy pundits, in the nicer comforts offered by a country house.

Nonetheless, the workings of the mind industry have been analyzed, in part, over and over again, sometimes with great ingenuity and insight. So far as the capitalist countries are concerned, the critics have leveled their attacks mainly against the newer media and commercial advertising. Conservatives and Marxists alike have been all too ready to deplore their venal side. It is an objection which hardly touches the heart of the matter. Apart from the fact that it is perhaps no more immoral to profit from the mass production of news or symphonies than from the mass production of soap and tires, objections of this kind overlook the very characteristics of the mind industry. Its more advanced sectors have long since ceased to sell any goods at all. With increasing technological maturity, the material substrata, paper or plastic or celluloid, tend to vanish. Only in the more old-fashioned offshoots of the business, as for example in the book trade, does the commodity aspect of the product play an important economic role. In this respect, a radio station has nothing in common with a match factory. With the disappearance of the material substratum the product becomes more and more abstract, and the industry depends less and less on selling it to its customers. If you buy a book, you pay for it in terms of its real cost of production; if you pick up a magazine, you pay only a fraction thereof; if you tune in on a radio or television program, you get it virtually free; direct advertising and political propaganda is something nobody buys—on the contrary, it is crammed down our throats. The products of the mind industry can no longer be understood in terms of a sellers' and buyers' market, or in terms of production costs: they are, as it were, priceless. The capitalist exploitation of the media is accidental and not intrinsic; to concentrate on their commercialization is to miss the point and to overlook the specific service which the mind industry performs for modern societies. This service is essentially the same all over the world, no matter how the industry is operated: under state, public, or private management, within a capitalist or a socialist economy, on a profit or nonprofit basis. The mind industry's main business and concern is not to sell its product: it is to "sell" the existing order, to perpetuate the prevailing pattern of man's domination by man, no matter who runs the society, and by what means. Its main task is to expand and train our consciousness—in order to exploit it.

Since "immaterial exploitation" is not a familiar concept,

it might be well to explain its meaning. Classical Marxism has defined very clearly the material exploitation to which the working classes have been subjected ever since the industrial revolution. In its crudest form, it is a characteristic of the period of the primary accumulation of capital. This holds true even for Socialist countries, as is evident from the example of Stalinist Russia and the early stages of the development of Red China. As soon as the bases of industrialization are laid, however, it becomes clear that material exploitation alone is insufficient to guarantee the continuity of the system. When the production of goods expands beyond the most immediate needs, the old proclamations of human rights, however watered down by the rhetoric of the establishment and however eclipsed by decades of hardship, famine, crises, forced labor, and political terror, will now unfold their potential strength. It is in their very nature that, once proclaimed, they cannot be revoked. Again and again, people will try to take them at their face value and, eventually, to fight for their realization. Thus, ever since the great declarations of the eighteenth century, every rule of the few over the many, however organized, has faced the threat of revolution. Real democracy, as opposed to the formal façades of parliamentary democracy, does not exist anywhere in the world, but its ghost haunts every existing regime. Consequently, all the existing power structures must seek to obtain the consent, however passive, of their subjects. Even regimes which depend on the force of arms for their survival feel the need to justify themselves in the eyes of the world. Control of capital, of the means of production, and of the armed forces is therefore no longer enough. The self-appointed elites who run modern societies must try to control people's minds. What each of us accepts or rejects, what we think and decide is now, here as well as in Vietnam, a matter of prime political concern: it would be too dangerous to leave these matters to ourselves. Material exploitation must camouflage itself in order to survive; immaterial exploitation has become its necessary corollary. The few cannot go on accumulating wealth unless they accumulate the power to manipulate the minds of the many. To expropriate manpower they have to expropriate the brain. What is being abolished in today's affluent societies, from Moscow to Los Angeles, is not exploitation, but our awareness of it.

It takes quite a lot of effort to maintain this state of affairs. There are alternatives to it. But since all of them would inevitably overthrow the prevailing powers, an entire industry is engaged in doing away with them, eliminating possible futures and reinforcing the present pattern of domination. There are several ways to achieve this end: on the one hand we find downright censorship, bans, and a state monopoly on all the means of production of the mind industry; on the other hand, economic pressures, systematic distribution of "punishment and reward," and human engineering can do the job just as well and much more smoothly. The material pauperization of the last century is followed and replaced by the immaterial pauperization of today. Its most obvious manifestation is the decline in political options available to the citizen of the most advanced nations: a mass of political nobodies, over whose heads even collective suicide can be decreed, is opposed by an ever-decreasing number of political moguls. That this state of affairs is readily accepted and voluntarily endured by the majority is the greatest achievement of the mind industry.

To describe its effects on present-day society is not, however, to describe its essence. The emergence of the textile industry has ruined the craftsman of India and caused widespread child labor in England, but these consequences do not necessarily follow from the existence of the mechanical loom. There is no more reason to suppose that the industrialization of the human mind must produce immaterial exploitation. It would even be fair to say that it will eventually, by its own logic, do away with the very results it has today. For this is the most fundamental of all its contradictions: in order to obtain consent, you have to grant a choice, no matter how marginal and deceptive; in order to harness the faculties of the human mind, you have to develop them, no matter how narrowly and how deformed. It may be a measure of the overwhelming power of the mind industry that none of us can escape its influence. Whether we like it or not, it enlists our participation in the system as a whole. But this participation may very well veer, one day, from the passive to the active, and turn out to threaten the very order it was supposed to uphold. The mind industry has a dynamic of its own which it cannot arrest, and it is not by chance but by necessity that in this movement there are currents which run contrary to its present mission of stabilizing the status quo. A corollary of its dialectical progress is that the mind industry, however closely supervised in its individual operations, is never completely controllable as a whole. There are always leaks in it, cracks in the armor; no administration will ever trust it all the way.[5]

In order to exploit people's intellectual, moral, and political faculties, you have got to develop them first. This is, as we have seen, the basic dilemma faced by today's media. When we turn our attention from the industry's consumers to its producers, the intellectuals, we find this dilemma aggravated and intensified. In terms of power, of course, there can be no question as to who runs the business. Certainly it is not the intellectuals who control the industrial establishment, but the establishment which controls them. There is precious little chance for the people who are productive to take over their means of production: this is just what the present structure is designed to prevent. However, even under present circumstances, the relationship is not without a certain ambiguity, since there is no way of running the mind industry without enlisting the services of at least a minority of men who can create something. To exclude them would be self-defeating. Of course, it is perfectly possible to use the whole stock of accumulated original work and have it adapted, diluted, and processed for media use, and it may be well to remember that much of what purports to be new is in fact derivative. If we examine the harmonic and melodic structure of any popular song hit, it will most likely turn out to employ inventions of serious composers centuries ago. The same is true of the dramaturgical clichés of mediocre screenplays: watered down beyond recognition, they repeat traditional patterns taken from the drama and the novel of the past. In the long run, however, the parasitic use of inherited work is not sufficient to nourish the industry. However large a stock, you cannot sell out forever without replenishment; hence the need "to make it new," the media's dependence on men capable of innovation, in other words, on potential troublemakers. It is inherent in the process of creation that there is no way to predict its results. Consequently, intellectuals are, from the point of view of any power structure bent on its own perpetuation, a security risk. It takes consummate skill to "handle" them and to neutralize their subversive influence. All sorts of techniques, from the crudest to the most sophisticated, have been developed to this end: physical threat, blacklisting, moral and economic pressure on the one hand, overexposure, star-cult, co-optation into the power elite on the other, are the extremes of a whole gamut of manipulation. It would be worthwhile to write a manual analyzing these techniques. They have one thing in common, and that is that they offer short-term, tactical answers to a problem which, in principle, cannot be resolved. This is an industry which has to rely, as its primary source, on the very minorities with whose elimination it is entrusted: those whose aim it is to invent and produce *alternatives*. Unless it succeeds in exploiting and manipulating its producers, the mind industry cannot hope to exploit and manipulate its consumers. On the level of production, even more than on the level of consumption, it has to deal with partners who are potential enemies. Engaged in the proliferation of human consciousness, the media proliferate their own contradictions.

Criticism of the mind industry which fails to recognize its central ambiguities is either idle or dangerous. It is a measure of their limitations that many media critics never seem to reflect on their own position, just as if their work were not itself a part of what it criticizes. The truth is that no one can nowadays express any opinion at all without making use of the industry, or rather, without being used by it.[6]

Anyone incapable of dialectical thinking is doomed as soon as he starts grappling with this subject. He will be trapped to a point where even retreat is no longer possible. There are many who feel revolted at the thought of entering a studio or negotiating with the slick executives who run the networks. They detest, or profess to detest, the very machinery of the industry, and would like to withdraw into some abode of refinement. Of course, no such refuge really exists. The seemingly exclusive is just another, slightly more expensive line of styling within the same giant industrial combine.

Let us rather try to draw the line between intellectual integrity and defeatism. To opt out of the mind industry, to refuse any dealings with it may well turn out to be a reactionary course. There is no hermitage left for those whose job is to speak out and to seek innovation. Retreat from the media will not even save the intellectual's precious soul from corruption. It might be a better idea to enter the dangerous game, to take and calculate our risks. Instead of innocence, we need determination. We must know very precisely the monster we are dealing with, and we must be continually on our guard to resist the overt or subtle pressures which are brought to bear on us.

The rapid development of the mind industry, its rise to a key position in modern society, has profoundly changed the role of the intellectual. He finds himself confronted with new threats and new opportunities. Whether he knows it or not, whether he likes it or not, he has become the accomplice of a huge industrial complex which depends for its survival on him, as he depends on it for his own. He must try, at any cost, to use it for his own purposes, which are incompatible with the purposes of the mind machine. What it upholds he must subvert. He may play it crooked or straight, he may win or lose the game; but he would do well to remember that there is more at stake than his own fortune.

Translated by the author.

Constituents of a Theory of the Media

> If you should think this is Utopian, then I
> would ask you to consider why it is Utopian.
>
> Brecht: *Theory of Radio*

With the development of the electronic media, the industry that
shapes consciousness has become the pacemaker for the social and
economic development of societies in the late industrial age. It
infiltrates into all other sectors of production, takes over more and
more directional and control functions, and determines the
standard of the prevailing technology.

In lieu of normative definitions, here is an incomplete list of new
developments which have emerged in the last twenty years: news
satellites, color television, cable relay television, cassettes, videotape,
videotape recorders, video-phones, stereophony, laser techniques, electrostatic reproduction processes, electronic high-speed printing, com-
posing and learning machines, microfiches with electronic access,
printing by radio, time-sharing computers, data banks. All these new
forms of media are constantly forming new connections both with
each other and with older media like printing, radio, film, television,
telephone, teletype, radar, and so on. They are clearly coming together to form a universal system.

The general contradiction between productive forces and
productive relationships emerges most sharply, however, when
they are most advanced. By contrast, protracted structural

crises, as in coal mining, can be solved merely by getting rid of a backlog, that is to say, essentially they can be solved within the terms of their own system, and a revolutionary strategy that relied on them would be shortsighted.

Monopoly capitalism develops the consciousness-shaping industry more quickly and more extensively than other sectors of production; it must at the same time fetter it. A socialist media theory has to work at this contradiction, demonstrate that it cannot be solved within the given productive relationships—rapidly increasing discrepancies, potential destructive forces. "Certain demands of a prognostic nature must be made" of any such theory (Benjamin).

A "critical" inventory of the status quo is not enough. There is danger of underestimating the growing conflicts in the media field, of neutralizing them, of interpreting them merely in terms of trade unionism or liberalism, on the lines of traditional labor struggles or as the clash of special interests (program heads/executive producers, publishers/authors, monopolies/medium sized businesses, public corporations/private companies, etc.). An appreciation of this kind does not go far enough and remains bogged down in tactical arguments.

So far there is no Marxist theory of the media. There is therefore no strategy one can apply in this area. Uncertainty, alternations between fear and surrender, mark the attitude of the socialist Left to the new productive forces of the media industry. The ambivalence of this attitude merely mirrors the ambivalence of the media themselves without mastering it. It could only be overcome by releasing the emancipatory potential which is inherent in the new productive forces—a potential which capitalism must sabotage just as surely as Soviet revisionism, because it would endanger the rule of both systems.

THE MOBILIZING POWER OF THE MEDIA

2. The open secret of the electronic media, the decisive political factor, which has been waiting, suppressed or crippled, for its moment to come, is their mobilizing power.

When I say *mobilize* I mean *mobilize*. In a country which has had direct experience of fascism (and Stalinism) it is perhaps still necessary to explain, or to explain again, what that means—namely, to make men more mobile than they are. As free as dancers, as aware as football players, as surprising as guerillas. Anyone who thinks of the masses only as the object of politics cannot mobilize them. He wants to push them around. A parcel is not mobile; it can only be pushed to and fro. Marches, columns, parades, immobilize people. Propaganda, which does not release self-reliance but limits it, fits into the same pattern. It leads to depoliticization.

For the first time in history, the media are making possible mass participation in a social and socialized productive process, the practical means of which are in the hands of the masses themselves. Such a use of them would bring the communications media, which up to now have not deserved the name, into their own. In its present form, equipment like television or film does not serve communication but prevents it. It allows no reciprocal action between transmitter and receiver; technically speaking, it reduces feedback to the lowest point compatible with the system.

This state of affairs, however, cannot be justified technically. On the contrary. Electronic techniques recognize no contradiction in principle between transmitter and receiver. Every transistor radio is, by the nature of its construction, at the same time a potential transmitter; it can interact with other receivers by circuit reversal. The development from a mere distribution medium to a communications medium is technically not a problem. It is consciously prevented for understandable political reasons. The technical distinction between receivers and transmitters reflects the social division of labor into producers and consumers, which in the consciousness industry becomes of particular political importance. It is based, in the last analysis, on the basic contradiction between the ruling class and the ruled class—that is to say, between monopoly capital or monopolistic bureaucracy on the one hand and the dependent masses on the other.

This structural analogy can be worked out in detail. To the programs offered by the broadcasting cartels there correspond the politics offered by a power cartel consisting of parties constituted along authoritarian lines. In both cases marginal differences in their platforms reflect a competitive relationship which on essential questions is nonexistent. Minimal independent activity on the part of the voter/viewer is desired. As is the case with parliamentary elections under the two-party system, the feedback is reduced to indices. "Training in decision making" is reduced to the response to a single, three-point switching process: Program 1; Program 2; Switch off (abstention).

"Radio must be changed from a means of distribution to a means of communication. Radio would be the most wonderful means of communication imaginable in public life, a huge linked system—that is to say, it would be such if it were capable not only of transmitting but of receiving, of allowing the listener not only to hear but to speak, and did not isolate him but brought him into contact. Unrealizable in this social system, realizable in another, these proposals, which are, after all, only the natural consequences of technical development, help towards the propagation and shaping of that *other* system." [1]

THE ORWELLIAN FANTASY

3. George Orwell's bogey of a monolithic consciousness industry derives from a view of the media which is undialectical and obsolete. The possibility of total control of such a system at a central point belongs not to the future but to the past. With the aid of systems theory, a discipline which is part of bourgeois science—using, that is to say, categories which are immanent in the system—it can be demonstrated that a linked series of communications or, to use the technical term, switchable network, to the degree that it exceeds a certain critical size, can no longer be centrally controlled but only dealt with statistically. This basic "leakiness" of stochastic systems admittedly allows the calculation of probabilities based on sampling and extrapolations; but blanket supervision would de-

mand a monitor that was bigger than the system itself. The monitoring of all telephone conversations, for instance, postulates an apparatus which would need to be n times more extensive and more complicated than that of the present telephone system. A censor's office, which carried out its work extensively, would of necessity become the largest branch of industry in its society.

But supervision on the basis of approximation can only offer inadequate instruments for the self-regulation of the whole system in accordance with the concepts of those who govern it. It postulates a high degree of internal stability. If this precarious balance is upset, then crisis measures based on statistical methods of control are useless. Interference can penetrate the leaky nexus of the media, spreading and multiplying there with the utmost speed, by resonance. The regime so threatened will in such cases, insofar as it is still capable of action, use force and adopt police or military methods.

A state of emergency is therefore the only alternative to leakage in the consciousness industry; but it cannot be maintained in the long run. Societies in the late industrial age rely on the free exchange of information; the "objective pressures" to which their controllers constantly appeal are thus turned against them. Every attempt to suppress the random factors, each diminution of the average flow and each distortion of the information structure must, in the long run, lead to an embolism.

The electronic media have not only built up the information network intensively, they have also spread it extensively. The radio wars of the fifties demonstrated that in the realm of communications, national sovereignty is condemned to wither away. The further development of satellites will deal it the *coup de grâce*. Quarantine regulations for information, such as were promulgated by fascism and Stalinism, are only possible today at the cost of deliberate industrial regression.

Example. The Soviet bureaucracy, that is to say the most widespread and complicated bureaucracy in the world, has to deny itself almost entirely an elementary piece of organizational equipment, the duplicating machine, because this instrument potentially makes everyone a printer. The political risk involved, the possibility of a leakage in the information network, is accepted only at the highest levels, at exposed switchpoints in political, military, and scientific areas. It is clear that Soviet society has to pay an immense price for the suppression of its own productive resources—clumsy procedures, misinformation, *faux frais*. The phenomenon incidentally has its analogue in the capitalist West, if in a diluted form. The technically most advanced electrostatic copying machine, which operates with ordinary paper—which cannot, that is to say, be supervised and is independent of suppliers—is the property of a monopoly (Xerox), on principle it is not sold but rented. The rates themselves ensure that it does not get into the wrong hands. The equipment crops up as if by magic where economic and political power are concentrated. Political control of the equipment goes hand in hand with maximization of profits for the manufacturer. Admittedly this control, as opposed to Soviet methods, is by no means "watertight" for the reasons indicated.

The problem of censorship thus enters a new historical stage. The struggle for the freedom of the press and freedom of ideas has, up till now, been mainly an argument within the bourgeoisie itself; for the masses, freedom to express opinions was a fiction since they were, from the beginning, barred from the means of production—above all from the press—and thus were unable to join in freedom of expression from the start. Today censorship is threatened by the productive forces of the consciousness industry which is already, to some extent, gaining the upper hand over the prevailing relations of production. Long before the latter are overthrown, the contradiction between what is possible and what actually exists will become acute.

CULTURAL ARCHAISM IN THE LEFT CRITIQUE

4. The New Left of the sixties has reduced the development of the media to a single concept—that of manipulation. This

concept was originally extremely useful for heuristic purposes and has made possible a great many individual analytical investigations, but it now threatens to degenerate into a mere slogan which conceals more than it is able to illuminate, and therefore itself requires analysis.

The current theory of manipulation on the Left is essentially defensive; its effects can lead the movement into defeatism. Subjectively speaking, behind the tendency to go on the defensive lies a sense of impotence. Objectively, it corresponds to the absolutely correct view that the decisive means of production are in enemy hands. But to react to this state of affairs with moral indignation is naive. There is in general an undertone of lamentation when people speak of manipulation which points to idealistic expectations—as if the class enemy had ever stuck to the promises of fair play it occasionally utters. The liberal superstition that in political and social questions there is such a thing as pure, unmanipulated truth seems to enjoy remarkable currency among the socialist Left. It is the unspoken basic premise of the manipulation thesis.

This thesis provides no incentive to push ahead. A socialist perspective which does not go beyond attacking existing property relationships is limited. The expropriation of Springer is a desirable goal but it would be good to know to whom the media should be handed over. The Party? To judge by all experience of that solution, it is not a possible alternative. It is perhaps no accident that the Left has not yet produced an analysis of the pattern of manipulation in countries with socialist regimes.

The manipulation thesis also serves to exculpate oneself. To cast the enemy in the role of the devil is to conceal the weakness and lack of perspective in one's own agitation. If the latter leads to self-isolation instead of mobilizing the masses, then its failure is attributed holus-bolus to the overwhelming power of the media.

The theory of repressive tolerance has also permeated discussion of the media by the Left. This concept, which was formulated by its author with the utmost care, has also, when whittled away in an undialectical manner, become a vehicle for resignation. Admittedly, when an office-equipment firm can attempt to recruit sales staff with the picture of Che Guevara and the text *We would have hired him*, the temptation to withdraw is great. But fear of handling shit is a luxury a sewerman cannot necessarily afford.

The electronic media do away with cleanliness; they are by their nature "dirty." That is part of their productive power. In terms of structure, they are antisectarian—a further reason why the Left, insofar as it is not prepared to re-examine its traditions, has little idea what to do with them. The desire for a cleanly defined "line" and for the suppression of "deviations" is anachronistic and now serves only one's own need for security. It weakens one's own position by irrational purges, exclusions, and fragmentation, instead of strengthening it by rational discussion.

These resistances and fears are strengthened by a series of cultural factors which, for the most part, operate unconsciously, and which are to be explained by the social history of the participants in today's Left movement—namely their bourgeois class background. It often seems as if it were precisely because of their progressive potential that the media are felt to be an immense threatening power; because for the first time they present a basic challenge to bourgeois culture and thereby to the privileges of the bourgeois intelligentsia—a challenge far more radical than any self-doubt this social group can display. In the New Left's opposition to the media, old bourgeois fears such as the fear of "the masses" seem to be reappearing along with equally old bourgeois longings for pre-industrial times dressed up in progressive clothing.

At the very beginning of the student revolt, during the Free Speech Movement at Berkeley, the computer was a favorite target for aggression. Interest in the Third World is not always free from motives based on antagonism towards civilization which has its source in conservative culture critique. During the May events in Paris the reversion to archaic forms of production was particularly characteristic. Instead of carrying out agitation among the workers with a modern offset press, the students printed their posters on the hand presses of the École des Beaux Arts. The political slogans were hand-painted; stencils would certainly have made it possible to produce them *en masse*, but it would have offended the creative imagination of the authors. The ability to make proper strategic use of the most advanced media was lacking. It was not the radio headquarters that were seized by the rebels, but the Odéon Theatre, steeped in tradition.

The obverse of this fear of contact with the media is the fascination they exert on left-wing movements in the great cities. On the one hand, the comrades take refuge in outdated forms of communication and esoteric arts and crafts instead of occupying themselves with the contradiction between the present constitution of the media and their revolutionary potential; on the other hand, they cannot escape from the consciousness industry's program or from its esthetic. This leads, subjectively, to a split between a puritanical view of political action and the area of private "leisure"; objectively, it leads to a split between politically active groups and subcultural groups.

In Western Europe the socialist movement mainly addresses itself to a public of converts through newspapers and journals which are exclusive in terms of language, content, and form. These newssheets presuppose a structure of party members and sympathizers and a situation, where the media are concerned, that roughly corresponds to the historical situation in 1900; they are obviously fixated on the *Iskra* model. Presumably the people who produce them listen to the Rolling Stones, watch occupations and strikes on television, and go to the cinema to see a Western or a Godard; only in their capacity as producers do they make an exception, and, in their analyses, the whole media sector is reduced to the slogan of "manipulation." Every foray into this territory is regarded from the start with suspicion as a step towards integration. This suspicion is not unjustified; it can however also mask one's own ambivalence and insecurity. Fear of being swallowed up by the system is a sign of weakness; it presupposes that capitalism could overcome any contradiction—a conviction which can easily be refuted historically and is theoretically untenable.

If the socialist movement writes off the new productive forces of the consciousness industry and relegates work on the media to a subculture, then we have a vicious circle. For the Underground may be increasingly aware of the technical and esthetic possibilities of the disc, of videotape, of the electronic camera, and so on, and is systematically exploring the terrain, but it has no political viewpoint of its own and therefore mostly falls a helpless victim to commercialism. The politically active groups then point to such cases with smug *Schadenfreude*. A process of unlearning is the result and both sides are the losers. Capitalism alone benefits from the Left's antagonism to the media, as it does from the depoliticization of the counterculture.

DEMOCRATIC MANIPULATION

5. Manipulation—etymologically, "handling"—means technical treatment of a given material with a particular goal in mind. When the technical intervention is of immediate social relevance, then manipulation is a political act. In the case of the media industry, that is by definition the case.

Thus every use of the media presupposes manipulation. The most elementary processes in media production, from the choice of the medium itself to shooting, cutting, synchronization, dubbing, right up to distribution, are all operations carried out on the raw material. There is no such thing as unmanipulated writing, filming, or broadcasting. The question is therefore not whether the media are manipulated, but who manipulates them. A revolutionary plan should not require the manipulators to disappear; on the contrary, it must make everyone a manipulator.

All technical manipulations are potentially dangerous; the manipulation of the media cannot be countered, however, by old or new forms of censorship, but only by direct social control, that is to say, by the mass of the people, who will have become productive. To this end, the elimination of capitalistic property relationships is a necessary but by no means sufficient condition. There have been no historical examples up until now of the mass self-regulating learning process which is made possible by the electronic media. The Communists' fear of releasing this potential, of the mobilizing capabilities of the media, of the interaction of free producers, is one of the main reasons why even in the socialist countries, the old bourgeois culture, greatly disguised and distorted but structurally intact, continues to hold sway.

As a historical explanation, it may be pointed out that the consciousness industry in Russia at the time of the October Revolution was extraordinarily backward; their productive capacity has grown enormously since then, but the productive relationships have been artificially preserved, often by force. Then, as now, a primitively edited press, books, and theater were the key media in the Soviet Union. The development of radio, film, and television is politically arrested. Foreign stations like the BBC, the Voice of America, and the *Deutschland Welle,* therefore, not only find listeners, but are received with almost boundless faith. Archaic media like the handwritten pamphlet and poems orally transmitted play an important role.

6. The new media are egalitarian in structure. Anyone can take part in them by a simple switching process. The programs themselves are not material things and can be reproduced at will. In this sense the electronic media are entirely different from the older media like the book or the easel painting, the exclusive class character of which is obvious. Television programs for privileged groups are certainly technically conceivable—closed-circuit television—but run counter to the structure. Potentially, the new media do away with all educational privileges and thereby with the cultural monopoly of the bourgeois intelligentsia. This is one of the reasons for the intelligentsia's resentment against the new industry. As for the "spirit" which they are endeavoring to defend against "depersonalization" and "mass culture," the sooner they abandon it the better.

PROPERTIES OF THE NEW MEDIA

7. The new media are orientated towards action, not contemplation; towards the present, not tradition. Their attitude to time is completely opposed to that of bourgeois culture, which aspires to possession, that is to extension in time, best of all, to eternity. The media produce no objects that can be hoarded and auctioned. They do away completely with "intellectual property" and liquidate the "heritage," that is to say, the class-specific handing-on of nonmaterial capital.

That does not mean to say that they have no history or that they contribute to the loss of historical consciousness. On the contrary, they make it possible for the first time to record historical material so that it can be reproduced at will. By making this material available for present-day purposes, they make it obvious to anyone using it that the writing of history is always manipulation. But the memory they hold in readiness is not the preserve of a scholarly caste. It is social. The banked information is accessible to anyone, and this accessibility is as instantaneous as its recording. It suffices to compare the model of a private library with that of a socialized data bank to recognize the structural difference between the two systems.

8. It is wrong to regard media equipment as mere means of consumption. It is always, in principle, also means of production and, indeed, since it is in the hands of the masses, socialized means of production. The contradiction between producers and consumers is not inherent in the electronic media; on the contrary, it has to be artificially reinforced by economic and administrative measures.

An early example of this is provided by the difference between telegraph and telephone. Whereas the former, to this day, has remained in the hands of a bureaucratic institution which can scan and file every text transmitted, the telephone is directly accessible to all users. With the aid of conference circuits, it can even make possible collective intervention in a discussion by physically remote groups.

On the other hand, those auditory and visual means of communication which rely on "wireless" are still subject to state control (legislation on wireless installations). In the face of technical developments, which long ago made local and international radio-telephony possible, and which constantly opened up new wavebands for television —in the UHF band alone, the dissemination of numerous programs in one locality is possible without interference, not to mention the possibilities offered by wired and satellite television—the prevailing laws for control of the air are anachronistic. They recall the time when the operation of a printing press was dependent on an imperial license. The socialist movements will take up the struggle for their own wavelengths and must, within the foreseeable future, build their own transmitters and relay stations.

9. One immediate consequence of the structural nature of the new media is that none of the regimes at present in power can release their potential. Only a free socialist society will be able to make them fully productive. A further characteristic of the most advanced media—probably the decisive one—confirms this thesis: their collective structure.

For the prospect that in future, with the aid of the media, anyone can become a producer, would remain apolitical and limited were this productive effort to find an outlet in individual tinkering. Work on the media is possible for an individual only insofar as it remains socially and therefore esthetically irrelevant. The collection of transparencies from the last holiday trip provides a model of this.

That is naturally what the prevailing market mechanisms have aimed at. It has long been clear from apparatus like miniature and 8-mm movie cameras, as well as the tape recorder, which are in actual fact already in the hands of the masses, that the individual, so long as he remains isolated, can become with their help at best an amateur but not a producer. Even so potent a means of production as the short-wave transmitter has been tamed in this way and reduced to a harmless and inconsequential hobby in the hands of scattered radio hams. The programs which the isolated amateur mounts are always only bad, outdated copies of what he in any case receives.

Private production for the media is no more than licensed cottage industry. Even when it is made public it remains pure compromise. To this end, the men who own the media have developed special programs which are usually called "Democratic Forum" or something of the kind. There, tucked away in the corner, "the reader (listener, viewer) has his say," which can naturally be cut short at any time. As in the case of public-opinion polling, he is only asked questions so that he may have a chance to confirm his own dependence. It is a control circuit where what is fed in has already made complete allowance for the feedback.

The concept of a license can also be used in another sense—in an economic one; the system attempts to make each participant into a concessionaire of the monopoly that develops his films or plays back his cassettes. The aim is to nip in the bud in this way that independence which video equipment, for instance, makes possible. Naturally, such tendencies go against the grain of the structure, and the new productive forces not only permit but indeed demand their reversal.

The poor, feeble, and frequently humiliating results of this licensed activity are often referred to with contempt by the professional media producers. On top of the damage suffered by the masses comes triumphant mockery because they clearly do not know how to use the media properly. The sort of thing that goes on in certain popular television shows is taken as proof that they are completely incapable of articulating on their own.

Not only does this run counter to the results of the latest psychological and pedagogical research, but it can easily be seen to be a reactionary protective formulation; the "gifted" people are quite simply defending their territories. Here we have a cultural analogue to the familiar political judgments concerning a working class which is presumed to be "stultified" and incapable of any kind of self-determination. Curiously, one may hear the view that the masses could never govern themselves out of the mouths of people who consider themselves socialists. In the best of cases, these are economists who cannot conceive of socialism as anything other than nationalization.

A SOCIALIST STRATEGY

10. Any socialist strategy for the media must, on the contrary, strive to end the isolation of the individual participants from the social learning and production process. This is impossible unless those concerned organize themselves. This is the political core of the question of the media. It is over this point that socialist concepts part company with the neo-liberal and technocratic ones. Anyone who expects to be emancipated by technological hardware, or by a system of hardware however structured, is the victim of an obscure belief in progress. Anyone who imagines that freedom for the media will be established if only everyone is busy transmitting and receiving is the dupe of a liberalism which, decked out in contemporary colors, merely peddles the faded concepts of a preordained harmony of social interests.

In the face of such illusions, what must be firmly held on to is that the proper use of the media demands organization and makes it possible. Every production that deals with the interests of the producers postulates a collective method of production. It is itself already a form of self-organization of social needs. Tape recorders, ordinary cameras, and movie cameras are already extensively owned by wage-earners. The question is why these means of production do not turn up at factories, in schools, in the offices of the bureaucracy, in short, everywhere where there is social conflict. By producing aggressive forms of publicity which were their own, the masses could secure evidence of their daily experiences and draw effective lessons from them.

Naturally, bourgeois society defends itself against such prospects with a battery of legal measures. It bases itself on the law of trespass, on commercial and official secrecy. While its secret services penetrate everywhere and plug in to the most intimate conversations, it pleads a touching concern for confidentiality, and makes a sensitive display of worrying about the question of privacy when all that is private is the interest of the exploiters. Only a collective, organized effort can tear down these paper walls.

Communication networks which are constructed for such purposes can, over and above their primary function, provide politically interesting organizational models. In the socialist movements the dialectic of discipline and spontaneity, centralism and decentralization, authoritarian leadership and anti-authoritarian disintegration has long ago reached deadlock. Networklike communications models built on the principle of reversibility of circuits might give indications of how to overcome this situation: a mass newspaper, written and distributed by its readers, a video network of politically active groups.

More radically than any good intention, more lastingly than existential flight from one's own class, the media, once they have come into their own, destroy the private production methods of bourgeois intellectuals. Only in productive work and learning processes can their individualism be broken down in such a way that it is transformed from morally based (that is to say, as individual as ever) self-sacrifice to a new kind of political self-understanding and behavior.

11. An all too widely disseminated thesis maintains that present-day capitalism lives by the exploitation of unreal needs. That is at best a half-truth. The results obtained by popular American sociologists like Vance Packard are not un-useful but limited. What they have to say about the stimulation of needs through advertising and artificial obsolescence can in any case not be adequately explained by the hypnotic pull exerted on the wage-earners by mass consumption. The hypothesis of "consumer terror" corresponds to the prejudices of a middle class, which considers itself politically enlightened, against the allegedly integrated proletariat, which has become petty bourgeois and corrupt. The attractive power of mass consumption is based not on the dictates of false needs, but on the falsification and exploitation of quite real and legitimate ones without which the parasitic process of advertising would be redundant. A socialist movement ought not to denounce these needs, but take them seriously, investigate them, and make them politically productive.

That is also valid for the consciousness industry. The electronic media do not owe their irresistible power to any sleight-of-hand but to the elemental power of deep social needs which come through even in the present depraved form of these media.

Precisely because no one bothers about them, the interests of the masses have remained a relatively unknown field, at least insofar as they are historically new. They certainly extend far beyond those goals which the traditional working class movement represented. Just as in the field of production, the industry which produces goods and the consciousness industry merge more and more, so too, subjectively, where needs are concerned, material and nonmaterial factors are closely interwoven. In the process old psycho-social themes are firmly embedded—social prestige, identification patterns—but powerful new themes emerge which are utopian in nature. From a materialistic point of view, neither the one nor the other must be suppressed.

Henri Lefèbvre has proposed the concept of the *spectacle*, the exhibition, the show, to fit the present form of mass consumption. Goods and shop windows, traffic and advertisements, stores and the world of communications, news and packaging, architecture and media production come together to form a totality, a permanent theater, which dominates not only the public city centers but also private interiors. The expression "beautiful living" makes the most commonplace objects of general use into props for this universal festival, in which the fetishistic nature of the commodities triumphs completely over their use value. The swindle these festivals perpetrate is, and remains, a swindle within the present social structure. But it is the harbinger of something else. Consumption as spectacle contains the promise that want will disappear. The deceptive, brutal, and obscene features of this festival derive from the fact that there can be no question of a real fulfillment of its promise. But so long as scarcity holds sway, use-value remains a decisive category which can only be abolished by trickery. Yet trickery on such a scale is only conceivable if it is based on mass need. This need—it is a utopian one—is there. It is the desire for a new ecology, for a breaking down of environmental barriers, for an esthetic which is not limited to the sphere of "the artistic." These desires are not—or are not primarily—internalized rules of the game as played by the capitalist system. They have physiological roots and can no longer be suppressed. Consumption as spectacle is—in parody form—the anticipation of a utopian situation.

The promises of the media demonstrate the same ambivalence. They are an answer to the mass need for nonmaterial variety and mobility—which at present finds its material realization in private car ownership and tourism—and they exploit it. Other collective wishes, which capital often recognizes more quickly and evaluates more correctly than its opponents, but naturally only so as to trap them and rob them of their explosive force, are just as powerful, just as unequivocally emancipatory: the need to take part in the social process on a local, national, and international scale; the need for new forms of interaction, for release from ignorance and tutelage; the need for self-determination. "Be everywhere!" is one of the most successful slogans of the media industry. The readers' parliament of *Bild-Zeitung** was direct democracy used against the interests of the *demos*. "Open spaces" and "free time" are concepts which corral and neutralize the urgent wishes of the masses.

There is corresponding acceptance by the media of utopian stories: e.g., the story of the young Italo-American who hijacked a passenger plane to get home from California to Rome was taken up without protest even by the reactionary mass press and undoubtedly correctly understood by its readers. The identification is based on what has become a general need. Nobody can understand why such journeys should be reserved for politicians, functionaries, and businessmen. The role of the pop star could be analyzed from a similar angle; in it the authoritarian and emancipatory factors are mingled in an extraordinary way. It is perhaps not unimportant that beat music offers groups, not individuals, as identification models. In the productions of the Rolling Stones (and in the manner of their production) the utopian content is apparent. Events like the Woodstock Festival, the concerts in Hyde Park, on the Isle of Wight, and at

* The Springer press mass publication.

Altamont, California, develop a mobilizing power which the political Left can only envy.

It is absolutely clear that, within the present social forms, the consciousness industry can satisfy none of the needs on which it lives and which it must fan, except in the illusory form of games. The point, however, is not to demolish its promises but to take them literally and to show that they can be met only through a cultural revolution. Socialists and socialist regimes which multiply the frustration of the masses by declaring their needs to be false, become the accomplices of the system they have undertaken to fight.

12. SUMMARY.

Repressive use of media	Emancipatory use of media
Centrally controlled program	Decentralized program
One transmitter, many receivers	Each receiver a potential transmitter
Immobilization of isolated individuals	Mobilization of the masses
Passive consumer behavior	Interaction of those involved, feedback
Depoliticization	A political learning process
Production by specialists	Collective production
Control by property owners or bureaucracy	Social control by self-organization

THE SUBVERSIVE POWER OF THE NEW MEDIA

13. As far as the objectively subversive potentialities of the electronic media are concerned, both sides in the international class struggle—except for the fatalistic adherents of the thesis of manipulation in the metropoles—are of one mind. Frantz Fanon was the first to draw attention to the fact that the transistor receiver was one of the most important weapons in the Third World's fight for freedom. Albert Hertzog, ex-Minister of the South African Republic and the mouthpiece of the right wing of the ruling party, is of the opinion that

"television will lead to the ruin of the white man in South Africa." [2] American imperialism has recognized the situation. It attempts to meet the "revolution of rising expectations" in Latin America—that is what its ideologues call it— by scattering its own transmitters all over the continent and into the remotest regions of the Amazon basin, and by distributing single-frequency transistors to the native population. The attacks of the Nixon Administration on the capitalist media in the USA reveal its understanding that their reporting, however one-sided and distorted, has become a decisive factor in mobilizing people against the war in Vietnam. Whereas only twenty-five years ago the French massacres in Madagascar, with almost one hundred thousand dead, became known only to the readers of *Le Monde* under the heading of "Other News" and therefore remained unnoticed and without sequel in the capital city, today the media drag colonial wars into the centers of imperialism.

The direct mobilizing potentialities of the media become still more clear when they are consciously used for subversive ends. Their presence is a factor that immensely increases the demonstrative nature of any political act. The student movements in the USA, in Japan, and in Western Europe soon recognized this and, to begin with, achieved considerable momentary success with the aid of the media. These effects have worn off. Naive trust in the magical power of reproduction cannot replace organizational work; only active and coherent groups can force the media to comply with the logic of their actions. That can be demonstrated from the example of the Tupamaros in Uruguay, whose revolutionary practice has implicit in it publicity for their actions. Thus the actors become authors. The abduction of the American ambassador in Rio de Janeiro was planned with a view to its impact on the media. It was a television production. The Arab guerillas proceed in the same way. The first to experiment with these techniques internationally were the Cubans. Fidel appreciated the revolutionary potential of the media correctly from the first (Moncada, 1953). Today illegal political action demands at one and the same time maximum security and maximum publicity.

14. Revolutionary situations always bring with them discontinuous, spontaneous changes brought about by the masses in the existing aggregate of the media. How far the changes thus brought about take root and how permanent they are demonstrates the extent to which a cultural revolution is successful. The situation in the media is the most accurate and sensitive barometer for the rise of bureaucratic or Bonapartist anticyclones. So long as the cultural revolution has the initiative, the social imagination of the masses overcomes even technical backwardness and transforms the function of the old media so that their structures are exploded.

"With our work the Revolution has achieved a colossal labor of propaganda and enlightenment. We ripped up the traditional book into single pages, magnified these a hundred times, printed them in color and stuck them up as posters in the streets. . . . Our lack of printing equipment and the necessity for speed meant that, though the best work was hand-printed, the most rewarding was standardized, lapidary and adapted to the simplest mechanical form of reproduction. Thus State Decrees were printed as rolled-up illustrated leaflets, and Army Orders as illustrated pamphlets." [3]

In the twenties, the Russian film reached a standard that was far in advance of the available productive forces. Pudovkin's *Kinoglas* and Dziga Vertov's *Kinopravda* were no "newsreels" but political television magazine programs *avant l'écran*. The campaign against illiteracy in Cuba broke through the linear, exclusive, and isolating structure of the medium of the book. In the China of the Cultural Revolution, wall newspapers functioned like an electronic mass medium—at least in the big towns. The resistance of the Czechoslovak population to the Soviet invasion gave rise to spontaneous productivity on the part of the masses, which ignored the institutional barriers of the media. Such situations are exceptional. It is precisely their utopian nature, which reaches out beyond the existing productive forces (it follows that the productive relationships are not to be permanently overthrown), that makes them precarious, leads to reversals and defeats. They demonstrate all the more clearly what enormous political and cultural energies are hidden in the enchained masses and with what imagination they are able, at the moment of liberation, to realize all the opportunities offered by the new media.

THE MEDIA: AN EMPTY CATEGORY
OF MARXIST THEORY

15. That the Marxist Left should argue theoretically and act practically from the standpoint of the most advanced productive forces in their society, that they should develop in depth all the liberating factors immanent in these forces and use them strategically, is no academic expectation but a political necessity. However, with a single great exception, that of Walter Benjamin (and in his footsteps, Brecht), Marxists have not understood the consciousness industry and have been aware only of its bourgeois-capitalist dark side and not of its socialist possibilities. An author like George Lukács is a perfect example of this theoretical and practical backwardness. Nor are the works of Horkheimer and Adorno free of a nostalgia which clings to early bourgeois media.

Their view of the cultural industry cannot be discussed here. Much more typical of Marxism between the two wars is the position of Lukács, which can be seen very clearly from an early essay on "Old Culture and New Culture." [4] "Anything that culture produces" can, according to Lukács, "have real cultural value only *if it is in itself* valuable, if the creation of each individual product is from the standpoint of its maker a single, finite process. It must, moreover, be a process conditioned by the *human* potentialities and capabilities of the creator. The most typical example of such a process is the work of art, where the entire genesis of the work is exclusively the result of the artist's labor and each detail of the work that emerges is determined by the individual qualities of the artist. In highly developed mechanical industry, on the other hand, any connection between the product and the creator is abolished. *The human being serves the machine, he adapts to it.* Production becomes completely independent of the human potentialities and capabilities of the worker." These "forces which destroy culture" impair the work's "truth to the material," its "level," and deal the final blow to the "work as an end in itself." There is no more question of "the organic unity of the products of culture, its harmonious, joy-giving being." Capitalist culture must lack "the simple and natural harmony and beauty of the old culture—culture in the true, literal sense of the word." Fortunately things need not remain so. The "culture of proletarian society," although "in the context of such scientific research as is possible at this time" nothing more can be said about it, will certainly remedy these ills. Lukács asks himself "which are the cultural values which, in accordance with the nature of this context, *can be taken over from the old society* by the new *and further developed.*" Answer: Not the inhuman machines but "the idea of mankind as an end in itself, the basic idea of the new culture," for it is "the inheritance of the classical idealism of the nineteenth century." Quite right. "This is where the philistine concept of *art* turns up with all its deadly obtuseness—an idea to which all technical considerations are foreign and which feels that with the provocative appearance of the new technology its end has come." [5]

These nostalgic backward glances at the landscape of the last century, these reactionary ideals, are already the forerunners of socialist realism, which mercilessly galvanized and then buried those very "cultural values" which Lukács rode out to rescue. Unfortunately, in the process, the Soviet cultural revolution was thrown to the wolves; but this esthete can in any case hardly have thought any more highly of it than did J. V. Stalin.

The inadequate understanding which Marxists have shown of the media and the questionable use they have made of them has produced a vacuum in Western industrialized countries into which a stream of non-Marxist hypotheses and practices has consequently flowed. From the Cabaret Voltaire to Andy Warhol's Factory, from the silent film comedians to the Beatles, from the first comic-strip artists to the present managers of the Underground, the apolitical have made much more radical progress in dealing with the media than any grouping of the Left. (Exception—Münzenberg.) Innocents have put themselves in the forefront of the new productive forces on the basis of mere intuitions with which communism —to its detriment—has not wished to concern itself. Today this apolitical avant-garde has found its ventriloquist and prophet in Marshall McLuhan, an author who admittedly lacks any analytical categories for the understanding of social processes, but whose confused books serve as a quarry of undigested observations for the media industry. Certainly his little finger has experienced more of the productive power of the new media than all the ideological commissions of the CPSU and their endless resolutions and directives put together.

Incapable of any theoretical construction, McLuhan does not present his material as a concept but as the common denominator of a reactionary doctrine of salvation. He admittedly did not invent but was the first to formulate explicitly a mystique of the media which dissolves all political problems in smoke—the same smoke that gets in the eyes of his followers. It promises the salvation of man through the technology of television and indeed of television as it is practiced today. Now McLuhan's attempt to stand Marx on his head is not exactly new. He shares with his numerous predecessors the determination to suppress all problems of the economic base, their idealistic tendencies, and their belittling of the class struggle in the naive terms of a vague humanism. A new Rousseau—like all copies, only a pale version of the old—he preaches the gospel of the new primitive man who, naturally on a higher level, must return to prehistoric tribal existence in the "global village."

It is scarcely worthwhile to deal with such concepts. This charlatan's most famous saying—"the medium is the message" —perhaps deserves more attention. In spite of its provocative idiocy, it betrays more than its author knows. It reveals in the most accurate way the tautological nature of the mystique of the media. The one remarkable thing about the television set, according to him, is that it moves—a thesis which in view of the nature of American programs has, admittedly, something attractive about it.

The complementary mistake consists in the widespread illusion that media are neutral instruments by which any "messages" one pleases can be transmitted without regard for their structure or for the structure of the medium. In the East European countries the television newsreaders read fifteen-minute-long conference communiqués and Central Committee resolutions which are not even suitable for printing in a newspaper, clearly under the delusion that they might fascinate a public of millions.

The sentence "The medium is the message" transmits yet another message, however, and a much more important one. It tells us that the bourgeoisie does indeed have all possible means at its disposal to communicate something to us, but that it has nothing more to say. It is ideologically sterile. Its intention to hold on to the control of the means of production at any price, while being incapable of making the socially necessary use of them, is here expressed with complete frankness in the superstructure. It wants the media *as such* and *to no purpose*.

This wish has been shared for decades and given symbolical expression by an artistic avant-garde whose program logically admits only the alternative of negative signals and amorphous noise. Example: the already outdated "literature of silence," Warhol's films in which everything can happen at once or nothing at all, and John Cage's forty-five-minute-long *Lecture on Nothing* (1959).

THE ACHIEVEMENT OF BENJAMIN

16. The revolution in the conditions of production in the superstructure has made the traditional esthetic theory unusable, completely unhinging its fundamental categories and destroying its "standards." The theory of knowledge on which it was based is outmoded. In the electronic media, a radically altered relationship between subject and object emerges with which the old critical concepts cannot deal. The idea of the self-sufficient work of art collapsed long ago. The long-drawn discussion over the death of art proceeds in a circle so long as it does not examine critically the esthetic concept on which it is based, so long as it employs criteria which no longer

correspond to the state of the productive forces. When constructing an esthetic adapted to the changed situation, one must take as a starting point the work of the only Marxist theoretician who recognized the liberating potential of the new media. Thirty-five years ago, that is to say, at a time when the consciousness industry was relatively undeveloped, Walter Benjamin subjected this phenomenon to a penetrating dialectical-materialist analysis. His approach has not been matched by any theory since then, much less further developed.

"One might generalize by saying: the technique of reproduction detaches the reproduced object from the domain of tradition. By making many reproductions it substitutes a plurality of copies for a unique existence and in permitting the reproduction to meet the beholder or listener in his own particular situation, it reactivates the object reproduced. These two processes lead to a tremendous shattering of tradition which is the obverse of the contemporary crisis and renewal of mankind. Both processes are intimately connected with the contemporary mass movements. Their most powerful agent is the film. Its social significance, particularly in its most positive form, is inconceivable without its destructive, cathartic aspect, that is, the liquidation of the traditional value of the cultural heritage.

"For the first time in world history, mechanical reproduction emancipates the work of art from its parasitical dependence on ritual. To an ever greater degree the work of art reproduced becomes the work of art designed for reproducibility. . . . But the instant the criterion of authenticity ceases to be applicable to artistic production, the total function of art is reversed. Instead of being based on ritual, it begins to be based on another practice—politics. . . . Today, by the absolute emphasis on its exhibition value, the work of art becomes a creation with entirely new functions, among which the one we are conscious of, the artistic function, later may be recognized as incidental." [6]

The trends which Benjamin recognized in his day in the film and the true import of which he grasped theoretically, have become patent today with the rapid development of the consciousness industry. What used to be called art, has now, in the strict Hegelian sense, been dialectically surpassed by and in the media. The quarrel about the end of art is otiose so long as this end is not understood dialectically. Artistic productivity reveals itself to be the extreme marginal case of a much more widespread productivity, and it is socially important only insofar as it surrenders all pretensions to autonomy and recognizes itself to be a marginal case. Wherever the professional producers make a virtue out of the necessity of their specialist skills and even derive a privileged status from them, their experience and knowledge have become useless. This means that as far as an esthetic theory is concerned, a radical change in perspectives is needed. Instead of looking at the productions of the new media from the point of view of the older modes of production we must, on the contrary, analyze the products of the traditional "artistic media from the standpoint of modern conditions of production.

"Earlier much futile thought had been devoted to the question of whether photography is an art. The primary question—whether the very invention of photography had not transformed the entire nature of art—was not raised. Soon the film theoreticians asked the same ill-considered question with regard to the film. But the difficulties which photography caused traditional esthetics were mere child's play as compared to those raised by the film." [7]

The panic aroused by such a shift in perspectives is understandable. The process not only changes the old burdensome craft secrets in the superstructure into white elephants, it also conceals a genuinely destructive element. It is, in a word, risky. But the only chance for the esthetic tradition lies in its dialectical supersession. In the same way, classical physics has survived as a marginal special case within the framework of a much more comprehensive theory.

This state of affairs can be identified in individual cases in all the traditional artistic disciplines. Their present-day developments remain incomprehensible so long as one attempts to deduce them from their own prehistory. On the other hand, their usefulness or otherwise can be judged as soon as one regards them as special cases in a general esthetic of the media. Some indications of the possible critical approaches which stem from this will be made below, taking literature as an example.

THE SUPERSESSION OF WRITTEN CULTURE

17. Written literature has, historically speaking, played a dominant role for only a few centuries. Even today, the predominance of the book has an episodic air. An incomparably longer time preceded it in which literature was oral. Now it is being succeeded by the age of the electronic media, which tend once more to make people speak. At its period of fullest development, the book to some extent usurped the place of the more primitive but generally more accessible methods of production of the past; on the other hand, it was a stand-in for future methods which make it possible for everyone to become a producer.

The revolutionary role of the printed book has been described often enough and it would be absurd to deny it. From the point of view of its structure as a medium, written literature, like the bourgeoisie who produced it and whom it served, was progressive. (See the *Communist Manifesto*.) On the analogy of the economic development of capitalism, which was indispensable for the development of the industrial revolution, the nonmaterial productive forces could not have developed without their own capital accumulation. (We also owe the accumulation of *Das Kapital* and its teachings to the medium of the book.)

Nevertheless, almost everybody speaks better than he writes. (This also applies to authors.) Writing is a highly formalized technique which, in purely physiological terms, demands a peculiarly rigid bodily posture. To this there corresponds the high degree of social specialization that it demands. Professional writers have always tended to think in caste terms. The class character of their work is unquestionable, even in the age of universal compulsory education. The whole process is extraordinarily beset with taboos. Spelling mistakes, which are completely immaterial in terms of communication, are punished by the social disqualification of the writer. The rules that govern this technique have a normative power attributed to them for which there is no rational basis. Intimidation through the written word has remained a widespread and class-specific phenomenon even in advanced industrial societies.

These alienating factors cannot be eradicated from written literature. They are reinforced by the methods by which society transmits its writing techniques. While people learn to speak very early, and mostly in psychologically favorable conditions, learning to write forms an important part of authoritarian socialization by the school ("good writing" as a kind of breaking-in). This sets its stamp forever on written communication—on its tone, its syntax, and its whole style. (This also applies to the text on this page.)

The formalization of written language permits and encourages the repression of opposition. In speech, unresolved contradictions betray themselves by pauses, hesitations, slips of the tongue, repetitions, anacoluthons, quite apart from phrasing, mimicry, gesticulation, pace, and volume. The esthetic of written literature scorns such involuntary factors as "mistakes." It demands, explicitly or implicitly, the smoothing out of contradictions, rationalization, regularization of the spoken form irrespective of content. Even as a child, the writer is urged to hide his unsolved problems behind a protective screen of correctness.

Structurally, the printed book is a medium that operates as a monologue, isolating producer and reader. Feedback and interaction are extremely limited, demand elaborate procedures, and only in the rarest cases lead to corrections. Once an edition has been printed it cannot be corrected; at best it can be pulped. The control circuit in the case of literary criticism is extremely cumbersome and elitist. It excludes the public on principle.

None of the characteristics that distinguish written and printed literature apply to the electronic media. Microphone and camera abolish the class character of the mode of production (not of the production itself). The normative rules become unimportant. Oral interviews, arguments, demonstrations, neither demand nor allow orthography or "good writing." The television screen exposes the esthetic smoothing-out of contradictions as camouflage. Admittedly, swarms of liars appear on it, but anyone can see from a long way off that they are peddling something. As at present constituted, radio, film, and television are burdened to excess with authoritarian characteristics, the characteristics of the monologue, which they have inherited from older methods of production—and that is no accident. These outworn elements in today's media esthetics are demanded by the social relations. They do not follow from the structure of the media. On the contrary, they go against it, for the structure demands interaction.

It is extremely improbable, however, that writing as a special technique will disappear in the foreseeable future. That goes for the book as well, the practical advantages of which for many purposes remain obvious. It is admittedly less handy and takes up more room than other storage systems, but up to now it offers simpler methods of access than, for example, the microfilm or the tape bank. It ought to be integrated into the system as a marginal case and thereby forfeit its aura of cult and ritual.

This can be deduced from technological developments. Electronics are noticeably taking over writing: teleprinters, reading machines, high-speed transmissions, automatic photographic and electronic composition, automatic writing devices, typesetters, electrostatic processes, ampex libraries, cassette encyclopedias, photocopiers and magnetic copiers, speedprinters.

The outstanding Russian media expert El Lissitsky, incidentally, demanded an "electro-library" as far back as 1923—a request which, given the technical conditions of the time, must have seemed ridiculous or at least incomprehensible. This is how far this man's imagination reached into the future:

"I draw the following analogy:

Inventions in the field of verbal traffic	Inventions in the field of general traffic
Articulated language	Upright gait
Writing	The wheel
Gutenberg's printing press	Carts drawn by animal power
?	The automobile
?	The airplane

"I have produced this analogy to prove that so long as the book remains a palpable object, i.e. so long as it is not replaced by auto-vocalizing and kino-vocalizing representations, we must look to the field of the manufacture of books for basic innovations in the near future.

"There are signs at hand suggesting that this basic innovation is likely to come from the neighborhood of the collotype." [8]

Today, writing has in many cases already become a secondary technique, a means of transcribing orally recorded speech: tape-recorded proceedings, attempts at speech-pattern recognition, and the conversion of speech into writing.

18. The ineffectiveness of literary criticism when faced with so-called documentary literature is an indication of how far the critics' thinking has lagged behind the stage of the productive forces. It stems from the fact that the media have eliminated one of the most fundamental categories of esthetics up to now—fiction. The fiction/nonfiction argument has been laid to rest just as was the nineteenth century's favorite dialectic of "art" and "life." In his day, Benjamin demonstrated that the "apparatus" (the concept of the medium was not yet available to him) abolishes authenticity. In the productions of the consciousness industry, the difference between the "genuine" original and the reproduction disappears —"that aspect of reality which is not dependent on the apparatus has now become its most artificial aspect." The process of reproduction reacts on the object reproduced and alters it fundamentally. The effects of this have not yet been adequately explained epistemologically. The categorical uncertainties to which it gives rise also affect the concept of the documentary. Strictly speaking, it has shrunk to its legal di-

mensions. A document is something the "forging"—i.e. the reproduction—of which is punishable by imprisonment. This definition naturally has no theoretical meaning. The reason is that a reproduction, to the extent that its technical quality is good enough, cannot be distinguished in any way from the original, irrespective of whether it is a painting, a passport, or a bank note. The legal concept of the documentary record is only pragmatically useful; it serves only to protect economic interests.

The productions of the electronic media, by their nature, evade such distinctions as those between documentary and feature films. They are in every case explicitly determined by the given situation. The producer can never pretend, like the traditional novelist, "to stand above things." He is therefore partisan from the start. This fact finds formal expression in his techniques. Cutting, editing, dubbing—these are techniques for conscious manipulation without which the use of the new media is inconceivable. It is precisely in these work processes that their productive power reveals itself—and here it is completely immaterial whether one is dealing with the production of a reportage or a play. The material, whether "documentary" or "fiction," is in each case only a prototype, a half-finished article, and the more closely one examines its origins, the more blurred the difference becomes.

THE DESACRALIZATION OF ART

19. The media also do away with the old category of works of art which can only be considered as separate objects, not as independent of their material infrastructure. The media do not produce such objects. They create programs. Their production is in the nature of a process. That does not mean only (or not primarily) that there is no foreseeable end to the program—a fact which, in view of what we are at present presented with, admittedly makes a certain hostility to the

media understandable. It means, above all, that the media program is open to its own consequences without structural limitations. (This is not an empirical description but a demand. A demand which admittedly is not made of the medium from without; it is a consequence of its nature, from which the much-vaunted open form can be derived—and not as a modification of it—from an old esthetic.) The programs of the consciousness industry must subsume into themselves their own results, the reactions and the corrections which they call forth, otherwise they are already out-of-date. They are therefore to be thought of not as means of consumption but as means of their own production.

20. It is characteristic of artistic avant-gardes that they have, so to speak, a presentiment of the potentiality of media which still lie in the future. "It has always been one of the most important tasks of art to give rise to a demand, the time for the complete satisfaction of which has not yet come. The history of every art form has critical periods when that form strives towards effects which can only be easily achieved if the technical norm is changed, that is to say, in a new art form. The artistic extravagances and crudities which arise in this way, for instance in the so-called decadent period, really stem from art's richest historical source of power. Dadaism in the end teemed with such barbarisms. We can only now recognize the nature of its striving. Dadaism was attempting to achieve those effects which the public today seeks in film with the means of painting (or of literature)." [9] This is where the prognostic value of otherwise inessential productions, such as happenings, flux, and mixed-media shows, is to be found. There are writers who in their work show an awareness of the fact that media with the characteristics of the monologue today have only a residual use-value. Many of them admittedly draw fairly shortsighted conclusions from this glimpse of the truth. For example, they offer the user the opportunity to arrange the material provided by arbitrary permutations. Every reader as it were should write his own book. When carried to extremes, such attempts to produce interaction, even when it goes against the structure of the medium employed, are

nothing more than invitations to freewheel. Mere noise permits of no articulated interactions. Short cuts, of the kind that Concept Art peddles, are based on the banal and false conclusion that the development of the productive forces renders all work superfluous. With the same justification, one could leave a computer to its own devices on the assumption that a random generator will organize material production by itself. Fortunately, cybernetics experts are not given to such childish games.

21. For the old-fashioned "artist"—let us call him the author—it follows from these reflections that he must see it as his goal to make himself redundant as a specialist in much the same way as a teacher of literacy only fulfills his task when he is no longer necessary. Like every learning process, this process too is reciprocal. The specialist will learn as much or more from the nonspecialists as the other way round. Only then can he contrive to make himself dispensable.

Meanwhile, his social usefulness can best be measured by the degree to which he is capable of using the liberating factors in the media and bringing them to fruition. The tactical contradictions in which he must become involved in the process can neither be denied nor covered up in any way. But strategically his role is clear. The author has to work as the agent of the masses. He can lose himself in them only when they themselves become authors, the authors of history.

22. "Pessimism of the intelligence, optimism of the will" (Antonio Gramsci).

Translated by Stuart Hood

Towards a
Theory of Treason

Our laws are not widely known. They are the secret of the small group of nobles that rules us. . . . It is a tradition that the laws exist and are entrusted to the nobility as a secret, but it is no more and cannot be more than an ancient tradition which has become credible through its very age, for the character of these laws also requires that their content be kept secret.

Franz Kafka
On the Question of the Law

1. TRAITORS—THOSE ARE THE OTHERS

No one wants to be considered a traitor. No matter who their legislator is, no matter under what social arrangements they live, most everyone is firmly convinced that he does not deserve that name—but just as firmly convinced, however, that there are traitors and that they should be punished as harshly as possible, preferably by the death penalty, but in any case with the strongest penalty the law knows.

2. EVERYONE AS TRAITOR

These convictions are puzzling to the point of stupefaction. They evidently stand in stark contrast to the historical experiences everyone could, and can still, have during his lifetime. If, for the time being, one places in abeyance the question of what actually constitutes treason—scarcely one of those who believe in it can give a definition—that is, if one orients one-self for the present by the legal systems that were in effect for the past thirty years, at least on the European continent, then there is no doubt whatever that almost every inhabitant of this continent was at some point in his life a traitor in the eyes of the state. However, not all these treasonable acts were discovered, prosecuted, and punished; that would only have been possible at the price of the depopulation of our part of the earth.

3. INEVITABILITY OF TREASON

It seems superfluous to offer proof of a fact that is so well known. However, to establish the fact that everyone *can* become a traitor is insufficient. To be decisive for the argument it must be shown that under certain historical conditions everyone *must* become a traitor. For example, the entire populations of Norway, Holland, France, Greece, and Yugoslavia consisted of traitors (always in the technical-legal sense of the word) during the German occupation of these countries. No matter which government each individual considered to be his, there existed always another in whose eyes he was committing treason. Similar mirrorlike compulsory situations come about in all partitioned countries, such as, for example, Germany since 1948.

4. DIALECTIC OF TREASON

Each radical change in sovereignty makes millions of people into traitors vis-à-vis the valid laws, and this event is as simple as the flip of a coin. Those who weren't, previously, become potential traitors now, and vice versa. The only thing that can protect one from this reversal is the immediate relinquishment of the previously maintained position and lightning-quick adaptation to the new principles that now obtain. Whoever doesn't want to be considered a traitor has to betray without delay what he was previously attached to.

On March 8, 1943, the seventy-five-year-old pensioner Wilhelm Lehmann was condemned to death in Berlin for instigating high treason because he had written on˙ the wall of a public toilet: "Hitler, you mass murderer, must be murdered."[1] Ten years later it would have approximated a treasonable act to express the opposite view. A reversal in the other direction has taken place in Spain. Margaret Boveri reports that the word *loyalist* described the republicans between 1936 and 1945, whereas today, in the United States, it is generally used to designate the followers of Franco.[2] The concept of treason of course undergoes a corresponding reversal. One can produce any number of analogous examples. The different phases of the Algerian conflict made every Frenchman between 1954 and 1962 into a traitor at one point or another. The same holds true for the inhabitants of all African and Asian countries who liberated themselves by force from colonialism, not to speak of the history of the Soviet Union under Stalinism.

5. ANTIQUATEDNESS

Under these circumstances it is a wonder that treason has been able to maintain itself at all as a consistent concept in legal practice. What it means scarcely anyone knows, least of all those who defend themselves most vehemently against it or most eagerly call for its persecution. Even professional jurists aren't capable of rational clarification of the matter. They confine themselves to a purely formal interpretation of whatever legal text happens to fit. In striking contrast to this general puzzlement stands the consistent outrage over the traitor and the general agreement to use the sharpest sanctions against him. The conception of treason is so firm that no historical experience can shake it, and so irrational that it seems above and beyond every scrutiny, every doubt, both of which point to its old age, its antiquity. In fact, the oldest European code of law, the Roman twelve-table law, already names a crime of treason (*perduellio*), and the oldest permanent court of law of Roman history was a special court which only acted in cases of treason (the *duumviri perduellionis*).

6. TREASON AS LAESA MAIESTAS

The archaic kernel of the crime is obscured in the twelve-table law, as under all republican, not to speak of democratic, constitutions. In Roman law it steps out of its obscurity again at the time of the emperors. Treason from now on is called *crimen maiestatis* or *laesa maiestas*, a term which has maintained itself through the history of European law. The English *Treason Act* of 1351, which is still valid today, designates as high treason "to compass or imagine the death of the king, the queen, or their eldest son and heir." The lawbooks of all European monarchies begin with similar definitions; for example, paragraphs 80 and 81 of the first German penal code, which invokes the death penalty for murder or attempt to murder the emperor or head of the country. The *laesa maiestas* lives on in nineteenth-century laws in the form of prohibiting insult to majesties. In contemporary republican legislation the murder of the head of state has apparently been edged to the periphery of the concept of treason; but not a single lawbook is without it. It is not possible to omit it, because it points to the secret basic thought behind treason. The German word *verraten*, to betray, etymologically has the root meaning "to reach a decision to undo someone." This someone is no other than the one who holds power.

7. THE RULER TABOO AND ITS
   DOUBLE MEANING

The archaic and irrational kernel of treason is a magic prohibition whose source has to be sought beyond all written laws in the ruler taboo. The "violation" of this taboo finds very clear expression in the Roman word for treason: *laesa*.[3]

Taboo is, as we know, a prohibition against touching. The person to whom it is attached may not be touched, is therefore protected against all aggression. The actual accomplishment of the taboo however lies in its double meaning. The ruler taboo not only protects the ruler from the ruled, but also the ruled from the ruler. "He must not only be guarded, he must also be guarded against."[4] This twin purpose is achieved by means of a highly complicated system of rules. What is admirable in these limitations is their complete symmetry and mutuality.

This taboo constitutes the prerequisite of the possibility of ruling per se, which is proved by the extreme sanctions that go with it. They alone guarantee the security of the ruler, as well as of his subjects, and neutralize the deadly threat in their fear of each other.

The ruler's *mana*, a magic "charge" which is the raison d'être for the taboo and supposedly makes touching dangerous, is to be regarded as the actual substance of his power. This *mana*, like an electric potential, allows of gradations and therefore of intermediaries between the ruler and the ruled. Thus a subchief or lesser adviser with lesser *mana* can touch the ruler without danger to himself and can himself afford to be touched by underlings. This conception allows the creation of hierarchies. One characteristic of a taboo is its transferability: it is, so to speak, infectious. What the ruler has touched becomes itself taboo. What counts is the principle of contiguity, something that, in any case, is a primary trait of magical thought. Freud has pointed out its close resemblance to association. This has remained the determining principle of treason to this day. We encounter it in the principle of *guilt by association* and invariably in the laws which deal with treason.

8. TREASON AS SACRILEGE

The relationship between the ruler and his subjects changes with the birth of the high religions. There exists a particular relationship between gods and kings of which the ruled do not partake. *Mana* is replaced by consecration; might becomes sacred; violating it verges on sacrilege. In Roman imperial law treason and sacrilege were already two aspects of one and the same phenomenon; they are called *laesa maiestas* and *laesa maiestas divina*. The automatic sanction accompanying the taboo, which revenges its violation, is replaced by persecution through the worldly organs. The identification of sovereignty with divinity, which goes far and beyond the "By God's Grace" of absolutism, leads to the point where treason and blasphemy become one and the same thing: in classic Roman law the profession of faith in Christianity was regarded as *crimen maiestatis*, that is, as treason.

In other words, the wrong opinion is enough to violate the ruling majesty. The importance of this development is self-evident. Simultaneously, the religious consecration of power endangers the greatest achievement of the ruler taboo, which lies in its double meaning. A remnant of it is retained in the concept of loyalty, still deemed to be a reciprocal relationship. Institutionally, it finds expression in the oath which only makes sense as long as it is kept by both parties. The double sense of the taboo is maintained under conditions as they obtained for a long time in the feudal system: the feudal lord was just as capable of treason as his vassal, and if he broke the oath he was, in principle, threatened with the same sanctions as his vassal. However, the more the sacredness of a sacred rule is consolidated, the less reciprocity appears necessary. Its erosion becomes progressively greater, a process which can be observed down to the smallest detail in the laws. The subjects of treason now are the people, its object the ruler. A reversal of this relationship has become almost legally unthinkable, it can only be theoretically imagined. The archaic taboo that imbues treason has turned into a pure implement of sovereign rule.

9. UNCERTAINTY AND INFECTION

"A government only needs to leave uncertain what treason is and it becomes despotic."[5] If one takes this Montesquieu observation at its word, one will scarcely find a government devoid of despotic traits. The concept of treason contained the tendency toward rank proliferation from its very beginning, that is, in its very taboo character which constituted the effectiveness of the prohibition. Simultaneously, it allows the arbitrary spread of the indicated crime through transference and infection. Its indeterminacy is not accidental. Rather, it represents the treason taboo's usefulness in the hands of rulers. Roman law already contains its core—the prohibition against killing the ruler—which is overgrown to such an extent by secondary and tertiary considerations that it has become nearly invisible. At the time of Justinian treason not only included all acts against the honor and security of the Roman people, but also desertion, criticism of the succession, the occupation of public places, the freeing of prisoners, the falsification of public documents, and the acceptance of illegal oaths. Intention was sufficient for a guilty verdict; traitors were beheaded. The oilspot-like spreading of the definition of treason finally led jurists to codify what did *not* constitute treason. Someone was *not* a traitor who restored an emperor's weatherbeaten statue, who melted down an unconsecrated metal statue, who unintentionally tossed a stone at such a statue.

Holding treasonable convictions was an even greater crime.

It spread over all of Europe and led to monstrous results already in the late Middle Ages and in the Renaissance. Henry VIII of England, for example, had two daughters who had claims to the throne. Englishmen became guilty of high treason, according to the law of 1534, by doubting Mary's claim or considering Elizabeth's justified; according to a law of 1536, to support either of these claims was treason; and finally, according to the law of 1543, to doubt either one of these claims.

The treason taboo is treated in a completely modern manner in the above instance: the ruler defines arbitrarily and one-sidedly who is to be considered a traitor. This method corresponds precisely to the procedure of our present-day rulers, who just as arbitrarily determine what deviations from official doctrine are to be regarded as treasonable. Treason is, as it were, imposed on the traitor without any act on his part; the victim becomes an "objective opponent," in the language of Stalinism.[6] The circle of these "objective traitors" can not only be immeasurably enlarged by means of new definitions of the crime; it also enlarges itself of its own accord through the taboo principle of infection. Not only relatives and acquaintances of the traitor are considered "inadmissible," "security risks," potential traitors, but also everyone who has knowledge of the treasonable crime or suspects it or fails to denounce the culprit. The magic "infectious" character of the crime becomes clearly apparent in the term "contact person." The advantage of the taboo as an instrument for ruling, and not just as an avoidable side effect or symptom of degeneration, consists of its capacity to make everyone a potential traitor and every action potentially traitorous.

10. PARANOID STRUCTURE

The indiscriminate growth of treason crimes and the bestial sanctions—from disembowelment of living persons and drawing and quartering customary during the Christian Middle

Ages, to the "special treatment" in modern concentration camps—indicate the degree to which rulers regard their domain as threatened. As the reciprocity of the old taboo falls into disuse, so does their sense of security become undermined. Because every act of their subjects seems a threat, they reply with a counter threat to punish each act, no matter what, and every possible belief as treason. Loyalty cannot be presumed among his subjects when it is alien to the ruler himself. The ruler considers himself constantly pursued, which lends him the justification to pursue all others at all times: the consequence is a vicious circle.

This pattern of treason and the war against it manifests a conformation we recognize from psychiatry, the structure of paranoia. A classic example of this structure is provided by the report of the Arab scholar Ibn Batuta from his stay at the court of the Sultan of Dehli, Mohammed Tughlak. He recounts the following arguments by the ruler: "Today there are far more evil and unruly people than there used to be. I punish them as soon as I have the slightest suspicion or presumption of their rebellious and traitorous intention, and the slightest act of disobedience I punish by death. I will continue to do this until the people start to behave decently and give up rebellion and disobedience . . . I punish the people because they all suddenly became my enemies and opponents."[7]

By the logic of paranoia no one is innocent, there are only those who haven't yet been convicted of treason—that is, masked traitors. Paranoia senses conspiracies everywhere: it becomes only a question of exposing them, "of tearing the masks off their faces." That is the language of Hitler's *Völkische Beobachter*, of today's Chinese press, and the language of fanatic anticommunism.

What is required to fight the "world conspiracies" of the paranoid delusionary system are counterconspiracies. Wherever the treason taboo is employed as a means for ruling, an organized system of informers makes its appearance. The profession of the informer, the *delator*, came into existence in Rome at the time of Tiberius. The corresponding modern version is the secret police, which becomes *the* central political organ as the number of treasonable acts and therefore the number of potential traitors increases.

11. PROJECTION

Such an interpretation of treason meets with the objection that it neglects the role of the enemy. Indeed, the enemy appears very early, in the legal codes which refer to treason, as the interested third party who benefits from the crime; yes, one can say that the reference to the outside enemy is indispensable for these laws. Moreover, the term is ascribed without regard for what is probable: thus, in the Union of South Africa every act directed against the government's apartheid policy is considered high treason; this interdiction is justified by reference to the Soviet Union, for whose benefit—yes, in whose service—this treasonable act is being committed. On the other hand, Stalin's regime interpreted every oppositional act as treason for the benefit and in the service of the capitalist powers. The German "stab in the back" legend after World War I, which was the psychological prerequisite for many treason trials during the Weimar Republic, had a similar function. Of course, there is nothing easier to find than some third party to cheer any internal criticism and each opposition move, and therefore every country always has a plethora of "enemies" from all sorts of other countries. That is the logic of paranoia.

The psychic mechanism at work here is called *projection*. The unresolved conflict between the ruler and his subject is shifted to the outside opponent; the threat to the rule from inside is transposed outside. It is well known the role that projection plays during the start of wars, and without projection the treason taboo would collapse. As soon as one has seen through this projection, it turns out that the enemy whom it conjures up is none other than the internal one. The only thing that is feared and called treason is the threat to the rule which emanates from the subjects themselves. High treason is nothing but the juristic name for revolution.

12. REVOLUTION AND TREASON

The magic infectious power of the treason taboo also extends to those who break it. Everywhere the history of revolutionary conspiracy shows the traces of this infection. The oath by means of which the ruler seeks to protect himself against treason corresponds to the oath which the conspirators swear. The revolutionaries fight a traitor in their own ranks more relentlessly than their actual enemy. Thus the paranoid structure of the old order is transposed onto the new one even before it has been erected. The conspiracies of Netchajev and the Fighting Organization of the Social Revolutionaries offers an excellent illustration of this. Their structural similarities to their opponent, the secret police, are striking; they are what makes possible a double game like that of Asev, who remained unrecognized as a traitor for the very reason that the habits of revolutionary activity resembled those of the counterrevolution to the point where both became practically indistinguishable from one another.

13. NEW TREASON TABOOS

After the revolution is victorious its achievements are secured against the *ancien régime* in the same manner as the *ancien régime* initially secured itself against the revolution. The treason taboo thus is not removed, but only reversed, a process during which, however, the central figure to whom one could be traitorous vanishes. The *mana* of the sovereign ruler is transferred to abstract "values," "goods," doctrines and their administrators, the anonymous state apparatus. The result is an enormous extension of potential treason crimes. Aspects of the taboo which were of secondary importance until now move into the foreground: the sovereignty and the territorial integrity of the national state, for example. Completely new touch prohibitions are added. The private ownership of the means of production, the party "line," the socialist achievement, the interests of a "race" or a class are now considered untouchable. The treason taboo serves in each instance whatever rule has been established.

Bourgeois democracy, with its rules about betraying the constitution, made an attempt to reestablish the original reciprocity of the treason taboo. These regulations (paragraph 89 of the penal code of the Federal Republic of Germany) count on the possibility that a state apparatus itself can become traitorous and place a taboo on certain constitutional guarantees against intrusion by the rulers themselves. Meanwhile, scarcely half a dozen of the more than 150,000 investigations launched by the states attorneys of the Federal Republic for crimes against the state and treasonable acts have been against government politicians.[8] For a guilty verdict of high treason, it suffices if a worker distributes communist leaflets; but when an officeholding minister of the interior declares before parliament that the government is moving outside the bounds of legality, that does not constitute sufficient grounds. Someone who asks *Bundeswehr* soldiers to refuse to service atomic weapons can be prosecuted for "treasonable desiccation of the constitution." Four Adenauer government ministers, on the other hand, became trustees of an organization (The Occidental Academy) which openly supported the removal of parliamentary democracy; no one took them to task. The reciprocity of the taboo therefore remains fictitious, at least in West Germany. In fact, the interdiction of treason continues to serve as the one-sided instrument of the rulers.

14. THE STATE SECRET

The prohibition against delivering secrets to a foreign power is not part of the old core of the law against treason. This very aspect, which stands official propaganda in such useful stead, is completely peripheral and is based on a much later extension of the concept of treason. It plays no role in the older laws. In Anglo-Saxon law the betrayal of state secrets isn't called treason at all; the crime does not fall under the *Treason Act* but under the *Official Secrets Act* of 1889. *State secret* and *espionage* as legal concepts are inventions of the late nineteenth century. They were born out of the spirit of imperialism. Their victorious march begins in 1894 with the Dreyfus affair.

Since that time the state secret has been raised to an instrument for ruling of the first rank. Its productivity is nearly unlimited. Its success and its arbitrariness derive from the fact that the magic conceptions which have always been part and parcel of the treason taboo are joined in a single complex. The old *mana* of the chiefs and priest-kings objectifies itself once more in the state secret—palpable and immaterial at the same time; this is the secret of power per se. Its presence evokes shudders of respect, its exposure hysterical outrage. No longer is there need of aggression for violation of the taboo; a question suffices. That is a degree of remoteness the likes of which no ruler has ever enjoyed before. The *mana* of the state secret communicates itself to its bearers and immunizes them, each according to the degree of his initiation, against the question; therefore they are free not to answer and, in the real sense of the word, are irresponsible. How many state secrets someone knows becomes the measure of his rank and his privilege in a finely articulated hierarchy. The mass of the governed is without secrets; that is, it has no right to partake of power, to criticize it and watch over it.

15. UNCERTAINTY AND INFECTIOUSNESS OF THE SECRET TABOO

Part of the state secret's magic character is that it allows of no definition. This uncertainty, indeterminability, which was always peculiar to the treason taboo is not merely an external feature; it constitutes its essence. At first a simple rubber stamp will do to declare something secret. But even this is not absolutely necessary and by no means binding. German law, for example, is being quite consistent in assuming that the official designation does not completely guarantee the character of the secret; something that lacks it can at any time, even retroactively, be made secret by means of a simple and unilateral government act. Nor is the taboo limited to state organs such as the government apparatus or the military: according to German law, a party's foreign policy program can also be considered secret, even its "mood." According to the so-called mosaic theory, such a secret can moreover be created in a certain sense through spontaneous generation by means of the simple compilation of information, none of which is secret by itself.

The infectiousness of the secret taboo is unlimited. It is transferred onto each and every thing that comes into contact with it. The one who betrays the secret infects his "contact persons" with it. The court action against him itself becomes secret in turn. Organizations that protect secret matters go underground themselves. Someone who carries secrets can be considered secret, as can someone who doesn't. *But what is primarily secret is what is a secret and what isn't; that is perhaps the actual state secret.* In German law it is guarded by means of a particular protective rule which one may regard as the culmination of the entire system. It threatens to penalize whoever "intentionally publicizes as true or genuine or lets get into unauthorized hands facts, objects, or news about them which are false, falsified or untrue but which if they were genuine and true *would* be state secrets."

In other words, what is liable to be punished here is the betrayal of state secrets which are nothing of the kind; it suffices that they might be. The taboo infects its negation. With this step the system is letter-perfect. If something (p) is the case, not only is giving out information about it treason (q), but also giving out its negation (q̄) is treason. If something isn't the case (p̄), the situation is the same: (q̄) as well as (q) are considered treason. With the sophistic logical precision of the calculus of propositions every imaginable utterance about arbitrarily determined cases is prohibited.

16. PROJECTION, ONCE AGAIN

The logic of paranoia is manifested with clinical purity in the delusionary system which is developed out of the secret taboo. The "tapping of thoughts," the aura of secretiveness by which the patient feels surrounded, the feeling of being watched and overheard, are classic features of the physiognomy of this illness. Therefore the state secret is more useful than any personal taboo as a crystallizing agent for a delusionary system. This system owes its enormous success to a mechanism with which we have already become familiar, namely projection.

In every instance is the secret taboo based on and justified by the existence of an external enemy. This enemy is portrayed as boundlessly ignorant and craving for knowledge; he is opposed by an appeal to national solidarity. The model situation which lies in back of this is war. Only in the military secret does the state secret come into full flower. Since war is posited a priori as a permanent and total condition, any matter at all may be subsumed under military categories: vis-à-vis the enemy, everything has to be considered secret and every citizen a potential traitor.

What this principle accomplishes in internal politics is obvious: it renders taboo the military as an instrument of the rulers and removes it from control by the subjects. Since modern war reaches into every aspect of life and can no longer be isolated from social existence, all imaginable secrets also have military character, no matter whether it is a question of weapons or food supplies, the economic conditions or the civilian population's "frame of mind."

Those who establish the secret and treason taboos doubtless do so with a clear conscience and the best of intentions. Not only those for whom it is intended, but its authors too, fall victim to the delusionary system. What constitutes the achievement of the system is that those who employ this form of projection cannot see through it. One cannot expect an administrator to have greater insight into the delusionary aspect of the taboo than a paranoid into his illness. Each attempt to enlighten him must fail for this very reason; no insight, no matter how lucid, into the unreality of their convictions can convince them. The perception that the secret taboo is by no means meant for the external but invariably for the internal population can therefore expect to meet with violent objections. For this there is no lack of evidence.

First of all, informing the public is usually made commensurate with betrayal to the external enemy. At any event, according to German law it is irrelevant whether the secret was known to the enemy at time of publication or not. Yes, even the highest court of the Weimar Republic punished the reprinting of foreign newspaper comments about internal German conditions. And with that it merely expressed the actual sense of the taboo: the keeping secret of political matters not from the external but from the internal enemy, namely the public. The trials of Dreyfus, Ebert, and Ossietzky, as well as the espionage trials in Stalinist Russia and the treason trials of the German resistance in the Third Reich, were exclusively directed against internal political enemies.

17. THE MYTHOLOGY OF ESPIONAGE

During World War II Goebbels began a propaganda campaign in Germany which stood under the motto: "Watch out! The enemy is listening!" On all walls and wherever else one could post bills there appeared a Black Man on a yellow background. This figure is the phantom of espionage. Like other taboo-protected phantoms, such as sovereignty, the less reality it possesses the more zealously is it conjured up. In not a single modern war has espionage or the betrayal of secrets played a decisive role of any kind. Hitler's defeat is not due to ransacked wastepaper baskets or notes written with invisible ink. Mata Hari and the secret courier in the Orient Express belong to the realm of political yellow journalism. The traditional spy legends flesh up the delusions of the official taboo, popularize them, and make them acceptable.

Espionage in this sense has an exclusively mythological function: it helps preserve the internal political taboo of the state secret. If it ever contained a trace of reality, it has long since become an anachronism. It has nothing whatever in common with the kind of work that the information services of the superpowers are capable of. This work is part of regular military routine, is so to speak a fourth branch of the service. Significantly, it is handled in an atmosphere of extreme sobriety. The opponents maintain certain rules of the game, so that one can almost speak of "playing into each other's hands" on the part of the opposing services, which of course maintain constant contact with each other. For example, if one takes a prisoner, one exchanges him at the first opportune moment. Hysterical and paranoid features are entirely absent. Men who perform this kind of work have perfectly normal, respected jobs. The leading heads of these information, defense, and planning staffs are usually firmly convinced that their mutual efforts serve solely the keeping of the peace.

The primary data which these services process derive almost exclusively from two sources: first of all from the normal internal flow of information of a modern industrial society which cannot be suppressed without doing grave harm to the society itself, and secondly as a result of technological observation of the opponent by means of airplanes and satellites. Compared to this, bedtime secrets and hidden microphones no longer provide much worthwhile information. Coinciding with this is the appearance of the expert, who has replaced the spy with dark glasses: they are mostly mathematicians, statisticians, game theorists, and other data-processing experts. The concept of the secret has no room in their methodical work; each side not only knows precisely what the other side is doing, it also knows that this knowledge is based on reciprocity.

Besides, the strategy of deterrence which applies undisputed throughout the world today leads to a situation where the newest state of armament (that is, *the* military secret par excellence) has to be ostentatiously demonstrated to the opponent so as to be effective. In this respect this strategy finds itself in complete agreement with extreme pacifist theories: their effectiveness is based on the elimination of the secret.

18. TREASON AS CIRCUMSTANTIAL EVIDENCE

One can therefore draw two opposite conclusions from the threat of total war: either that everything is a state secret or that state secrets no longer exist. In a certain sense both sentences mean the same thing; the first changes into the second, but with the following result: the betrayal of such secrets is prosecuted ever more ruthlessly the more eagerly statesmen proclaim them. The absurdity of this situation is apparent; but the very delusionary character of the taboo prevents its dissolution. It cannot be combined with genuine democracy. Politics has to be conducted out in the open. If the political freedoms as they are guaranteed in the constitutions have any meaning, that meaning lies here.

The projections which the great taboo invokes implode before everyone's eyes. The kind of treatment accorded to those who dare touch it becomes a telling verdict on the internal conditions of the respective country. The more state secrets a government guards, the more it has to hide from those it pretends to represent. The more treason taboos it erects, the more it despises and fears the citizens of its own country, and the more it stinks.

Translated by Michael Roloff

Reflections Before a Glass Cage

1. DEFINITIONS

We know what a crime is, and yet we don't. The *Encyclopedia Britannica* defines it in the following way:

> (lat. *crimen*, accusation), the general term for offences against the criminal law (q.v.). Crime has been defined as "a failure or refusal to live up to the standard of conduct deemed binding by the rest of the community." Sir James Stephen described it as "some act of omission in respect of which legal punishment may be inflicted on the person who is in default whether by acting or omitting to act."[1]

Thomas Hobbes wrote in a similar vein three hundred years ago: "A crime is a sin, consisting in the committing, by deed or word, of that which the law forbiddeth, or the omission of what it has commanded."[2]

The tautological structure of these sentences is manifest, and like all tautologies they are reversible: what is punished is a crime, what is a crime is punished; everything deserving of punishment is punishable and vice versa. The linguistic model of such definitions can be found in the Biblical sentence: "I am the one I am." Such sentences place the legislator above reason and above argument, and the codified law acquires this syntactical attitude for itself. The German penal code simply says: "An act threatened with imprisonment of five or more years is a crime."

Defining concepts in such a way as to eliminate all discussion has definite advantages, because it relieves legal practice once and for all of the problem of what constitutes a crime, relegating it forthwith to the realm of theory as an amusement for particularly esoteric minds. A good deal of thought has been given, in seminars, to "the material concept of crime," but little of any validity has been discovered. No wonder then that the penal codes aren't a consistent system but at best a heterogeneous, frequently bizarre assemblage of historically deposited orders to protect the most varied kinds of legal prerogatives and interests, codified concepts of taboos and morality, and rules of the game which are value-free only from a purely pragmatic viewpoint.

Besides, legal scholars find themselves in a perfectly common bind: the more general and more fundamental something is, the less distinct its concept tends to be. No one (or everyone) can say what a nation is (but everyone in his way). Everyone knows what money is, and some people know how to handle it; the economists, however, can't agree on what it is. What is health? Medicine makes educated guesses. What is death? Biologists are full of suggestions.

In confusing cases such as these, it is perhaps best to go on the street and ask the first ten persons what they think. The most frequent reply will not be a definition but an example which, moreover, is strikingly often the same: "A crime, for example, is a murder." The frequency of this reply bears no relationship to criminal statistics, where entirely different infractions play the chief role. Although comparatively rare, murder plays a key role in the general public consciousness. It is due to the power of its example that one begins to understand the very nature of crime.

Crime novel and crime film, as reflections of this general consciousness, confirm that murder occupies a central role in it—yes, becomes synonymous with crime as such.

From its punishment, according to the *lex talionis*, one also gathers that murder is the actual and the oldest capital crime per se: certainly, the oldest and most severe penalty—and until deep into the Middle Ages also the chief penalty—is the death penalty which reflects what it wants to revenge, and that is murder.

2. NATURAL HISTORY OF CRIME

We have no certain knowledge of the ethnological origin of crime. Even the most primitive societies that are open to observation have "lawbreakers," even, that is, when they lack codified rules. Murder plays a significant role in the oldest documents of human society. Since the primordial condition of society is nowhere ascertainable, every attempt to discover its natural history must remain hypothetical. However, we have a number of aids available: biological behavior studies (which, however, only allow limited inferences for human behavior), ethnology, the study of myths, as well as psychoanalysis.

Sigmund Freud provides us with the classical description of the "original crime." It begins with Darwin's primal horde: "A violent, jealous father who keeps all women for himself and drives out the growing sons." The crime itself is described in the following way:

> One day the brothers who had been driven out banded together, killed and devoured the father, and thus put an end to the horde. United they dared and accomplished what had been impossible for them alone. . . . The violent original father had certainly been the envied and feared model of each member of the tribe of brothers. Their act of devouring completed their identification with him; each of them acquired a piece of his strength. The totem meal, perhaps humanity's first feast, would be the repetition and the memorial celebration of this memorable criminal act which was the beginning of so many things: the social organizations, the ethical limitations, and religion.[3]

This description is met with the facile objection that one can't speak of a crime where there is no law, but such a consideration is legalistic, not philosophical, and misses the point. Such a pseudo-objection resembles the question, which came first, the chicken or the egg? Law can only be defined by injustice, at its limit, to be recognized as law; the "ethical limitations" can only be taught as a reply to a challenge. And in that sense the original crime is undoubtedly a creative act. (Walter Benjamin treats of its legislative power in *Zur Kritik der Gewalt*.)

This hypothesis, which Freud established in his essay "The Infantile Return to Totemism," is both famous and unknown— and for a good reason. Freud had few illusions about the resistance which would meet his attempt "to trace back our cultural heritage, of which we are justly proud, to a horrible crime which is an insult to all our feelings." Aside from a number of specialists, people did not so much oppose his "scientific myth" as simply ignore it.[4] It is no longer the sexual taboos which block reception of Freud's theses, as in the thirties, but their social and political consequences. The more manifest these become in history, the more thoroughly they are repressed.

3. POLITICS AND MURDER

If we are to give credence to Freud, the original political act thus coincides with the original crime. An ancient, intimate, and dark connection exists between murder and politics, and it is retained in the basic structure of all sovereignty to date. For power is exercised by those who can have their underlings killed. The ruler is the "survivor." This definition is Elias Canetti's, who has provided us with an excellent phenomenology of sovereignty.[5]

To this day the language of politics reflects the criminal act of its origin. Even in the most harmless and civilized election campaign, one candidate "beats" the other (which actually means beats him to death); a government is "toppled" (to die); a minister is "shot down." The action that such expressions symbolically retain unfolds and realizes itself in extreme social situations. No revolution can do without killing the previous ruler. It has to break the taboo which forbids the underlings to touch him; for "only someone who has proved capable of transgressing such a prohibition has acquired the character of the forbidden."[6] The *mana* of the killed ruler is transferred to his murderers. All revolutions to date have infected themselves with the prerevolutionary conditions and have inherited the basic structure against which they fought.

4. CONTRADICTION

Even the more "progressive," "civilized" constitutions allow for the killing of people, and permit it—but only in "extreme" cases, such as war or revolutionary situations. In other respects the basic structure of the government remains concealed. Any command is still a "suspended death sentence," now as then (Canetti). But this verdict is expressed only as an infinitely mediated threat, it only exists virtually;[7] and throughout history we find this limitation institutionally anchored in the body of laws.

Every philosophy of law to date has sought to resolve the contradiction at the root of this law, which is that this law, like every social order, is based on the original crime, that it was created by means of injustice. For every body of laws to date simultaneously protects against the ruler and is his instrument. Perhaps the entire history of law can be interpreted as its removal from the political sphere. This immense process can only be unravelled by someone with the calling for it; yet it seems as though it has been unable to resolve the inner contradictions at its root. The separation of the executive from the legislative and judiciary powers; the independence and permanence of the judge; the separation of the state's attorney's office from the court and its institutionalization as a "party"; the multifarious procedural safeguards during a trial —all of these mediations are invaluable, but nonetheless the ruler always remains the supreme judge; and the judge, the impartial arbitrator, always stands in the service of the state.

The ambiguous nature of the legal order is most clearly discernible from the problematic nature of punishment. If every command is a "suspended death sentence," then punishment constitutes its execution, no matter in how attenuated a form. Death is the oldest, most powerful, the actual punishment. If the death penalty is taken away, the duty and right of the state to mete out punishment moves from the magic darkness of religious conceptions into the field of rational reflection. Once the death penalty is questioned, punishment as such becomes questionable; and that is why opinions and constitutions diverge at this point, and this alone explains the passion with which the question of the death penalty is argued. What nourishes this quarrel is neither the possibility of a miscarriage of justice nor simple pity for the condemned, not to mention the intention to protect society from the criminal. No matter what the argument of those who call for the death penalty, a hysterical undertone gives evidence of their longing for an all-powerful authority with which they can identify. What is forbidden to the individual—that is, to kill —is permitted to him as a member of the collective, through the execution. Therefore its characteristic mystique: that of a ritual. It is completely consistent with this mystique that the death penalty used to be performed in public: killing in the name of everyone can only occur in public, because then everyone partakes in it; the hangman is only our deputy.

If thought through to its ultimate consequence, the removal of the death penalty would change the nature of the state; it would be the anticipation of a social order from which we are far removed, because it deprives the state of the permission to decide the death or life of the individual. This power, however, constitutes the actual heart of sovereignty.

5. SOVEREIGNTY

"Sovereignty in the judicial sense," wrote the German historian Heinrich von Treitschke, "the complete independence of the state from any other power on earth, constitutes the state's nature to such an extent that one can say that it represents the very criterion of the state."[8] The power of this concept remains unbroken, although it is obvious that such kind of sovereignty has never existed. It follows from this conception of the state that it is above and beyond any legal order, and anyone who maintains this idea can never believe in the existence of international law. National sovereignty and international law are mutually exclusive.

A reference work published in 1959 maintains quite appropriately that "it is very doubtful whether such a thing as international law actually exists . . . the so-called 'international law' has limited itself to date essentially to the development of diplomatic rules for the exchange of declarations and rules for the eventuality of war. . . . There exists no binding social norm between states as yet."[9]

The purest way in which a state expresses its sovereignty, as Treitschke understands this word, is in its internal politics, in the intercourse with its individual antagonist, by means of the death penalty; in foreign politics, in its relationship with other states, this sovereignty is expressed by means of war. If the state, as the overlord of the legal order, is permitted to kill one individual, it is also permitted to kill many or if necessary everyone, in its and its people's name, and to make the execution of this sovereign act a duty to its citizens.

Sigmund Freud wrote of World War I:

> In this war the individual member of a state can notice with horror what had perhaps occurred to him already in peacetime: that the state has forbidden all acts of injustice to him not because it wants to eliminate injustice but because it wants to monopolize it like salt and tobacco. The war-making state allows itself every injustice, every act of violence which would dishonor the individual. . . . One should not interject that the state cannot do without committing injustice because this would put it at a disadvantage. The obedience of ethical norms and the relinquishment of the use of brute power is usually very disadvantageous to the individual too.[10]

What surprises us even more than the violence which the states unleashed during World War I is the astonishment of the bourgeois world in face of its accomplishments and its catastrophe. The simplest reflection shows that private murder throughout history has never been comparable to public murder. All individual acts of violence, from Cain to Landru, do not add up to the injustice caused by the Wars of Succession in eighteenth-century Europe alone or the sovereign actions of a colonial power during a single decade.

Such reflections of course are considered amateurish. At least, influential statesmen and influential jurists have never paid particular attention to them, and this reluctance is understandable. However, the connection between crime and politics has never been entirely forgotten. The nineteenth century, too, retained a sense of it. Pushed to the edge of consciousness, and therefore to the edge of society, the problem became the domain of outsiders. Anyone who, like Freud, paid attention to it found himself in mixed company, among the disadvantaged and exploited, among iconoclasts and oddballs, among peculiar holy men and sectarians of every ilk. The more self-confident a society feels of its foundations, the more it allows these outsiders to call them into question. The bourgeois nineteenth century throttled every armed attack on its form of society, but it allowed the most radical examination of its basic structure . . . as a pastime for world-improvers. It is not for nothing that, to this day, it is regarded as the ultimate folly to want to improve the world, whereas the contrary effort can always depend on meeting with a certain respect. Anyone who wants to take the lessons of World War II seriously is met with especial ridicule, which serves as repression: however, ridicule no longer kills, not by itself, as the rubber truncheons and police files, which are meant to assist it, go to prove.

6. EPOCH

Anyone wanting to know in what age he lives only needs to open the nearest newspaper. There he will find out that he lives in the age of synthetic fiber, tourism, professional sports, or of the theater of the absurd. The information industry has also reduced to this level the knowledge that we live in the age of Hiroshima and Auschwitz. Twenty years after our baptism with this phrase, it already sounds like a cliché. Valid sentences today become threadbare before they have had an opportunity to take full effect, and are treated like consumer articles which can be discarded at will and replaced by newer models. Everything that is said appears to be at the mercy of an artificial aging process; people believe they are done with a sentence once it has been scrapped. But it is easier to get rid of a consumer article than of a truth.

What happened in the 1940s does not age; instead of becoming more remote, it inches up on us and forces us to revise all human forms of thinking and of relating to each other; only at the price of mortal future danger to us and everyone else can we maintain our conceptions of justice and injustice, of crime and of state.

Although it is scarcely a recent discovery that the modern nation state and its adherents are capable of everything—the spokesmen of imperialism already announced this proudly in the nineteenth century—we now know that it is also technically capable of everything. The age-old connection between crime and politics, the internal contradictions of law, the delusionary conceptions of sovereignty must as a consequence become more and more prominent and become, literally, explosive.

Nothing can remain as it was and is. However, as everyone knows (at the price of suicide), the revision we are forced to make has hardly begun and already is about to be choked off by the highly specialized propaganda about "overcoming guilt." The reality of the name Auschwitz is to be exorcised as though it belonged only to the past, and even an exclusively national one at that—not a collective present and future. What assists in this development is a complicated ritual of inconsequential self-accusation, which wants to have done with an event that laid bare the roots of all politics to date (and that finally means: wants to forget) without drawing the consequences to which it forces the participants (and there are no nonparticipants). It is obvious that such an "overcoming" must remain sterile, that it cannot even heed the most superficial and most proximate consequences; not to speak of being able to eliminate the prerequisites which made the event possible in the first place.

The compulsive notion of sovereignty has undergone practically no revision at all. The "nature of the state" continues to consist of its "inability to endure a power higher than itself" (Treitschke); now as then, sovereignty of this kind continues to be "the criterion for the existence of the state," except that, fifteen years after the German defeat and the destruction of Hiroshima the criterion for this criterion has become—in the eyes of leading German politicians and military men—the power to dispose over nuclear weapons.

But this implement is the present and future of Auschwitz. How can one condemn the genocide of yesterday, or even try to "overcome" it, while carefully preparing with all scientific and industrial means at one's command the genocide of tomorrow? Every reason with which the parties have armed themselves from each other's respective ideological arsenal is struck out of its master's (and its servants') hands by the implement. It cannot serve as the defense of freedom and rights; rather, the very existence of the implement suspends all human rights; from the right to go for a walk, the right to found parties, to the right to work or eat. They all exist under its protection—that is, under its threat; exist only upon recall and become a mere exercise in mercy which can be revoked at any moment. Simultaneously the "implement" rescinds all political freedoms and only permits democracy under a proviso which gradually emaciates it. As the Cuban missile crisis demonstrated to the blindest, the bomb withdraws the genuine decisions once and for all from parliament and places it in the hands of a few individuals, each of whom is more powerful, and is able and is forced to make lonelier and more irrevocable decisions than any despot in history.

Every invocation of the strategy of deterrence is impotent.

The Nazis too, had their analogy. (Hannah Arendt, among others, has described it with all imaginable precision.) No less paranoid than the delusionary notion of the "Jewish world conspiracy." is the principle of an armaments race whose objective is too well known for anyone even to bother to inquire after it. The implement is not a weapon in class warfare; it is neither a capitalist nor a communist weapon; it is no weapon at all, just as little as the gas chamber.

Someone who wants to legislate or adjudicate finds himself in an odd position under conditions as they have prevailed for the past twenty years. This situation can be easily illustrated. There is no lack of examples.

7. FIRST EXAMPLE: ANIMAL PROTECTION

Statute about the killing and keeping of live fish and other cold-blooded animals, of January 14, 1936:

> # 2(1) Crabs, lobsters, and other crustaceans whose meat is designed for human consumption are to be killed, if possible, by being tossed singly into strongly boiling water. It is prohibited to put the animals into cold or lukewarm water and bring the water to a boil afterwards.

Telex Berlin Nr. 234 404 of November 9, 1938, to all Gestapo offices and headquarters:

> 1. VERY SHORTLY ACTIONS AGAINST JEWS, PARTICULARLY AGAINST SYNAGOGUES, WILL OCCUR IN ALL OF GERMANY. THESE ACTIONS ARE NOT TO BE INTERFERED WITH. . . . 3. PREPARATIONS ARE TO BE MADE FOR THE ARREST OF ROUGHLY 20 TO 30 THOUSAND JEWS IN THE REICH. PARTICULARLY WEALTHY JEWS ARE TO BE SELECTED. FURTHER INSTRUCTIONS WILL FOLLOW THIS NIGHT. . . .
> GESTAPO II. SIGNED: MÜLLER"[11]

Statute for the protection of wild plants and nonhuntable animals, of March 18, 1936:

16. (1) Property owners, those permitted the use of property, or their representatives are permitted to catch cats and take them into custody during the period of March 15 to August 15 and as long as snow covers the ground if the cats are found in gardens, orchards, cemeteries, parks and similar grounds. Cats taken into custody are to be properly cared for. . . .

Telex Warsaw Nr. 663/43 of May 24, 1943, to the SS and Police Chief/East:

RE NUMBER 1. OF THE 56,065 JEWS SEIZED SO FAR, ROUGHLY 7000 HAVE BEEN DESTROYED IN WAKE OF THE ACTION IN THE FORMER JEWISH QUARTER. 6929 JEWS WERE DESTROYED BY MEANS OF TRANSPORT TO T. II, SO THAT A TOTAL OF 13,929 JEWS HAVE BEEN DESTROYED. ABOVE AND BEYOND THE FIGURE OF 56,065, ROUGHLY FIVE TO SIX THOUSAND JEWS WERE DESTROYED THROUGH DETONATION AND FIRE. . . .
THE SS AND POLICE CHIEF IN THE WARSAW DISTRICT. SIGNED: STROOP.[12]

From Heinrich Himmler's conversation with his masseur:

"Herr Karsten, how can you possibly shoot out of ambush at the poor animals which are grazing so innocently, defenselessly and unawares at the edge of the woods? If you take the right view of your action, it is murder pure and simple. Nature is very beautiful, and after all, every animal has a right to live. It is this point of view which I admire so much in our ancestors. Respect for animals is something you find in all Indo-Germanic people. It interested me terribly to hear the other day that Buddhist monks still wear little bells when they walk through the forest, so that the animals on whom they might step have a chance to get out of the way. But here everyone steps on worms and snails without giving it a second thought."[13]

Speech by Heinrich Himmler to the SS Group Leaders in Posen, on October 3, 1943:

". . . most of you will know what it means when you see one hundred corpses lying in one spot, three hundred, or a thousand. To have seen this through to the end and—aside from exceptions of human weakness—to have remained decent, that is what has made us hard. This is an unwritten and never to be written page of honor in the annals of our history."[14]

Statute for the protection of wild plants and nonhuntable animals:

No. 23 (I) For the protection of the remaining nonhuntable animals it is prohibited:
1. To catch them en masse without a reasonable or justified purpose or to kill them en masse.

8. SECOND EXAMPLE—GAME PLAN

In April, 1961, the trial of the former Obersturmbannführer A. Eichmann opened at a court in Jerusalem. The indictment did not say that the accused had personally operated the gas chambers, but that Eichmann conscientiously and in detail *planned* the murder of 6 million people.

Also in the year 1961, in Princeton, New Jersey, there appeared a work by the mathematician, physicist, and military theoretician Herman Kahn, *On Thermonuclear War*. This work contains the following table:

Tragic but distinguishable postwar statistics.

DEAD:	ECONOMIC RECUPERATION
2,000,000	1 year
5,000,000	2 years
10,000,000	5 years
20,000,000	10 years
40,000,000	20 years
80,000,000	50 years
160,000,000	100 years

Will the survivors envy the dead?[15]

Objective investigations show that the sum of human tragedy (sic) would rise considerably in the postwar period, but this rise would not exclude the possibility of a normal happy existence for the majority of survivors and their progeny.[16]

But will the survivors be in a position to lead the kind of life Americans are used to living? That is with cars, country homes, iceboxes, etc.? No one can say for sure, but I believe that even if we make no preparation for our recovery—disregarding the acquisition of radiation detection equipment, the distribution of handbooks and the practice of certain counter measures—the country would get back on its feet fairly quickly.

[The death of embryos] is of limited significance. . . . Presumably there will be five million such cases during the first generation, and 100 million in the course of subsequent generations. I regard the last-named figure as not all that serious, disregarding that minority of cases of obvious abortions or stillbirths. However that may be, humanity is so fertile that a slight decrease of this fertility does not need to be taken that seriously, not even by the individuals affected.

[What price] should the Russians be made to pay as punishment for their aggression? I have discussed this question with many Americans, and after talking for about a quarter of an hour they usually arrive at an acceptable price of between ten and sixty million. Usually one agrees on a figure somewhat closer to the higher of the two figures. . . . The ways and means how the upper limit seems to be reached is rather interesting. Namely, one mentions a third of the total population of a country, in other words something less than half.

A. Eichmann was condemned to death in December, 1961, and was hanged.

H. Kahn is advisory member of the Scientific Advisory Committee of the U.S. Air Force, of the technical committee of the Atomic Energy Commission, evaluator for the office of Civil Defense, and head of the Hudson Institute in White Plains, N.Y., which provides expert opinions for the U.S. military planning. Kahn is married, has two children, and is known as a gourmet.

A question: can one compare K. and E.? Is there such a

thing as the "objective investigation" of "the sum of human tragedy"? What moral cogency has a language which can call 6o million killed "an acceptable price"? Can genocide be the object of "impartial observation and calculation"? Where lies the difference between observation and planning, between calculation and preparation? Do such differences exist? Can one prevent genocide by planning it? Can prevention and planning be entrusted to "experts"? To whom do these experts offer their services? Does their advice have any consequences? Do their predispositions play a role? Who gave them their orders, who judges them?

9. THIRD EXAMPLE—
UNDERSTANDABLE EXCITEMENT

How many people are prepared to obey, unconditionally and of their own accord, even when they know that the execution of an order will put another person to considerable pain?

Setup for an experiment: Two rooms, with a switchboard in one and an electric chair in the other. It is explained to subject A that an experiment is being conducted to find out to what degree an adult's capacity to memorize can be increased by administering corporal punishment. A is asked to take over the role of the tester while someone else assumes the role of the learner. The leader of the experiment places a memory test in front of B and fastens him onto the electric chair in front of A's eyes. A goes to the adjacent room with the switchboard, where he turns a lever whenever B makes a mistake. The shocks are graded according to a scale which is attached to the implement that administers the punishment. The chastisement begins with a 15-volt shock and is increased with each memorization mistake that B makes. At the twentieth shock, which has a power of 300 volts, B drums against the wall. At 375 volts a warning lights up on the switchboard: "Danger. Heavy shocks." The last lever, for 435 and 450 volts, merely has the designation XXX. The arrangement of the experiment is fictitious. There is no connection between the switchboard and the electric chair; the electrodes are not activated. The person in the chair only simulates his reactions, something the person administering the test cannot know: he finds himself in the role of a genuine torturer.

A series of experiments of this kind were conducted in 1963 at Yale University under the guidance of the psychologist Dr. Stanley Milgram. The subjects were volunteers, all of them citizens in good standing; 65 percent of the guinea pigs performed all the orders the leader of the experiment gave them and worked all levers according to instructions.[17]

In 1964 in Kempten in the Allgäu (Bavaria) the former Feldwebel L. Scherer was put on trial. He was accused of having captured fifteen men, women, and children whom he encountered while searching a forest in the Brjansk region during World War II, locking them in a wooden shed, setting fire to the shed, and throwing hand grenades into it. Professor Maurach of the University of Munich presented the court with expert testimony to the effect that the verdict would have to take account of the defendant's "boiling excitement" while he committed these acts. Maurach did not regard the killing of fifteen men, women, and children "illegal." The court delivered a not-guilty verdict; the accused, it said, had been placed in an acute state of distress by his orders.

At the same time, however, the German legal code still punished people:

> who drive a sled in the cities without a firm shaft or without a bell or ringing mechanism (# 366, section 4);
> whoever tears off public notices, orders or advertisements posted by officials or official bodies (#134);
> whoever intentionally and illegally damages objects which serve the beautification of public thoroughfares (#304, section I);
> whoever advertises means for birth control or for the prevention of venereal diseases in a manner injurious to public mores and good behavior (# 184, section 3a);

whoever defaces officially affixed signs of the sovereignty of the Federal Republic of Germany (#96, section 2).

10. ARTIFICIAL FIGURE

The criminal in the traditional sense of the word, as one still finds him at court trials, belongs to the mythological substratum of the present age. He has long since assumed the traits of an artistic creation, for he claims a place in our imagination which is incommensurable with his real significance, his deeds, and the actuality of his existence. It remains extraordinary and puzzling how much passionate interest we bring to bear on him and what an enormous apparatus we keep up to fight him off. He enjoys an irrational publicity. It can be gleaned from our headlines that a simple murder interests us more than a war which is taking place far enough away—and much more than a war which hasn't started yet but is just being prepared. One is tempted to think the reason for this zealousness has something to do with the tenacity of our legal institutions. Undoubtedly justice holds on more tenaciously than any other social institution—not excepting churches—to old ideas and forms, even when they no longer correspond to anything in reality (the worse for reality). Even the newest reasons for the so-called reform of the penal code reflect the cultural lag which dominates the whole legal sphere. The language of our lawbooks is rife with turns of phrase so old-fashioned it requires recourse to philosophy to understand them. *Breach of peace, ringleader, workhouse, torts, armed rabble*, and the like are linguistic fossils which preserve historical conditions that have long since passed. In a certain sense it is almost admirable how the legal code has maintained itself unchanged in an alien world.

The role of the criminal in our world, however, is not to be explained solely by means of institutions. Taking a closer look, one finds that an entire system of roles has been entrusted to him which makes him indispensable and raises him to the rank of a mythological figure.

11. PALLIATIVE

The primary function of the "ordinary criminal" is to pacify. Although his appearance in society evokes fear, this fear is of an extraordinarily harmless kind. Moreover, in contrast to the far more real political and military threats to society, it is readily identifiable. The perpetrator of the cause for this fear appears on *Wanted* posters on every wall. His behavior, in contrast to that of the ruling powers, is comprehensible and overseeable. His act can be morally categorized without the slightest difficulty. The lawbooks tell us what we are to think of the act. The murderer's fate makes it apparent to us that there "are still judges," and to his figure there is attached the wished-for illusion that killing is indeed prohibited. By punishing the criminal, society supports its conviction that its legal order is intact. All of this has a pacifying effect.

12. SCAPEGOAT

For the individual, each condemnation of another—and the criminal is regarded as the Other, per se—constitutes an acquittal of himself. Whoever is guilty is punished; therefore, anyone who is not punished isn't guilty. It is instructive to observe the glee with which the collective citizenry participates in the pursuit of an escaped convict. The vocabulary from the hunting world is employed at once: the criminal is "fair game," and is allowed to be "shot down." The police practice of shooting at criminals, which is appalling in any event, can be encouraged at any given moment by means of a referendum. The demand for the death penalty also enjoys extreme popularity; especially after the discovery of so-called sex crimes, which always enjoy incredible publicity, does this call break out in hysterical waves. The role of the criminal as scapegoat for society is age-old; however, it is becoming particularly distinct under present conditions.

13. DEPUTY

The criminal not only receives his punishment in everyone's stead—he also acts in everyone's name, if not on their instruction. For he only does what everyone would like to do, and he does it on his own without a concession from the state. The outrage over the fact that he takes upon himself to do what everyone else forbids himself as long as it is prohibited and not ordered—this outrage expresses itself by demanding an eye for an eye and by revisiting the criminal's act upon himself. However, this repetition occurs at the hands of the state, therefore is again performed through deputies. What the individual foregoes, in reality he partakes of twice symbolically, through vicarious participation in the criminal's act and through participation in his punishment. Murderer and hangman relieve us of what we wish and yet don't wish to do, thus providing us not only with moral alibis but also with a sense of moral superiority. Perhaps this helps explain that undercurrent of gratitude which the public occasionally manifests toward some criminal, particularly toward the "successes" in their field. They are respected, as experts. Evil is their specialty, and the criminal practices it; thus, the society which practices division of labor delegates this area to him.

14. COMPETITION

The criminal is not only the deputy for the individual but for society as a whole, which he confronts by assuming its preroga-

tives: that is, he regards himself, in the words of Paule Acker-
mann, the lumberjack from Alaska, as a man who "has permission to permit himself everything." With this claim he puts
himself in the same position as, and consequently against the
state, and becomes its competitor; he questions the state's
monopoly on violence. This is an old role, too. The robbers
and pirates of times past have given the purest performances
of it, and every rebel assumes their features, if not of his own
accord then by default; they are attributed to him by the
world either through its disgust or admiration.[18]

Although the state's superior power vis-à-vis the criminal is
never in doubt, although the criminal's means of exercising
force stands in no relationship whatsoever to the state's capacity, the latter considers itself directly threatened by the individual's or the gang's actions. The state loves to claim that
its "foundations are endangered." And it does not take a
holdup murder to "shake" them—a simple pickpocket or the
writing of an article can be quite sufficient. However, what
seems to irritate modern legislators more than anything else is
"resistance to the power of the state." Wherever this crime is
mentioned, the text gladly abandons its anachronistic equanimity. Foam begins to form at the guardians' mouths, the
harmless get-together becomes a "conspiracy," the trespasser a
delinquent. The fury with which his crime is punished shows
the other side of the coin of overwhelming power: the insecurity of our public order. Not even a diamond or oil monopoly
will appear so strong yet so susceptible, so hypersensitive yet
so brutal; and scarcely a one of them will go to battle against
an outsider with such resounding righteousness.

15. PARODY

As soon as criminals organize themselves they tend to form a
state within the state, and the structure of such criminal societies gives a fairly faithful reflection of the rules of govern-

ment employed by their rivals and competitors. The robber bands of the Late Middle Ages imitated the feudal constitution, and a form of vassalage has been maintained by gangs to this day. The forms of military organizations were frequently copied too. The *Carbonari* of the nineteenth century counted royalist bandits among them. Other secret societies, such as the Camorra, had something of a republican organization; but Salvatore Giuliano considered himself the liberator of Sicily "by the grace of God." The Sicilian Mafia has imitated the structure of the patriarchal government down to its smallest detail and has actually replaced the government in large areas of the country: it possessed an intricate administration, collected duties and taxes, and had its own court system.

Similar symmetries can be observed between the secret police of Czarist Russia, the Ochrana, and the conspiratorial groups it had been designed to combat. Rival organizations always tend to resemble each other. It is difficult to distinguish between the physical behavior and physiognomy of the bodyguards of gangsters and the guards of statesmen.

Specific capitalist organizational forms have found their criminal correspondence too. Modern American gangster organizations are called "crime syndicate" or "Murder, Inc." They are constructed on the pattern of the large corporations, have their own tax advisers, accounting and legal departments, and afford their employees the same social benefits as a legal company. Fascism as a "racket"—from Peachum's "middle class" center for harboring criminals to the Cauliflower Trust—has been described by Brecht. Thus the criminal societies appear as parodies of the general social and political arrangements, and vice versa. However, the criminals usually lag behind the development of the country as a whole, and that lends them a romantic aura. Fascism soon surpassed Brecht's description of it, which was perhaps accurate of a traditional basher-of-heads such as Röhm, even Göring possibly, but looks quite anachronistic when confronted with figures such as Heydrich, Bormann, or Höss, who manifest a far more abstract structure of the social "order."

The criminals already lagged far behind fascism. Today, when fascism itself is superannuated, since the nuclear implement makes even the accomplishments of an Eichmann look paltry by comparison, the most advanced criminal gang looks like an heirloom of former times, and it is unjust when the scholasticists of atomic strategy, authors such as Morgenstern, Brodie, Kahn, and their Soviet counterparts, speak of a "two-gangster situation" during their dry runs: their calculations far exceed the imagination of a criminal. After all, the ambition of two antagonistic gangsters is to kill each other off, whereas the above-mentioned scholars have their eye trained on the millions who are left out of their dry runs.

16. PHRASEOLOGY

The delinquent in our world therefore cuts a comparatively harmless, almost sympathetic and humane figure. His motives are comprehensible. As a victim and accomplice of the now-illusory moral division of labor, he is fitted out by society in a mythological costume. The gangster has been unable to follow the inexorable progress of society; the technological development liquidated his artisan's methods of liquidation and replaced them by industrial methods. Even figures like Trujillo and many "benefactors" of his kind, who are still holding power in dozens of countries, testify—no matter how actual their rule—to the historical lag of the countries which they govern rather than to the future of their metier. The old-time gangster, as well as the criminal traitor, is superannuated.

This explains the semantic difficulties one encounters as soon as one tries to apply traditional legal concepts to the misdeeds of the middle of the twentieth century. *Instigator, culprit, aiding and abetting, accomplice, accessory to the crime* —useful terms all when used to describe a robbery—have become vague and senseless. As it says in the Jerusalem verdict:

With a huge and complicated crime of the kind with which we are dealing here, a crime in which many people participated on many different levels and through different acts—as planners, as organizers and as executors, depending on their individual rank —with a crime such as this the normal concepts of instigation and conspiracy make little sense. For these crimes were committed massively, not only with respect to the number of victims but also with respect to the number of perpetrators; and the remove of a particular perpetrator from the one who actually killed the victim, or his proximity to him, is not a significant yardstick of his responsibility. Quite on the contrary, this responsibility generally increases the further we get away from the one who actually wielded the deadly instrument with his own hands.

But it is not only the concept of justice and its classifications, but even the concept of crime itself, which becomes self-defeating when applied to figures such as those who stand before our courts today or who man the planning staffs for the crimes of tomorrow. Whoever calls Hitler a common criminal belittles him and transfigures him into the realm of the comprehensible. (Brecht's Arturo Ui is nothing but *understatement*: the playwright vainly seeks to make the figure commensurable with the gangster.) Similarly, all the talk about "war criminals" amounts to prettification, as unintentional as that may be—as though modern war could be given the same denominator as petty crime. Crime, having become total, explodes its concept.

This too is just one more example of the impotence of our habits of mind and speech in the face of the atomic situation. It was a well-intentioned but absurd attempt which some American citizens made some years ago when they brought suit against the continuation of atomic tests to the Supreme Court. The court declared itself incompetent. Our concepts, too, have become incompetent. Günter Anders was the one who showed most clearly that our military implement can no longer be understood as a weapon. A political decision which would eliminate all further political decisions no longer deserves that name. There can be no responsibility—in the traditional sense of that word—for an act that would not leave anyone to ask any questions.

17. FINAL SOLUTION

> "I can build a device—I think I know how to do it to-day, I doubt that it would take me ten years to do and I doubt that it would cost me 10 billion dollars—and this device which I could bury, say, 2000 feet under-ground and, if detonated, it would destroy everybody in the world—at least all unprotected life. It can be done, I believe. In fact, I know it can be done." (Herman Kahn at the Centenary Celebration of M.I.T., 1961)[19]

With quantum mechanics mathematics has brought forth a discipline which permits the scientist to calculate with the modification of the infinitely small and infinitely large. A moral quantum mechanics does not exist. Whoever seeks to make distinctions within the unspeakably evil is not just deal-ing with semantic difficulties. The failure of language only manifests the failure of our moral capacities in the face of our own capabilities.

Legal casuistry is as incapable of handling the situation as political practice has been to date. Posterity, busy preparing its deadly birth, today seeks to judge those responsible for Hitler's "Final Solution." This is its inconsistency. This incon-sistency is our only hope . . . a tiny one. No future misdeed can be equal to those of the past; misdeeds do not allow of sub-traction, only of summation. (Doubtlessly there exists a form of moral impotence which believes Auschwitz can be dimin-ished. It is particularly prevalent in Germany, where some persons seriously use the word *Wiedergutmachung*—indemni-fication—even in official documents.) "Final Solutions" cannot be made good again and weighed, not even on the scale of justice. That is one further reason why the world must hold court over them; and one further reason why this court does not suffice.

There are differences between the "Final Solution" of yesterday and the "Final Solution" of tomorrow—that is, between two unimaginable acts:

(1) The Final Solution of yesterday was accomplished. The Final Solution of tomorrow is only being prepared. But it is a feature of the un-concept of this act that it can only be judged as long as it has not been accomplished, for it will leave no judges, no defendants, and no witnesses behind.

(2) The Final Solution of yesterday was not prevented. The Final Solution of tomorrow can be prevented, although society seeks to delegate its prevention, as well as its preparation, usually to one and the same specialist. The prevention of the Final Solution can be delegated no more than the Solution itself can be delegated. Neither one nor the other will be the work of a single individual, but the work of everyone; or it will not be at all. The mighty are impotent without the impotent ones.

(3) The Final Solution of yesterday was the work of a single nation, the German one. Four nations have possession of the implement for the Final Solution of tomorrow. The governments of many other nations are trying to obtain the implement. Some are not.

(4) The planning and realization of the Final Solution of yesterday was accomplished in secret. The planning of the Final Solution of tomorrow occurs in public. In 1943 there lived persons who were not accessories to the act. In 1964 there are only accessories.

(5) The perpetrators of the Final Solution of yesterday were recognizable. They wore uniforms, their victims wore a star. The perpetrators of the Final Solution of tomorrow can no longer be distinguished from their victims.

The Israeli psychiatrist who examined Eichmann called him "a completely normal man: he seems more normal to me than I do to myself after having examined him." Another expert considered him an exemplary family father. Eichmann busied himself primarily with statistics, traffic schedules, and paper work; still, he saw his victims with his own eyes. The planner of the last world war will be spared his sight.

For example, is Edward Teller guilty? Is the journalist guilty who writes an article supporting the demand of German politicians to have the implement? Is the unknown mechanic from Oklahoma or Magnitogorsk guilty? Is Mao Tsetung guilty? Are those guilty who believe in the chimera of "the relaxation of tension" while candidates like Strauss and Goldwater can campaign for the power over life and death? Is the construction firm owner guilty who builds a control bunker? Are there still guilty parties in the future? Are there still innocent ones? Or are there only family fathers, nature lovers, normal persons? The glass cage in Jerusalem stands empty.

Translated by Michael Roloff

Rafael Trujillo

Portrait of a Father of the People

It wasn't Santo Domingo that issued the first announcement on 1 June 1961. It was Washington, a city one and a half thousand miles away from the scene of the crime. An era had come to an end during the previous night, under the coconut palms of the George Washington highway on a Caribbean beach, six miles west of the Dominican capital going towards San Cristobal. Well that is how the news agencies put it. The industry to which we entrust the writing of daily history likes sounding epic notes and amidst the flurry of those 'historic moments' there's a Tacitus sitting at every Telex machine. The less ambitious amongst us might have more modestly referred to the last performance of a 'Whodunnit', which had been running for thirty-one years. The inevitable props of twentieth-century politics remained lying by the side of the road: props for a script 'telling it as it really was': an empty machine gun magazine, a pool of blood, a pile of splintered glass, and a peaked cap bearing the insignia of a general. The corpse, mutilated and barely recognizable, was not discovered until the next morning in the boot of a car parked in the garage of an empty house in the villa quarter of Santo Domingo.

The Benefactor of the Fatherland, the Honourable President, the Paladin of Democracy, First Doctor of the Republic, Bearer of the Great Cross of the Papal Order of St Gregory, the Boldest, Genius of Peace, Saviour of the Fatherland, Protector of All Workers, Most Honourable Knight of the Sovereign Order of Malta, First Teacher of the Republic, Father of the New Fatherland, the First and Greatest of all Dominican Heads of State, the Work-Hero, the Restorer of Economic Independence, First Journalist of the Republic, the Supreme Commander of the Armed Forces, bearer of a neck-ribbon of the Order of Isabella of the Catholics, as well as 87 other decorations of the highest order, His Excellency Generalissimo Professor Dr (Pittsburgh) Dr h.c. Dr h.c. Dr h.c. Dr h.c. Rafael Leonidas Trujillo Molina had finally met his end in a roadside grave.

A state funeral seemed inadvisable under the circumstances. It was only seven months after the demise of the Benefactor that a mahogony coffin bearing his embalmed remains arrived at Orly airport flown in by Pan American World Airways in a special plane. The burial at the Parisian cemetery of Père Lachaise was a very quiet affair. A £30,000 mausoleum preserves, to this day, the memory of the deceased.

LEGACY

The Benefactor left his country an inheritance which is very complex and not easy to assess. Most of the interest has been in his personal fortune, but even serious assessments of this part of his legacy differ widely. According to figures in the relevant literature, give or take a nought, they range from 750 million to 9,000 million dollars. The differences of opinion are partly due to the fact that chroniclers make practically no distinction between liquid assets, debts and material assets, and also to the fact that the imagination of a journalist is hardly capable of dealing with the amounts in question. One should also perhaps ask oneself whether a fortune of such enormousness can be represented in figures; today even a middle-sized concern can make use of accounting techniques capable of circumventing the best of controls, and Capital is organized in international labyrinths constructed with as much complexity as any electronic calculator.[1]

Added to these objectives, and to a certain extent inevitable, worries engendered by Trujillo's inheritance are a number of subjective differences of opinion. Nothing is known of a will. The Dominican Republic is laying strong claim to the inheritance though there is little evidence that the Benefactor had that particular inheritor in mind.

The man who restored economic independence to his country left his successors not only his fortune but also a family, scattered as far and wide as the branches of a firm. How many children he had cannot be ascertained: all that is certain is that it must have been more than forty. Correspondingly numerous are the widows—and brides—of the Benefactor, not to mention his brothers, half-brothers, sisters, uncles, aunts, in-laws, nephews and cousins. It is due to the efforts of these relations that 250 million dollars from the Benefactor's purse has found its way to Europe, although they would not have succeeded without the energetic help of various reputable European banks. The private bank of the French armament firm, Schneider-Creuzot, made itself particularly available 'for the welfare of the family'. At least thirty-one members of the clan have found a second home in the Old World: they are living in the Spanish capital as guests of another benefactor. Apart from the 1,887 Trujillo monuments, Raphael Leonidas Trujillo left the following legacy to the Dominican republic:

40% unemployed

55–70% illiterate

65% of all peasants without land of their own as well as an average income of 200 dollars per head per year.

CAREER

1891: the Benefactor came into the world in San Cristobal (not far from where he left it seventy years later); he was the son of a petty postal official by the name of Pepito.

1955: In the XXVth year of the Trujillo era the Dominican Congress passed a law declaring all public statements which did not fit in with the historical truth punishable falsifications of history. The historical Academy in Ciudad Trujillo was to decide what historical truth was. As a result it is not possible to find out anything definite about the Benefactor's early years; it is to be assumed that they would not stand up to a thorough criticism based on source material.

1901: Trujillo went to the high school in San Cristobal.

1905: Trujillo left the above institute of education, the only one he ever attended.

1910: he got a job as a telephonist.

1912–15: he acquired his first experiences as a horse thief and a pimp.

1916: he entered the services of a large American sugar firm and acted as an informer and 'agent provocateur', seeing to it that there was no unrest amongst the workforce on the plantation.

1918: Together with his brother Petan, Trujillo was sentenced to six months' imprisonment for falsification of documents and deception.

After his release, he was employed as a spy for the American occupying forces by Major James Mclean, the man who could well be said to have 'discovered' him.

1919: After a trial period he was taken on as a lieutenant in the Guardia Civil, one of the voluntary police forces set up by the Americans, where he did some 'very good work' and excelled himself in the guerilla war against his own people.

1921: He passed a course with honours at the Haina military college set up by the American military government.

1922: He was promoted to police captain and co-opted, along with the rest of the collaborators, into the service of the Dominican Republic.

1924 (March): After a bloody intrigue he became a major and in December of the same year a Lieutenant-Colonel on the General Staff.

1925: The President of the Republic made him Chief of the state police with the rank of Colonel.

1927: After the transformation of the police troops into a national army, Trujillo was made a Brigadier-General and C.-in-C. of the armed forces.

1930 (March): he stood as a candidate in the Presidential election and won in May of the same year.

The remaining thirty-one years of his life Trujillo spent as the absolute ruler and owner of his country.

THE PRINCIPLE

From a speech by Trujillo made at the Altar of the Fatherland on 16 August 1955 to mark the occasion of his acceptance of the Great Chain of the Order of the Fatherland presented to him by Congress on the 25th Anniversary of the start of the Trujillo era:

> Exalted Chamber:
>   Today, through my person, you are honouring the first 25 years of a work of patriotism, which has brought great prosperity to the Dominican people, and the certainty that they are now involved in a glorious destiny. . . .
>   It is my bounden duty to accept the judgement passed on my deeds and historic achievement by my fellow men. And thus it is that I welcome your decision, and accept with satisfaction, in this portentous hour, the gratitude of the nation. Without doubt you have made a judgement that anticipates the judgement yet to be made by posterity. You have seen me involved in this work. You know the nature of my struggle. You are my most reliable and legitimate witnesses.
>   I am very human and it is only natural that I should be deeply moved by such a magnificent ceremony; and even as a statesman, duty bound daily to make his country grander and greater and deeply attached to his fellow citizens, I must, at this moment in time, speak of my personal feelings and convictions. We are standing at the Altar of the Fatherland. Altars have always been places of great sacrifice. In the future I would like to do even more for my Fatherland and for my people than I have up to now. Thus before these stones, which cover the ashes of the founders of our state, I make this solemn pledge and vow: as long as my

heart is still beating, it will be devoted to the service of our republic . . .
25 years ago I promised my fellow countrymen—and I have kept this
promise—I promised that as long as there was purity of soul and a clear
understanding of duty, freedom would remain an untouched virgin,
which no brutality could ravish . . .

The future is our laurel wreath. It crowns only the bold, industrious,
idealistic peoples. Let us march towards it full of trust, armed with our
unsullied patriotism and with the most noble commitment that we can
make to serve humanity in a Christian manner.[2]

THE PRECONDITIONS

The Dominican Republic (three and a half million inhabitants, two-
thirds mulatto, one-sixth negro, one-sixth white, about the size of
Wales, seventy people per square kilometre, Catholic, excess of
births over deaths thirty per thousand) is, like all republics in the
Caribbean area with the single exception of Cuba, a semi-colonial
agricultural country whose fate is decided by the political and
economic interests of the United States and not by its own.

The country produces raw materials and foodstuffs especially
sugar, cocoa, coffee, tobacco, bananas, and hardwoods. Of these
products which account for nine-tenths of total exports, sugar is the
most important. For selling its stock the Dominican Republic relies
on the American internal market, which is 'oligopolitically'
administered and politically regulated by import clauses. In return
American importers dominate the Dominican market for industrial
goods from toothbrushes to power stations.

Despite periodic announcements from the White House of some
new guiding principle—a 'policy of good neighborliness' or
'partners for progress'—the same old semi-colonial exploitation
continues in the classic manner: complicity between domestic and
foreign capital, which, with wages of a dollar a day, can get hold of
cheap labour; dependence on politically and economically vastly
superior partners and opponents; periods of short-term prosperity
and periods of chronic crisis dictated by the rising and sinking of
prices of raw materials; economic and political stability guaranteed
only through 'imperialistic' intervention from outside.

Only five years after the Spanish crown had finally given up all claim to her oldest colony (Columbus discovered the island Hispaniola—Little Spain—on his first voyage and made it the centre for futher colonization) and after the withdrawal of the last Spanish batallion, President Buenaventura Baez suggested to the American government that his country become part of the Union. In 1872 the application was turned down by the American senate by a majority of one.

American interests preferred a less binding form of annexation. By the turn of the century they had all but eliminated European competition from the Dominican market. By the time the first world war broke out the sugar planations and refineries were firmly in the hands of American monopolies. Even at that time the country was effectively ruled from the diplomatic mission of the USA. This state of affairs was ratified by the American–Dominican Convention of 1907: to protect the interests of large American banks, the United States authorities took over control of customs and thus, simultaneously, the main source of income of the Dominican state.

In 1919 American policy went a step further. As it had become clear that the stability of the country could no longer be guaranteed without some direct intervention, units of the American marines (the so-called 'leathernecks') landed on the sugar island Hispaniola on 15 May. As no Dominican government was prepared to fulfil the conditions of the invaders, a United States military government took over the reins of power in Santo Domingo in November: it dismissed Parliament, suspended the Supreme Court, banned all political organizations, disarmed the population and set aside the system of community self-government in favour of local military commanders. For support the military régime could rely on the large landowners, the lumpenproletariat, and part of the petty bourgeoisie; in opposition were the agricultural workers, who organized themselves into partisan groups.

Today the form that occupation took is no longer open to debate. The American diplomat Benjamin Sumner Welles, United States High Commissioner in Santo Domingo from 1922 to 1924, put it this way:

It is an indisputable fact that in the eastern provinces of the Dominican Republic the occupying power imposed a régime of oppression for some considerable period of time; a régime that was politically inept, that took it out on a peaceful, law-abiding population and undoubtedly committed many atrocities.[3]

The American Senate decided to set up a commission of its own to investigate the murders, torturing and shooting of hostages which the leathernecks and their allies the *guardia civil* (made up of native gangsters) had perpetrated. Of those summoned to appear it is worth mentioning a certain Captain Merckle, one of the most deeply incriminated officers: he was Rafael Trujillo's superior and 'patron'. 'The marines', writes American journalist John Gunter, 'had a special liking for Trujillo. They used to say, "He thinks just like one of us".'[4]

In June 1924 the marines left the island, but only after American pressure had brought the Vasquez government into being, a typical puppet régime propped up by patronage, protection and the police. A few years later Vice-Admiral Thomas Snowden was succeeded by another native benefactor: an obscure police captain from a provincial town in the north who had decided to 'become a politician'.

DIARY OF A SEIZURE OF POWER

We don't need no hurricane
We don't need no typhoon
'Cause what they do to cause pain,
We can do ourselves alone.

(Brecht, *Rise and Fall of the City of Mahagonny*)

Early 1929

A group of American financial experts headed by a former US vice-president carry out an investigation into the Dominican administration. The army budget, which accounts for one third of total expenditure, is found to contain irregularities. There is talk of a 500,000 dollar deficit. The payrolls are full of 'ghost soldiers' who have been regularly paid but are untraceable. The Commander-in-Chief of the army, Rafael Leonidas Trujillo, feels affronted by the investigating committee and secretly gets in touch with an opposition group in the province of Santiago de los Caballeros, the so-called Republican Party of lawyer Estrella Urena.

Late 1929

The worldwide depression has a disastrous effect on the Republic's economy. The political situation becomes tenser.

22 February 1930

On the basis of a confidential conversation with Estrella Urena, the American embassy in Santo Domingo reports to the State Department that a *putsch* attempt is imminent.

23 February 1930

After a mock battle with troops 'the stronghold of San Luis falls into the hands of the rebels'. The *putsch* led by Estrella Urena had been previously arranged with C.-in-C. Trujillo.

24 February 1930

Horacio Vasquez, the President of the Republic, along with his wife and leading members of his cabinet, calls on the American embassy and asks for asylum.

26 February 1930

The rebels march into the capital. The army offers no resistance. Estrella Urena goes to the American embassy to negotiate with Vasquez. The American chargé d'affaires chairs the meeting. Trujillo is called to the embassy. In the evening the Ambassador cables Washington:

> Despite solemn assurances given to his superiors and to the American embassy it has, today, become absolutely clear that Trujillo has been in conspiratorial alliance with the leaders of the *putsch* and that on repeated occasions he has deceived his government.[5]

29 February 1930

After tough negotiations in the embassy the following agreement is reached:

1. The previous government to step down voluntarily.
2. Estrella Urena to be provisional President of the Republic.
3. An election to be called by him for 16 May.
4. All weapons to be handed in to the army.
5. Trujillo to remain C.-in-C. but not to be allowed to stand as a presidential candidate; the American government to promise that, should the occasion arise, it will refuse recognition to any government set up by Trujillo.

3 March 1930

Inauguration of Estrella Urena in a legitimate and constitutional manner before the Dominican congress.

5 March 1930

First public appearance of Trujillo's storm troopers the '42-ers' (named after the 42nd company of the American marines). This is an economically independent organization that lives off its booty. Amongst its tasks are: the breaking up of meetings, the kidnapping of opposition candidates and the killing off of political enemies. Their most infamous tool is the 'carro de la muerte', a red Packard which operates on the American gangster principle. Several hundred opponents of Trujillo fall victims to the '42-ers' during the election campaign.

18 March 1930

Trujillo is nominated as a presidential candidate by a 'coalition of patriotic citizens'. On the same day the American ambassador cables the State Department:

> This afternoon I had an exhaustive and frank discussion with the President [Estrella Urena], and he disclosed to me that General Trujillo is determined to depose him. Taking the position of the army into account he said he could not guarantee a fair election. In other words manipulated results are to be expected. The President asked me to make publicly known what had been agreed between us, namely that the United States would refuse to recognize Trujillo as president. He said that if he himself were to oppose Trujillo's candidature it would be taken as a personal attack.[6]

19 March 1930
Washington replies to the telegram and says that the American government are reckoning with a Trujillo victory, that they are prepared to recognize him, and that they are anxious to 'foster the most cordial relations with him and his government'.[7]

21 April 1930
Estrella resigns. Home Affairs minister Peynado, one of Trujillo's henchmen, takes over the business of government.

7 May 1930
1930
The election committee for the coming general election resigns on the grounds that the whole election campaign had been made pointless by the activity of the army and the house-to-house searches by armed bands.

8 May 1930
Trujillo has his middleman, the acting president Peynado, appoint a new election committee, which is packed with his supporters.

14 May 1930
Two days before the election numerous opponents of Trujillo withdraw, since the terror campaign has made free elections impossible.

16 May 1930
Election day in the Dominican Republic.

18 May 1930
Letter from the American ambassador to the State department in Washington:

> I am honoured to be able to confirm my report concerning the peaceful passing off of election day. However, there is a certain tension in the air here . . . The 'Confederacion' reports that the provisional count shows 223,851 votes cast for General Rafael Leonidas Trujillo. As the above number is considerably higher than the total number of registered voters, any further comments regarding the honesty of these elections is superfluous.

19 May 1930

Frederico Velasquez, considered before the election to be the most hopeful opposing candidate, is arrested. Numerous other politicians flee to South American embassies and ask for asylum.[8]

30 May 1930

A raiding squad from the '42ers' carries out an armed attack on the buildings of the country's largest newspaper.

1 June 1930

The opposition politician Martinez Reyna is found murdered in his house. The perpetrators had beheaded the corpse and cut off the nose. A few days later Juan Paredes, Jose Brache and Eliseo Esteves are shot down in broad daylight. In the months that follow at least a thousand Dominicans on Trujillo's blacklist are killed off; thousands of others are thrown into prison and tortured.[9]

16 August 1930

Trujillo is ceremoniously inaugurated as President. Washington promptly recognizes his government.

3 September 1930

A hurricane devastates the capital, Santo Domingo. Parliament declares a state of emergency and grants the President sweeping special powers.

5 September 1930

Captain Paulino, chief of the '42ers' and a much-feared guerilla, has hundreds of corpses covered in petrol and set alight in the Plaza Colombia. Though this measure makes identification of victims difficult, it is welcomed by the President as a necessary act of public hygiene. In the President's opinion the danger of plague has thus been removed.

16 August 1931

Founding of President Trujillo's Unity party, the 'partido dominicano'. Within one year, according to the party's central office, 80 per cent of all eligible voters have registered as members.

CONCERN FOR LEGALITY

Speech in reply to an oration given by the Dominican judiciary, delivered on 9 January 1956.

> My Lord Judges:
> . . . I cannot conceal from you the fact that I have been deeply moved by the words of your address of homage. In it you declare that I have 'given the concept of justice a loftier meaning, and laid down the exalted principles by which a judge, in the execution of his office, must let himself be guided . . .
> I have, in fact, been striving to realize a civil freedom, that can act as an incentive to our institutions of justice. Towards this end it was necessary to secure respect for the bench. The behaviour of a judge must satisfy the most stringent of standards, so that each citizen can stand before him without fear or inner doubts.
> The majesty of justice, my lords, rests as much on its insight as on its austerity. The administration of justice requires intelligence for the making of judgements and conscience as its moral guide. Both these elements are vital if the spirit of justice is not to be betrayed, and if the passion for truth is to be strengthened. And how magnificent and sacred the seat of justice is when integrity is rooted in its representatives, who stand above all men and whose only ambition is to be fair and just.[10]

The constitution of the Dominican Republic is one of Liberalism's most delightful documents. It is a presidential constitution on the American pattern. It remains true to the classic principle of the division of powers, provides for a two-chamber system and contains an impressive list of civil rights and freedoms. It has never been suspended. The *coup d'état* of 1930 adhered strictly to its provisions. The Benefactor, too, was a conscientious respecter of the constitutional form.

For example, every four years the citizens of the country diligently turned out to vote. The results became neater and neater. In 1930, according to the official count, 1,883 votes were cast against the Benefactor. Four years later, on the other hand, Trujillo managed to outdo even Hitler and Stalin in the popularity stakes. Votes for: 256,423; invalidated: 0; abstentions: 0; votes against: 0.

Legislation in the Dominican Republic was carried out with perfect propriety. The Benefactor never neglected to provide the tiniest of his actions with a legal basis. In 1935, instead of just getting separated from his second wife or having her murdered, he asked Congress to pass a new law stating that a partnership which had remained childless for more than five years could be annulled simply by a declaration of will of one of the parties concerned. One day after the law had been passed the Benefactor became the first person to make use of it. He exercised a similar kind of care and respect with regard to his numerous titles, each of which went through due process. In fact under his auspices Congress was the most industrious legislative body in the world. The Benefactor saw to it that a mind-boggling number of laws was enacted. Walking barefoot in the capital, selling pictures of the Benefactor without a permit from the Ministry of Culture, wearing a shirt and trousers in the same shade of khaki—all these actions were punishable offences under the new system of justice.

> Parliament approves legislative proposals presented by the President with exemplary speed and it is not unusual for a pressing submission to pass through both houses in a day. I was a member of congress for two years [writes German Ornes, who later emigrated to the USA], and I can't remember one single law ever having been debated. Members only made submissions in exceptional cases (I myself was compelled to do so twice) and then it was always at the personal behest of the Generalissimo.[11]

The Benefactor even worked out judicially satisfactory solutions for dealing with the Executive. Ministers and officials were not simply removed, as is normal practice in a dictatorship. They always resigned voluntarily or simply took their leave. The same applied to members of Congress who were always quite prepared to resign their seats. To make things easier for them, the Benefactor got each one to sign a document of resignation before taking up office, seat or post and then, at the given moment, merely had to fill in the date.

What about justice? In the Dominican Republic the death penalty was abolished years ago. Prisoners not 'shot while trying to escape' or killed in one of the apparently frequent car crashes, usually hanged themselves in their cells 'out of remorse' as the national newspapers laconically put it. *Se perdio:* he's had it, people would say in such cases. Understandably there were hardly any political trials under the rule of the Benefactor. If it did ever come to legal proceedings, his opponents always turned out to be pathological criminals, who had to be condemned because of homosexuality, tax-fiddling, drug addiction or some other arbitrary failing.

What about the constitutionally guaranteed freedoms? Well, the Benefactor often enough bemoaned the fact that nobody ever seemed to want to make use of them. That the newspapers never wrote anything critical about him for thirty years, he could only put down to the fact that he was the Benefactor.

Throughout the decades Trujillo showed himself to be a good friend of the constitutional state. He never thought of doing away with it in the same way as he never thought of openly opposing the judiciary, rather, in a very perceptive manner, he recognized the possibilities of a systematic administration of justice. Fernando Fournier, former foreign minister for the Republic of Costa Rica, was sent to Santo Domingo by the International Law Commission to investigate the judicial practice of the Benefactor; he summed up his impressions in the following manner: 'In the Dominican Republic everything, literally everything, was possible. It was possible to be woken at 3 o'clock in the morning and be deported in your pyjamas. It was possible to be subjected to the most refined forms of torture, simply because of some anonymous denunciation or because somebody wanted to get their own back, perhaps just because of a passing remark about how everything had become dearer. . . . There were electric chairs which forced out confessions with the help of high voltage shocks; cigarettes pressed into the skin; women raped in front of their husbands; tanks filled with stinking water in which prisoners were immersed up to their necks for hours or even days; shark pools into which prisoners were thrown in the presence of Raphael Trujillo Junior and friends; vaults especially equipped for the purpose of torturing; dungeons with hunting dogs trained to bite off the genitals of their victims; and concentration camps on remote islands where there was practically nothing to eat.'[12]

THE HUMAN FACE

It would not be very productive to list the attributes of the Benefactor. There was nothing very special about him. He was five foot seven tall. His appetite was normal, his health excellent, his complexion ruddy, his deportment good. Trujillo was an early riser and an enthusiastic walker; he took care of himself physically, had a penchant for patent medicines, and in his later years was taking a special preparation for the purpose of restoring his potency. At the age of seventy he had all the hallmarks of a successful managing director.

All informants bear witness to his extraordinary industry and exemplary diligence. The routine for the day was strict; nine to ten hours at his desk was normal. A bad speaker, never very successful on public occasions, no charisma. Pragmatician. Very irritable. A great dissembler. A tough, practical intelligence. Excellent memory. An unusually gifted organizer. A strong sense of family.

The private life of the Benefactor was in line with contemporary people of his position and income: thirty-five cars, two private yachts, own racing stable. His residence, situated next to that of the American ambassador, included a dental clinic, a cosmetic salon, a gym, a cinema and a skating rink all made of marble and mahogany, as well as the inevitable swimming pools.

Trujillo was considered to be a good dancer. Since his own work left him little time for women, he employed a special adjutant to 'procure' for him. He made no secret of his numerous illegitimate children, and liked to hear his 'love' affairs being talked about in public; he was of the opinion that it proved his masculinity.

The Benefactor was a choosy dresser, preferring on the whole white suits; he wore jewellery, had his underwear initialled and sported hand-printed hundred-dollar ties in the style of American businessmen. His favourite uniform, worth about ten thousand dollars, was encrusted with gold and consisted of a jacket with heavy epaulettes and gold brocade tails, a silk sash in the national colours, blue trousers with gold stripes and a gold and white three-cornered hat covered in feathers.

An in-depth study of the desires of Rafael Trujillo would not bring to light anything very surprising; it can be omitted here. Nevertheless amongst his 'needs' there is one that is worth going into in more detail, namely his lust for recognition, which took on the most bizarre forms.

The Statesman dedicated a considerable amount of time and effort to his collection of titles, orders, medals and monuments. He introduced and made legal a system of telling the time named after him. In 1936 he had Santo Domingo, the oldest town in the Western Hemisphere, re-christened Ciudad Trujillo; after a short while the name was to be seen on countless streets, parks, schools, squares and hospitals. It was given to whole provinces and even to the highest mountain in the country. After having awarded himself all imaginable decorations—including a prize for literature—the Benefactor, guided by his strong sense of family, saw to it that the other members of the Trujillo clan were similarly provided for. For example, his son Ramfis was made a colonel in the national army at three years of age, and at the age of six Congress granted him the title of 'Protector of the Poor Children', at nine he became a brigadier-general and was awarded a medal for bravery—'for exceptional achievements at a tender age' as the official document put it.

The whole country was riddled with posters, pictures, banners and icons. On buses, housefronts, and handcarts: God and Trujillo; on shop-windows: Trujillo is my protector; on hospitals: Trujillo alone will cure me; on savings banks: All that I have, I have thanks to Trujillo; on village pumps: It is Trujillo who gives us our water. A bronze plaque, which was particularly useful in the likely event of your house being searched and which therefore hung in hundreds of thousands of homes, carried a colour portrait of the Benefactor with the inscription: In this house Trujillo commands. On the reverse side was the motto: Rectitud, Libertad, Trabajo, Moral (Honesty, Freedom, Work and Morality)—an acrostic from the initials 'Rafael Lenoidas Trujillo Molina. The plaque cost 30 dollars in the shops; the cost of its manufacture (a monopoly of Ferreteria AG) was 2 dollars. The majority shareholder in the company was Mrs Rafael Leonidas Trujillo Molina.

Very few stories about the Statesman have been handed down. He did not give away much about himself and merely confirmed that the Benefactor was well suited to his job. His weakness for acts of revenge was assisted by his elephant's memory. One of the first people he had killed off after seizing power was a man who, years before, had refused the Benefactor a loan.

If you asked a man like Trujillo about his sense of humour he probably would not understand what you were talking about. An instance from the year 1931 illustrates why. In that year he had the president of the Senate, Desiderio Arias, shot down. He turned up with the hearse at the widow's house and insisted on standing by her side for the whole of her night-long vigil; the next morning he called for three days of state mourning.

Again and again the psychologists amongst his biographers have made pointless attempts to analyse his personality and character. This sort of slandering cannot be firmly enough repudiated. The Benefactor was neither megalomaniac nor sadist. His character was one and the same as the politics which he carried out, he had no need of any other. His apparently helpless lust for recognition had nothing to do with an inferiority complex, but served a political purpose. The personality cult is not there to allay the doubts of the Statesman about himself, but to weed out the doubt of everybody else; an arbitrary act of revenge is not proof of an unhappy childhood, but a demonstration of political power; a sense of family is part of personality politics; cruelty the carefully groomed handmaid of deterrent. The most absurd action of the Benefactor, his most idiotic moods, all were politically motivated. Did he have a face? If he did have one it was dissolved by his function as a statesman, like an alka-seltzer in a glass of water. Like Eichmann you cannot reproach him for having been someone. The greatest thing about Trujillo was his banality.

THE ART OF THE POSSIBLE

The Benefactor of the Fatherland was one of the most talented and imaginative politicians of his time. He had only his own ability to thank for what was perhaps his most significant achievement as a statesman: remaining alive and in power for thirty years. In that he surpassed both Stalin and Franco as well as Hitler and Mussolini. There is only one other contemporary who could compete with him for honours in the fields of tenacity, skill, willpower and patience, and that is the Benefactor of China, Generalissimo Chiang-Kai-Shek. There were of course numerous attempts to overthrow Trujillo, and it is true to say that they failed as much because of his protectors as because of his circumspection; but many a less-talented man would never have managed to acquire such powerful allies.

At the root of Trujillo's method were the politics of personality. From the start he showed 'dynamic qualities of leadership' combined with 'an understanding of the problems of dealing with people'. He never trusted anybody. That required considerable self-discipline. He never showed gratitude. That is a sign of inner stability. He was an expert at blackmailing and betraying. That proves his versatility.

Rule number one in his personality politics was never to delegate power permanently. To counter the inevitable accumulation of power and control by those at the top in the administration, he continually reshuffled in a manner that was as arbitrary as it was systematic. Ministers, members of Congress and generals often learnt of their resignations from the newspapers. Yes-men, especially, often found themselves, after years of service, being suddenly eased out or arrested at their desks with no reason given. No one held the post of chief of police for longer than a year. The turnover of officials was enormous. Even in the Benefactor's immediate circle nobody was safe. You couldn't even be certain that someone who had 'resigned' was finished: Trujillo had a way of suddenly reinstating people or giving them a new job; but he was clever enough not to follow any hard and fast rules in the 'terror game'; he kept in practice, and worked on the principle of 'a bit of this and then a bit of that'. His 'cleansing bouts' were followed by long periods of calm, he proclaimed amnesties, made liberal gestures, smiled a hundred smiles; in this way he enticed political opponents into the open, and then he clamped down again as hard as ever.

So as to avoid the formation of cliques, he would on no account tolerate friendships amongst fellow-workers, soldiers or officials. One of his fundamental maxims was to break the moral fibre of his team. A favourite speciality of his was to cajole and entice potential opponents into the government: in part they were recruited straight from the prisons. Sometimes he won over good brains to his cause in this way. but at the same time he discredited them in the eyes of those on the outside. He carefully preserved evidence of their collaboration. After the inevitable dismissal these documents were published: the victims of this blackmail were then written off as collaborators by the émigré resistance and thus made harmless.

For similar reasons Trujillo did very little about general and traditional corruption in the administration, but did toughen up the laws against bribery. The discrepancy between regulation and reality did not worry him in the least, on the contrary he welcomed it: he had incriminating evidence against employees meticulously collected and filed, so that it could be used later to put the pressure on.

Though it did distinguish itself with original details, the Benefactor's version of personal politics kept to the classic maxims, on the whole. The same is true of his administrative methods. Spying and dossiers, physical terror and torture, bugging and censorship, propaganda and provocation, are nothing new in our enlightened century. That he was so experienced in these things the Benefactor owed to his years of apprenticeship as gangster and policeman. He developed the necessary bureaucratic mechanisms with an exemplary sense of order; for in a land of 3 million people law and order could not be based on the barrel of a gun forever. Every citizen had to carry an identity card, which was stamped at elections as a means of control and in which tax stamps had to be stuck. Party membership cards had to be presented to the authorities when contracts were signed, at graduation and in all banks. In addition references from the secret police were necessary for anyone wishing to open up a business, get hold of a passport, or work freelance.

The Benefactor's secret police were not just one single unit. The tasks were carried out by various organizations. At times there were as many as seven different state security authorities working alongside each other in Trujillo's empire: the Secretariat for State Security, the Army Counter-Intelligence Service, the Confidential Commissariat of the Unity Party, the President's Body Guard, the so-called 'Presidential Inspectorate' and the 'Spanish Police' (a unit of approximately one hundred well-tried experts handed over to Generalissimo Trujillo by Generalissimo Franco in 1956). In the main the secret services were recruited from the bourgeois intelligentsia, from domestic prisons, and from veterans of the FBI and CIA. This complicated network of different bodies illustrates another of the Benefactor's golden rules: the systematic duplication of authorities and institutions. This was a means of preventing unwelcome concentrations of power by playing off leading functionaries against one another and creating a continuous feeling of rivalry between the different set ups; the only person to benefit was the big boss.

Obviously it was not his methods alone that made Trujillo successful. However refined and up-to-date his techniques of exercising power might have been, he still needed the traditional supports if he was to develop that power. In fact the Benefactor never lost his respect for the institutional pillars of society. Only one of them was actually set up by him: the 'Partido dominicano', his Unity Party. The others he skilfully used for his own ends. They were: the church, the army, capital and the American government.

Of these five pillars the Unity Party was the weakest. Trujillo needed it only as a back-up for the fiction of a parliamentary democracy; though it was also useful as a propaganda weapon, as a spy network, as well as being a good little business. Since all state employees had to belong to it and since they were also legally bound to contribute 10 per cent of their wages to it, it soon began to show a handsome profit. The eight letters of Trujillo's name made up the essence of the party programme.

As President of a country in which Catholicism was and is the state religion and as a practising Catholic himself, the Benefactor made sure he had the support of the church at the very beginning. He had an excellent relationship with the Vatican; in 1954 this cooperation was crowned with a Concordat. A mass, or at least a Te Deum, was sung at every party rally and at every party meeting. Amongst Trujillo's most enthusiastic propagandists was Monsignore Ricardo Pittini, consecrated Archbishop of Santo Domingo in 1935; as late as 1957 he publicly declared that the 'totally anti-communist Dominican Republic' guaranteed its citizens 'the same freedom as those enjoyed by the citizens of the United States'. Cardinal Spellman, too, was only too happy to put in a good word for the Benefactor. Pope Pius XII showered him with decorations and never missed the opportunity of exchanging telegrams with him when there was something to be celebrated. On the 'Silver Wedding Anniversary' of Trujillo and the Fatherland (that was the official title given to the government's 25th anniversary celebrations) the Pope sent one of his personal legates, Monsignore Salvatore Siino, and through his emissary expressed his admiration for the 'Christian spirit and humanitarian qualities of the régime'.

It was the army, from which he himself had risen, that gave the Benefactor his monopoly of physical power. In 1952 the army (together with the police) accounted for 46 per cent of the budget; it was 40,000 strong, and equipped with the most up-to-date weapons. There was no strategic or foreign policy role for enormous military apparatus; apart from the massacre of 15,000 Haitian agricultural workers on its borders, the Dominican Republic had never experienced armed conflict. Rather Trujillo had quite consciously and deliberately built up an army of occupation, whose sole purpose was to hold the population in check.

For the Benefactor the army had been as indispensable as it had been dangerous, and thinking back on his own career meant that he took a lot of trouble to make sure that the army itself was kept in check. He recognized in good time the dialectic implicit in every rearmament: there is some indefinable border beyond which imposed oppression can suddenly turn into aggression against the imposer. It is true that Trujillo introduced conscription in 1947 but he was aware of its dangers; he never gave the recruits weapon training but merely drilled them. The officers were obliged to keep all firearms and ammunition permanently under lock and key. On the whole the army and especially the officer corps, bought with social and material privileges, proved itself to be one of the Benefactor's most reliable supports. Not only did it refrain from those periodic *coups d'état* against their protector, typical of Latin America, but it also remained faithful to him after his death and laments the passing of his régime to this day.

The sheer audacious simplicity and effectiveness of Trujillo's economic policy deserves a more thorough analysis, as do his relations with the USA.

GROW AND PROSPER

Speech on the occasion of a Banquet of Loyalty and Gratitude given by the country's businessmen in the hotel El Embajador on 18 February 1956:

> I am deeply touched by all that has been laid on in my honour by the employers and businessmen of my country to whom I have always given special attention. It is with great pleasure that I accept the medal you have awarded me for my achievements in building up the Dominican economy.
>
> I believe that spiritual values stand above all others and it is my ardent desire that my people should uphold them in their works of art, in their moral behaviour, and in their deeds of Christian good neighbourliness. On the other hand nations need material goods. . . .
>
> In this connection it should be mentioned that industry, trade, agriculture and mining have all supported my personal initiative and the efforts of the government for a better future in a forceful, responsible, enthusiastic and peaceable manner . . . And yet: A statesman such as I must speak with a firm and fatherly voice: some employers have been lacking in initiative and have been taking out their capital; others are not really businessmen in the Christian sense of the word, but rather feverish speculators . . . but people who are shortsighted and set in their ways will never discover the secrets of economic life. . . .
>
> Employers: Gentlemen: Raise up your hearts to those heights where today the banner of the cross billows in the breeze. Give flight to your

> thoughts with the wings of initiative and creative energy. I will be
> constantly by your side as you strive for the Fatherland. . . .[13]

There could be no doubt in the minds of the assembled Dominican employers that it was one of them, their boss, who spoke these words. It is in economic affairs that the Benefactor's genius really shines through. His strong points, industriousness, organizational ability, thoroughness, fantasy and enterprise all fuse together to form a vibrant whole. Not even in his original area of concern, the police, did he manage to scale such peaks of perfection. His brilliance can already be seen at work in the years 1928 and 1929 when he was Commander-in-Chief of the army. At that time the Benefactor arranged a very useful little concession for his girl-friend (later wife) Maria Martinez: henceforth all the army's dirty washing was to be sent to one concern owned by this woman. To simplify matters the relevant costs would merely be deducted from the soldiers' wages. Monthly wages were 15–20 dollars so that meant 8–10 dollars for Miss Martinez, or half as much as the entire army of the republic.

On taking power Trujillo discovered that the government's solvency left something to be desired. His lady-friend set up a debt collection agency, which in return for a modest commission of 60 per cent helped suppliers recover outstanding debts from the state. In the financial year 1930/31 alone this service brought her 800,000 dollars.

The Benefactor soon realized that in order to concentrate working capital it would be a good idea to set up his own finance institution. The collection agency was turned into 'El banquito' (the little bank). It soon won itself a solid position in the Dominican credit market. Since the government tended to be a bit slow in paying its employees the Little Bank advanced the wages in return for 5 per cent interest per month. For the sake of rationalization the government soon got into the way of paying the allotted wages directly into the Benefactor's bank. Even then, in his early creative period, the originality of his schemes and his determination were remarkable. But Trujillo did not neglect those more traditional sources of income, which the Chicago underworld had made their special metier, and early on he became involved in prostitution and gambling. His penchant for registering suitable firms in the name of one of his numerous relatives was not just a hallmark of his sense of family but was also a refinement considered by 'classical' racketeers to be the 'done thing'.

Nevertheless there was something 'small time' about these enterprises, even though the Benefactor may have set them going in a grand manner, and in the long run they could not do justice to the style of a Generalissimo. Much more was possible for a man who was a head of government, than for a mere gang leader; simple robbery, to which Trujillo owed a considerable part of his property holding, was something he had to move on from.

One of his first economic measures was the introduction of an unofficial turnover tax on all state contracts and public expenditure. Responsibilities were carefully shared out. Justice for example was in the hands of Brigadier-General Pedro Trujillo Molina. This particular brother of the Benefactor took an 8 per cent share out of the 20 allocated to the upkeep of every prisoner. More modest was the cut another brother, Hector Bienvenido Trujillo, got from all military purchases, from weapons, equipment and servicing facilities: it was a mere 10 per cent. In other areas of state expenditure, especially that of public building, the Benefactor himself had a stake of 10 or 20 per cent.

In this way Trujillo built up sufficient capital for his plans. An added convenience was a special law passed by the Dominican congress exempting the head of state and his family from all taxes. There was now little that stood in the way of a further development of his talents. Trujillo was not one of those employers who take their capital out of circulation or who are lacking in vision. He invested it, steadfastly believing in the future, in the economy of the Dominican Republic.

It is not easy to do justice to this enormous life-work. Apart from the difficulty of surveying such a vast enterprise, of unravelling the network of units, of having such a large number of family members involved, and of dealing with the enormous number of limited companies, subsidiaries and holding companies from which the whole is made up, apart from all this there is something else which gets in the way of an accurate assessment. When looking at this economic empire one is continually confronted with the question of where state wealth ends and the Benefactor's private wealth begins. As time went on this border became more and more hazy and was increasingly 'crossed'. For example Trujillo had a habit of selling off his share in a project to the state as soon as it proved unprofitable, and of taking over on favourable terms state enterprises which were flourishing. Many concerns obviously changed hands several times dependant on the state of the economy. It goes without saying that in these circumstances even the most painstaking assessment can only be approximate. It is generally assumed that on his death the Benefactor controlled one-third of the country's fixed assets; 80 per cent of the working population were directly dependent on him, that is 35 per cent as state employees and 45 per cent as workers and personnel in Trujillo's enterprises.[14]

There follows a list, which makes no claim to be comprehensive, of the most important sectors of Trujillo Enterprises:

1. Tobacco. Monopoly of the Tabaculara Dominicana Co.: majority share holder, Rafael Leonidas Trujillo.

2. Salt. Monopoly of the Compania Salinera Nacional. Annual net profit 700,000 to 1,000,000 dollars. Owner: Rafael Leonidas Trujillo.

3. Edible oil. Bonetti Burgos Co. Share of the market 80 per cent. Majority share holder: Hector Bienvenido Trujillo.

4. Beer. Monopoly of the Cervexceria Salinera Nacional Co. Majority of shares in the hands of groups of American capital. Minority shareholder with right of veto: Rafael Leonidas Trujillo.

5. Meat. Virtual monopoly of the state's own Matadera Industrial y Planta de Refrigeracion. Leaseholder: Ramon Savinon Luberes on behalf of his brother-in-law, Rafael Leonidas Trujillo.

6. Milk. Largest milk producer in the country: Hacienda Fundacion. Owner: Rafael Leonidas Trujillo. Central Lechera: Dairy produce monopoly owned by the state, controlled by members of the Trujillo family.

7. Matches. Monopoly of the Fabrica Nacional de Fosforos.

Majority of shares in the hands of a Swedish match-producing group. Holding with right of veto: Rafael Leonidas Trujillo.

8. Cocoa refining and export. Biggest firm in the business: Chocolatera Nacional. Majority shareholding: Rafael Leonidas Trujillo.

9. Cement. Monopoly of the Fabrica Dominicans de Cemento. Majority shareholder: Martinez Alba, a brother-in-law of Rafael Leonidas Trujillo.

10. Medicines and drugs. Monopoly of the Laboratorio Quimico Dominicano. President: Martinez Alba.

11. Iron. Virtual monopoly of the Ferreteria Read Co. Majority shareholder: Mrs Rafael Leonidas Trujillo.

12. Importing. Representation of the American market leaders in machine, automotive, steel and electrical products: holding of a group of firms, controlled by Martinez Alba.

13. Insurance. Virtual monopoly of the Compania de Seguros San Rafael. President: Pina Chevalier, an uncle of the chief shareholder, Rafael Leonidas Trujillo.

14. Press, radio, television. Various daily papers under the control of Trujillo enterprises. Virtual monopoly of radio and television.

15. Air and sea transport. Two Trujillo shipping companies sold to the state because of non-viability. The Compania Dominicana de Aviacion subsidiary of Pan American. Holding with right of veto under the control of Rafael Leonidas Trujillo.[15]

Not mentioned in the list are a whole number of other interests and involvements, especially in banking, building, mining, agriculture, and in the textile, armament, leather, flour, and wool producing industries.

The bold, adventurous methods of the Benefactor make it impossible to verify in detail the meagre and incomplete list of his concerns. But it shows us what it is all about. Trujillo's economic policies were ingeniously simple. They swept aside that age-old capitalist malaise, conflicts of interest, and created overnight—there is no other way of putting it—social peace. What one American Defence Secretary merely hinted at in a famous dictum, this life's work made a reality: What's good for Trujillo is good for the Dominican Republic. Enterprise and Nation were identical. Its leader was in every sense the boss: head of state, breadgiver, and proprietor rolled into one.

There is nothing ironical about the claim that the Benefactor's régime was progressive. The country he took over was way behind the big industrial nations in terms of capitalist development. Incompetent landowners and a parasitic petit-bourgeoisie were exploiting the working class; but they were not remotely capable of accumulating the necessary capital for industrialization or of taking on the historic role of the bourgeoisie. Foreign interests did not want to take it on either, and for their part regarded the Caribbean republics merely as objects for exploitation. The Benefactor, in contrast, brought progress to the country, albeit in the form of a parody. His enterprises leapfrogged whole phases of capitalist development, created an enormous concentration of capital and instituted a form of nationalization of nearly all means of production, which must be unique. His blackmail and bribery did away with the so-called middle-class in as cold-blooded a manner as any multi-national corporation or People's Democracy. Since Trujillo was the state, and *vice versa*, nationalization and privatization fused into a paradoxical *quid pro quo*.

Obviously this development produced some material progress. Justifiably Trujillo referred to himself as 'the restorer of the Republic's independence'. But the independence he achieved was independence for himself. In the thirty years of his rule he presented his country (and therefore also himself) with roads, bridges, ports, irrigation plants, a new university and many other wonderful things. But he had no choice in the matter. How could Trujillo, the Statesman, reject or ignore the wishes of Trujillo, the Chairman of the Board? It could not be helped, if, in the process, a few other people occasionally made a bit on the side. Anyway, the government's paternal hand ensured that such attendant symptoms were kept to a minimum. Problems of egalitarianism or even of prosperity could not possibly arise. At first glance an average yearly income of £140–160 might seem quite impressive for a semi-colonial country, but if one takes into account the share of this income taken by the Trujillo family then the figure sinks to £90 a year. So nobody can accuse the Benefactor of having betrayed the interests of the employer or of having wantonly changed the social structure of the Fatherland.

Even his education policy, which his numerous admirers always hold up as the régime's gem of progressiveness, does not fall into the latter category. It is true, he did genuinely concern himself with turning the Dominicans into a nation of readers, but only into readers of Trujillo. Amongst the branches of industry in which the Benefactor had a finger was publishing. This branch produced a bestseller, written by the Benefactor, which must be mentioned and quoted as final proof of his business acumen. The book in question is called *A Citizen's Primer*. It was written in 1933 and for decades has been used as a textbook in all schools throughout the country. Here are some of the salient points in the work.

> The President works unremittingly for the happiness of his people. He ensures that there is peace and order, supports the schools, builds roads, protects the worker, aids agriculture, helps industry, maintains and improves the ports, is concerned about hospitals, is in favour of studying and strengthens the army to protect all law-abiding citizens.
>
> Every Dominican must help him with these tasks, love his country above all else and obey the government, for that is the surest way to happiness. Every policeman is your best defender, every member of the government your best adviser and every judge your best friend.
>
> Should somebody walk past your house, who says he wants to change the way things are, report him. He is the evilest of all evil people. The criminal, who sits in prison, has perhaps killed one person or stolen one thing. But the revolutionary wants to kill everybody he meets and steal everything he can find, even those things which belong to you and your neighbour. He is the worst of all possible enemies.[16]

In later editions of *A Citizen's Primer* the word revolutionary was replaced with the word communist.

CONSEQUENCES OF A *FAUX PAS*

A communist? At least we can be certain that the Benefactor was not a communist. Was he an anti-communist? Was he for or against anything? Throughout his life the Benefactor was for the Benefactor, and against everything which was not for the Benefactor. This modest, realistic principle was also the guiding factor in Trujillo's foreign policy whilst in power. Until Castro appeared on the scene, the Central American countries had no significant role in world politics; therefore it is not really worth making an in-depth investigation of the Benefactor's ambitions and schemes in this area. Like all exponents of real-politik he collapsed as soon as the protection of the big power was taken away. A general summary account of his foreign affairs will suffice: a little flirtation with Hitler, an 'entente-cordiale' with Franco's Spain, excellent relations with the Vatican under Pius XII, a murderous action taken against neighbouring Haiti, a deeply-felt bond of understanding with Fulgencio Batista and similar colleagues, and the occasional intrigues against them, as well as an understandable distaste for the few democratically inclined Latin American governments.

On the whole, though, the Benefactor recognized in good time when and when not to act in foreign affairs. If there was any doubt the State Department in Washington advised him. For a country like the Dominican Republic all foreign policy revolves around its relationship with the United States; independent action can only take the form of a flourish here, a variation there, or the occasional tactical difference of opinion. In Trujillo's case that relationship was excellent for twenty-five years. In 1930 the declared wish of the American government was to foster the friendliest of relations with him and his government and this they did. When, in September 1939, Trujillo announced that the Dominican Republic would back United States policy whatever this might be, he was referring to the second world war, but, at the same time, he was formulating a general rule of Caribbean politics.

The Benefactor guaranteed his 'protector', what the State Department called 'political and social stability'. This basically meant American economic interests. Trujillo's army, the official mafia, saw to it that the workers remained 'quiet' on the American sugar plantations, and his enterprises saw to it that American imports dominated the market.

Secondly, he turned the Dominican Republic into a strategic-military base for the USA. His military build-up was carried out at the expense of American tax payers, firstly on the basis of a loan agreement and later on the basis of a bilateral Pact for Mutual Assistance entered into in 1953. His airforce was virtually a unit of the USAF. It was set up, trained and paid for by the USA, and by the end had two hundred jets at its disposal. The Benefactor also received propaganda support from the Americans. But here, apart from the Dominican-American cultural institute which was financed with taxes, it was the interest groups themselves, who came out in support of Trujillo. Whole-page advertisements in the *New York Times*, praising his achievements, were not uncommon, and in Dominican newspapers firms like Esso and Pan Am published whole-page messages of goodwill to the Benefactor.

For his part Trujillo did not rely on his professional diplomats (for the most part a bunch of well-tested thugs) when dealing with the government in Washington, but engaged American lawyers, journalists, politicians and advertising consultants. Trujillo should go down in history as one of the pioneers of public relations, at one time or another he made use of twelve leading PR firms. For years there was a gleaming three-foot high portrait of the smiling Benefactor stuck up in Lower Manhattan; every New Yorker must have been convinced of the reliability and friendliness of this cement face.

But it was not just a poster that won him his good reputation in New York boardrooms, rather it was his prompt payment of debts. In 1947 he paid off the last of his foreign debts and acquired for himself the title of 'Restorer of Financial Independence'; the State Department spoke of an example worthy of imitation. As things turned out that was a little short-sighted. The loyalty that Trujillo showed to his 'protector' was just as fickle as all the Benefactor's other emotions. Relations between agent and employer are always two-edged. Contradictions start to emerge when the agent begins to regard himself as his own employer, and when he is in a position to do so. At that moment he becomes a competitor.

It was at the time of the Korean War that Trujillo felt strong enough to switch roles. Having paid off all of his American debts, he was in a stronger position. A boom in the raw materials market made the situation even more favourable and tempting. The bitter struggle, in which he now got involved, was fought out on the sugar fields of the Dominican Republic.

Up until that time the country's sugar industry, which involved nearly 70 per cent of the working population, had been in American hands. For this reason sugar, the most important product in the country, did not feature amongst Trujillo interests. Before 1953 the Benefactor had not dared touch the monopoly of the American sugar firms, in particular the South Porto Rico Sugar Co. Ltd, the Ozona Sugar Co. Ltd, and the West Indies Sugar Corporation. His first moves to involve himself in the sugar business were very discreet and aimed at securing some small foothold in this key industry. Not until 1954 did he stage an all-out attack, by abruptly expropriating a number of key plantations. Six years later 60 per cent of the Dominican sugar industry was under his control. Here again 'independence' from the USA obviously did not mean independence for his country, but merely independence for the Benefactor. Here too his actions took on a paradoxically progressive quality, though in reality they were based entirely on the logic of greed.

His American 'bosses' never forgave Trujillo for this move. They did not, however, drop him at once. The influential sugar lobby had other interests to consider, and these interests were best served by a continuation of the régime. (The records show that, in 1956, the yield on American investments in the Dominican Republic was between 12 and 15 million dollars.)[17]

What finally drove the USA to drop the Benefactor, and what finally broke his neck, was his flirtation with communism, a poker game that even this experienced double-dealer was not up to.

Not that Trujillo was a beginner. In an earlier bout he had apparently won game, set and match. But perhaps it was just that experience of success that drove him to his last deadly bluff.

The Benefactor's régime was in a very bad way after the end of the second world war. The raw materials boom had collapsed. South America was experiencing a temporary wave of democratization and the USA was having to quietly stand by and acquiesce as several of the dictatorships typical of Latin America came to an abrupt end. After the defeat of fascism American liberal opinion also took a look at the situation in the Dominican Republic, and found a noticeable lack of any opposition party.

Trujillo reacted with skill, brashness and determination. In June 1945 he announced that the Dominican Republic was considering taking up diplomatic relations with the Soviet Union, a country which had shown itself to be 'one of the most reliable forces on the side of humanity and progress'. The soviets did not respond to Trujillo's advances.

On 27 August 1946, to everyone's astonishment, a manifesto of the 'Partido Socialista Popular' appeared in the daily paper *La Nacion*, one of the Trujillo Enterprises. From the manifesto it was to be assumed that the party was communist with Stalinist tendencies, and also that it was expecting to be allowed to operate legally in the Dominican Republic. Three weeks later the Benefactor himself made an announcement in the same newspaper.

> That communism now exists in our land is a fact of paramount importance. It has its roots in the USSR and when considering the role it can play in social and political matters, one should not forget the selfless co-operation of the Soviet Union with democratic countries in the last world war. Moreover, the party's presence in our midst is positive proof for those slanderers who, without foundation, accuse our state of not being a true democracy.

It goes without saying that the Benefactor merely waited for the first demonstrations, strikes, and meetings and then went over to the offensive. By late autumn 1946 the usual arrests, bans, and murders had already begun. In June 1947 the Congress set up a 'committee for the investigation of un-Dominican activities': five days later it decreed a total ban on all communist organizations.

This manœuvre showed Trujillo's tactical genius at its highest. He won on five counts. First of all he had trapped his most dangerous and best organized opponents. Secondly he had shown foreign public opinion the 'liberality' of his régime. Thirdly he had given the Americans to understand that the communists were the only opposition in his country. Fourthly he blackmailed the American government with the threat of giving, at the express wish of public opinion in the USA, this opposition a free hand. Fifthly, with his ban of the Communist Party he assured for himself a very favourable starting position in the cold war.

What is not clear is why the communists went along with this one-sided game. Perhaps it was a matter of making their presence felt at any cost. At any rate they must have been interested in establishing that they really were the only alternative to the ruling régime, and this is the point where the intentions of both sides coincide, for Trujillo was equally keen to prove it.

Having won the game the Saviour of the Fatherland let loose a no-holds-barred witch-hunt against the communists. Anyone who contradicted him, stood in the way of his enterprises, or even was just cool towards him (as was the case with some high-up State Department officials) was denounced as a stooge of Moscow. For twelve years Trujillo exploited the paranoid logic of the cold war and dubbed himself Number One Anti-communist of the World, Defender of the Christian Civilization Against the Red Peril, and Leader of the Crusade Against Bolshevism.

Towards the end of the fifties Trujillo's régime was hit by one of its periodic crises. The sugar market was depressed. The United States threatened to cut its import quota. Differences between Trujillo's enterprises and American capital got bigger. Pope John XXIII adopted a policy completely opposed to that of his predecessors. A Papal letter protesting against 'the continuous disregard for fundamental human rights' in the Dominican Republic was read from the nation's pulpits. In Venezuela, the left-liberal President Betancourt had come to power and started to heap invective on Trujillo with a venom that was almost hysterical. In June 1960 the Benefactor organized a crude and pointless assassination attempt on Betancourt. In Santo Domingo political unrest was on the increase. In July, Trujillo decreed a State of Emergency. In August, at a conference in San Jose (Costa Rica), the

Organization of American States decided to expel the Dominican Republic. It was then agreed by all American governments to break diplomatic relations with Trujillo and to impose an economic boycott on his country. There was unanimous approval for these resolutions. After thirty years the State Department had dropped its charge.

Not that some appeal to morality had changed American policy overnight. For the Benefactor to go around trying to murder people was nothing out of the ordinary, and a few protesting bishops could hardly have reversed policies, which had even survived an attack on the American sugar monopoly. No, the origins of the San Jose resolutions are to be found in an event which had radically changed the strategic situation in the Caribbean. This event was the victory of the Cuban revolution. Dropping Trujillo was the price the United States were prepared to pay for the isolation of Castro.

In this hopeless situation Trujillo made the only unforgivable faux pas of his career as the first and greatest of all Dominican heads of state. He tried to repeat the bluff that had succeeded so brilliantly fifteen years earlier.

Towards the end of 1960 the Benefactor legalized the 'Movimento Popular Dominicano', the country's communist party, started a campaign against American imperialism and promised agrarian reforms. Six months later, a few days after Trujillo's liquidation, Raul Castro made a speech in Havana. He said:

> In the end Trujillo was nothing more than a tiresome obstacle. They [the Americans] would have gladly got rid of him without bloodshed. We know they told him he had to go and we know why. It was probably through diplomatic channels that they let him know. Trujillo, in his turn, asked whether perhaps his brother could remain in his stead. He was told that all the Trujillos must disappear together and that a kind of 'democratic' election must take place, rather like in Guatemala.
>
> To this Trujillo replied, that under such conditions he could not possibly go.
>
> You remember then how he suddenly called off his attacks against Cuba, how a few of Fidel's speeches were allowed to be broadcast (audience laughter), how he threw out a few mercenaries (he is here referring to the American supported emigre Cubans), how he said he wanted to introduce agrarian reforms and set up co-operatives like us,

and how one day he even legalized the Communist Party? Naturally even the most stupid of communists knew that all Trujillo was interested in doing was manœuvring himself into a good position for blackmail. The problem for the imperialists was how to get rid of him.

That took a bit of time, Trujillo continued to play his games and then wham! it was all over, and who do you think was the first to report the strange case of murder that had taken place there? The American government.

Even today that strange case of murder has still not been cleared up. But, whoever instigated it carried it out, and whatever motives they might have had for doing it were rewarded with a sigh of relief and gratitude.

PARADIGM

The Benefactor is dead, his story just an excerpt from some exotic thriller, the Dominican Republic just one of those small insignificant countries, which people in Europe and America refer to, with a shrug of the shoulders, as a banana republic, temperamental communities where primitive traditions and strange political goings-on are the order of the day. Any similarity with living personages, with organization or events in developed nations, is purely coincidental.

Moreover, Rafael Leonidas Trujillo must be seen as a monster, as a greedy sadist with illusions of grandeur. In short: a pathological case.

And last but not least one must not forget the historical conditions out of which his régime developed, as the chicken from the egg; conditions that could not be repeated, at any time or in any place, because history does not repeat itself. Where, on the other hand, similar conditions are still extant they must be done away with; colonial exploitation and unscrupulous sugar owners must be finished off once and for all, and then the world will be safe from people like Trujillo, a mere 'lackey of imperialism' and nothing more, upon whom it is not worth wasting words or intellectual energy.

Thus in the eyes of the indifferent, in the judgement of the psychologists and in the conscientious analysis of the marxist critic, Trujillo's régime is relegated to history in a comforting and soothing manner.

I am afraid, however, we cannot just drop the matter like that. As far as the self-satisfied, priggish references to banana republics go, they merely show a poor knowledge of history and geography. How many of the ten dozen states, which currently consider themselves to be sovereign, cannot be characterized in this manner? How many communities, during the thirty-one years of Trujillo's rule, made it without a Benefactor? How many peoples were living or live in a banana republic? The exceptions can be counted on the fingers of your hands. (I make it eight.)

As far as 'historical conditions' are concerned, in 1930 in far off Santo Domingo, well they can be settled upon with great exactitude. Only, they are not unrepeatable. If, for example, Hispaniola lay on the Adriatic and was called Albania, it is unlikely that 'historical conditions' would be much of an obstacle to a thirty-nine-year-old police chief of Trujillo's calibre.

One could think of other examples not quite so out of the way.

The assurances of a poverty-stricken psychology that Trujillo was a pathological case are hardly worth countering seriously. He was something much more dangerous than a madman: he was a completely normal, run-of-the-mill human being.

Trujillo's system was a parody. Like all parodies it took the features of the original and exaggerated them, presented them in the purest of forms and in so doing exposed them. The original, in this case, is nothing less than politics up to now, all politics up to now, nothing less than the statesmanship of prehistory. The only unique quality of Trujillo's régime was its openness and logic which meant that there was no chance of the motivation behind it being covered up. This motivation is common to all power structures up to now, but in his case was devoid of ideology. Trujillo was quite happy to utilize different ideologies, but was never caught by any one in particular. He saw them as meaningless set-pieces in a game that was exclusively about power. And it is just this that gives his case such paradigmatic force, and that accounts for the opalescent generality, which is peculiar to him and which constantly invites comparison. Anybody who, from his standpoint, finds nothing criminal in this particular anthology of politics, must either be very far removed from or very close to the Trujillo model. Today some parts of the world are succumbing to the attraction of this model; and everywhere politics are open to the temptation to drop the mask, and show the face that has been there all the time, shorn of furtiveness and half-heartedness.

The Benefactor is dead, the Benefactor is living amongst us.

Translated by Richard Woolley

Dreamers of the Absolute

Part I: Pamphlets and Bombs

This is what the citizens of St. Petersburg read more than a hundred years ago one morning in April 1862 on a secretly published leaflet that had been pasted on the walls of public buildings at night:

> To the young Russia!
>
> The guilt of our rulers has brought our country into a horrible situation. It has only one way out: a bloody, pitiless Revolution which will radically eliminate the foundations of contemporary society and will destroy the adherents of the ruling system. We are not afraid of this revolution although we know that it will cost torrents of blood . . .
>
> First of all, we are going to settle accounts with the Royal house. The Romanovs are going to pay with their blood for the agony of their people, for the many years of despotism, for the disregard of the simplest human rights and needs of their subjects. The whole house of Romanov is going to lose its head. Let us move into the Winter Palace and exterminate its inhabitants.
>
> Our work may be completed with the destruction of the family of the Czar—perhaps. But more probably not: the entire imperial party will rise to a man for the Czar. In that case we will trust ourselves, our strength, the love of the people, the glorious future of Russia, which will be the first country in the world to realize the great

cause of Socialism, and we call out: to the axes! Strike
pitilessly at the Czarist party! Strike them on the plazas
when that pack of dogs dares show its face there! Strike
them in the streets of the provincial towns and on the
boulevards of the metropolises! Strike them in the villages
and in the hamlets!

But if we fail, if we have to pay with our lives for the
attempt to help mankind to its rights, we will step onto
the scaffold and put our head on the block without fear.
The Central Revolutionary Committee.[1]

The few libraries and institutes in the West with a copy of
this leaflet treat it with great care; yellow and crumbling, it is
kept under glass, like a relic. And like all relics it not only
evokes enthusiasm but also the doubts of those who were born
afterwards; yes, mostly doubt. It is worth examining thoroughly. The faded document is a declaration of war. It announced the last holy war against the old order in Europe and
simultaneously the first great act of modern resistance. This
twofold meaning can be gathered from the text of the proclamation. Its high-sounding language resounds with echoes of the
French Revolution. Its rhetoric is secondhand, its images a
reminiscence of the eighteenth century: the ultima ratio of the
St. Petersburg conspirators is the axe, the weapon of the
Jacobins. It is not the mitrailleuse of the Paris Commune nor
is it dynamite—the symbolic substance of the late nineteenth
century, which Alfred Nobel discovered at the same time in
his Stockholm laboratory as the court officials presented Czar
Alexander II with that crudely printed sheet that prophesied
his and his regime's execution.

For the man in the Winter Palace, the autocrat of all the
Russians, it cannot have been easy to take seriously this threat
and declaration of war. Who had uttered it and to whom had
it been addressed? The Central Revolutionary Committee of
1862 consisted of a handful of untested students and officers. It
had no organization to fall back upon; it had no power to call
its own and no experience. With empty hands they went in to
battle against a superpower and its absolute sovereign. Ar-

raigned against them they had: a mighty army, an immense bureaucracy, three police systems, which were independent of each other, one of which, the secret police, was under the Czar's direct command and enjoyed unlimited authority. They lacked a mass basis, a party, and financial resources. They had nothing but the words of their declaration of war.

Despite that, their words were not empty. The war that they declared was a fact. It had been waged for decades. The first Jacobin conspiracy, which wanted to do away with the Czar and his family, had been the Decembrists. It consisted of officers from the aristocracy and took the form of the traditional coup d'état. On the morning of December 14, 1825 two thousand mutineering guard soldiers had marched in front of the Senate Palace in St. Petersburg: a single salvo of grape-shot had ended the coup.

Nicholas I, who was Czar at the time, executed the five heads of the Decembrists conspiracy on his birthday, and simultaneously founded an institution that was to wage the cold civil war in Russia for ninety years and keep fanning it back to life repeatedly. That was the so-called "Third Section of his Majesty's Personal Chancellery." This secret police of the Czar had but one task: to choke off, ruthlessly, any sign of opposition. During the first forty years of its existence not a single shot was fired at the Czar. But these forty years were the incubation period of the revolutionary terror. The liberal historian Karl Oldenberg describes them in the following way:

> The Third Section of the Imperial Chancellery indeed became the mightiest authority of the realm to which even ministers had to subordinate themselves. The intolerance of the Censor became incredible. Almost all outstanding products of German, French and English literature and ninety per cent of all periodicals stood on the index. The indigenous newspapers were censored with the same severity. Besides needing permission from the very highest authority, anyone wanting to leave the country had to put 500 rubles in escrow . . . The ministry of education was given to a man who eliminated all academic chairs in philosophy and political science, limited the number of students

at each university to 300; and it is a fact that the Czar was planning to abolish all universities completely. The aging Czar's belief in his own infallibility, and his tyrannical nature became so boundless during his last years that even his most trusted advisers began to doubt the soundness of his mind.[2]

These antecedents, barely alluded to with information such as the above, are what lend the 1862 declaration its full weight. Certainly, it was nothing but a piece of paper with second-rate political prose printed on it. Saint-Just would have made far better formulations than that handful of nameless ones. Still, the printing press that had manufactured this leaflet stood in the Russian General Staff Building, and its authors were putting their heads on the line. Four years later, in the summer garden of St. Petersburg, an obscure member of the petty nobility by the name of Dimitri Karakosov took the first shot at the Czar. He missed. But the war in the dark had turned deadly serious.

It is difficult to describe this war—not only because it expresses itself in the wishes and ideas of its protagonists but also in the contradictions of nineteenth-century Russian society: the interests of the landowners and of the bourgeoisie in the cities, of the capitalists of trade and industry, of the nobility of the Czar's service and the awakening intellectuals. Dynastic pacts, foreign political entanglements, fluctuations of the grain prices on the world market and behind the scenes competition for railway construction and industrialization influenced it, yes perhaps decided it. The finest points of this war can only be understood by someone who has studied the entire political, social, and economic history of Russia in the nineteenth century.

This can only be mentioned in passing here, because another story is being told: the history of a desperate minority of a few dozen, a few hundred, a few thousand people who literally put their heads on the block. The meaning of this story cannot be completely grasped with sociological categories and

Marxist analysis. It does not deal with class warfare and production relationships but of dreamers and fanatics, of amok runners and bel esprits, of mountebanks and phantasts, missionaries and suicides, of bloody saints the likes of which the world has not seen again.

It is a dark and confused story, which plays in the underbrush of history and in the wilderness of illegality. Its showplaces are cellar apartments and fortresses, prisons and salons, shabby attics in Zurich and Geneva, miserable shelters in Ukrainian villages, courtrooms, factory halls, and palaces. Its main protagonists remain shadowy, twisted by memory lapses, and enveloped by a swarm of spies and agents. Its sources are untrustworthy and full of contradictions. Important evidence has been permanently lost or is rotting in secret archives. Anyone who wants to tell this story is dependent on the zeal of a few liberal compilers in the Germany of the 1880s and on the sparse information and memoirs that the few survivors of the conspiracy have left us.

The path of the action is labyrinthine and chaotic. Its logic is dialectical, not linear. It follows the fever curve of Russian society through the nineteenth century. The tactics of the revolt change from decade to decade with the climate of the regime. The play of the material interests, the moods of the Czar and his advisers, the atmosphere in the ten leading St. Petersburg salons are all unstable, change from one day to the next, from frenzied suppression to semiconcession, from half-reforms to ruthless reaction. One day the opposition press is allowed, and prohibited again the following night; political prisoners suddenly find themselves freed or pardoned; one year later they are beaten to death or banished by the thousands without trial.

And if that were not a surfeit of confusion, we see the heroes of our story fighting with each other for nights on end over glasses of punch or tea. They are never of one mind. They are always tugging at a hundred strings. They divide into innumerable groups and circles. They mistrust each other, even detest each other. Always in danger of being raided or betrayed, they overwhelm each other with suspicion. In St. Petersburg, Moscow, Odessa, London, Geneva, and Zurich the factions carry out embittered feuds. Loudmouths and traitors, mountebanks and madmen poison the conspiracy. That is how impoverished and disrupted the tiny fighting force looked that made the Czar, the absolute ruler, tremble, and to which he finally succumbed.

Not a single red thread, least of all a chronological one, leads through the labyrinth of this conspiracy. Anyone who wants to follow its progress must pursue it to the most important scenes. The first of these is the battlefield of theory.

Nothing, in retrospect, appears more harmless than the beginning of a revolution. This beginning is invariably unperspicuous, peaceful, occasionally touching. These are some of the first acts of the Russian conspirators: they founded Sunday schools; they dissected frogs; they read French books; they started reading circles; they put Hegel's *Logic* into verse; they got all hot over a new novel and they wrote reviews; they founded a health insurance plan for students; they helped each other and met for lunch; they played chess; one of their members, Feodor Dostoyevsky, designated their age, sociology, and mentality with the words: "We were a proletariat of graduates." For years on end this proletariat dissipated and renewed itself. Indiscriminately, impatiently, voraciously it ingested the ideas of Western Europe. The agenda of this euphoric reception contained the following items:

> In the 1830s, the French Utopians, particularly Henri de Saint-Simon and Charles Fourier;
> in the 1840s, the early socialists Owen and Proudhon;
> in the '60s, the *German Ideology*, Feuerbach and Friedrich Karl Büchner, plus the natural sciences, especially Darwinism;
> in the '70s, the positivism of Comte and the socialist teachings of Marx, Engels and Lasalle.

That was the curriculum of the progressive bourgeois intellectual all over Europe, except that the Russian students caught up with it only ten to twenty years later. This and nothing else earned them the appellation *nihilists*, a word that even then was as devoid of real meaning as now when it serves as bogeyman for the bourgeoisie. Of course at that time the nihilists recited their lesson with especial passion. Atheism, materialism, natural science, socialism—all of this only served as an ideological weapon for them in their fight against the gospel of the old autocracy. It was itself a gospel in its own right and was devoured without criticism, enthusiastically believed and ecstatically proclaimed. What is specifically Russian is the missionary zeal that simultaneously transfigured and distorted the imported ideas. The nihilists were apostles of the future but they preached the rationalistic credo with a fanatical evangelism that belied the coldness of their theses. One of those students is supposed to have been as presumptuous as to proclaim: "Each one of us is prepared to go to the gallows and lay down his head for Moleschott and Darwin."[3]

A ridiculous confession; but the Czar's regime took it at its word. The death sentence confirms its seriousness.

In March 1848 the chief of the "Third Section" in St. Petersburg received a denunciation: each Friday evening there was a gathering of young people, students, officials, and officers at the home of a certain Petrachevski, an official in the foreign office. Thereupon a spy from the secret police participated at the discussions of the so-called conspirators for one year.

On April 23, 1849, the police took action. Thirty-three of the participants—average age: twenty-five—were arrested, among them a student called Dostoyevsky. Twenty-one of them were condemned to death and pardoned only under the gallows—to long sentences in Siberian prisons. The others were banished from the country.

The "plots against the state" were more of a theoretical nature: the "conspirators" read books and discussed the ideas they found in these books. Not their actions, but their opinions were punished. The Petrachevskies were typical representatives of the revolutionary intellectuals of those years. They had no organization; undertook no political actions whatsoever; had no plans; performed no assassinations, not to speak of demonstrations. Their battlefield was theory. It was a bloody battlefield: for one platitude you could get ten years in prison, for one iota of utopianism the gallows. A peaceful uprising under such circumstances was a pipe dream. The opposition had no peaceful means. Its most harmless move was treated like a major crime. It can be said that in a certain sense the Czarist regime had bred and trained its opponents. The first effective secret society in Russia was the "Third Section" of the Czarist Chancellery. It was the merciless teacher of young Russia; it became the model for conspiratorial techniques and illegal methods. Its theory had been imported by young Russia; its practice had been acquired in the mother country and on its own body: the practice of the underground. Now they no longer founded sober debating societies and Sunday schools; it was "The Society of the People's Court or the Axe," "Hell";"The Central Union of Workers," "The South Russian Workers' Union"; "The Lawristi"; "The Buntari"; "The Society for Land and Freedom"; "The People's Will"; and with these groups the phantom conspiracy became real. The premises were clear, less so were the objectives and methods, less so the choice of weapons.

The Central Revolutionary Committee, which was calling for the axe in spring 1862 received a reply from Alexander Herzen, the leading head of the older generation, from his London exile: "I will not call for the axe, this *ultima ratio* of the oppressed, as long as there still exists the slightest hope for a solution without the axe. Russia needs brooms not axes . . . We have to take the evolutionary path of America and England. The artists of the revolution don't like this path, but that doesn't concern us. We decidedly prefer this path over the bloody one."[4]

And even seven years later he implored the wild Bakunin: "What sensible people will forgive Attila, the Committee for Public Welfare, even Peter the Great—they will not forgive us. We have not heard a voice from on high commanding us to fulfill a destiny, we haven't heard a voice from the depths to guide us. For us there exists only one voice and one leader: reason and understanding. Discarding these, we become apostates of civilization."[5]

That was not a choice between lawfulness and revolt, it was a choice of weapons—between pamphlet and bomb. The Czarist regime was justified in regarding both as equally dangerous. Herzen's *The Bell*, printed in London, was prohibited in Russia. But every devious means was used to smuggle it into the country: at the Novgorod Trade Fair the police confiscated a hundred thousand copies of a single issue. Nor was *The Bell* the only organ of the revolutionaries. The printing presses of the emigrants stood in Berlin and Geneva, in London and in Zurich, and all over Russia there were illegal primitive handpresses which issued a flood of leaflets and pamphlets: *The Free Word, The Worker, Forward, The Seed-kernel, The Storm Bell, The Subterranean Word, Freedom, The Community, Land and Freedom, the People's Will, The Beginning, The Harbinger of Truth, The Black Distribution, The People's Cause* . . .

The cheap and crude little issues, which went from hand to hand, are the first historical examples of the immeasurable effect of illegal political propaganda. They were published in ridiculously small editions, generally between 300 and 3000 copies were printed; but each copy found many readers, and before being read to shreds they were hand-copied and passed on. This procedure is instructive because it shows for the first time how political literature can work as a trace element and, with minimal investment, can effect enormous consequences.

However, the plethora of publications that sprouted spontaneously and indiscriminately in the underground does not only prove how widespread the revolutionary unrest was in the bourgeoisie and among the intellectuals. It is also an expression of the perplexity and splintering of the revolutionary forces. On the battlefield of theory they not only faced the Czar, they also decimated each other.

The common basis for their agitation was narrow. It consisted of the thesis that things would have to change in Russia.

Each proposition that exceeded this demand became the object of tenacious quarrels, bitter animosity, endless sophistry and idle speculation. The leaflets and handprinted papers of that time, printed at great sacrifice and disseminated at mortal danger, all accused each other, openly or secretly, of corruption, cowardice, incomprehension and treason. The tinier and more impotent it was, the more hysterical and dogmatic the illegal press sounded. Historians of ideas will neatly classify their directions, nuances and contradictions one of these days, in five-volume works—or perhaps they won't.

It was no wonder that this gibberish became a kind of permanent condition. What young Russia had imported from the West, feverishly and uninspected, was extremely heterogeneous material. It spanned the spectrum from insipid liberalism to the most extremist anarchist teachings. The fermentation of this material led to severe conflicts in Europe throughout the entire century; in Russia this fermentation process took place in a sharply confined area and under constant threat.

Besides, the uncritically absorbed teachings from Europe were by and large inappropriate to Russian conditions. The underdeveloped Czarist realm lacked every prerequisite for a bourgeois, not to speak of a proletarian, revolution. As though to spite these truths, these teachings were that much more stubbornly invoked, that much more irreconcilably did the partisans adhere to them.

The Russian contribution to revolutionary theory is therefore correspondingly small. Except for their attempt to solve the farmers' question, the Russian intellectuals occupied themselves primarily with the technique of revolution as such. In this process it developed radically new, in part horrible, new theses. These are the work of three men.

> The spirit, this old mole, has already done his subterranean work, and will soon re-appear, to hold court . . . All people are filled with a certain premonition, and everyone who still has a sense of life, looks with ominous anticipation toward the approaching future which will speak the liberating word. In Russia, which has perhaps a great future, dark thunderclouds are

gathering, and therefore we call to our blinded brothers: Do penance! do penance! The Kingdom of the Lord is near! Therefore let us trust the eternal spirit which only destroys and obliterates because he is the ineffable and ever-creative source of all life. The joy of destruction is also a creative joy.[6]

These sentences stood in the *Deutschen Jahrbüchern für Wissenschaft und Kunst* of 1842. Its author was a Russian of lionesque stature, the son of a noble family, educated in the fashionable St. Petersburg Artillery School, a brilliant and violent man with the characteristics of a Slavic Danton. "Bakunin the Giant," his friends called him. He sat in Hegel's classes and got mixed up in every European revolution of his time. In 1849 he was condemned to death in Saxony and Austria, pardoned, handed over to the Russian police and sent to Siberia. In 1861 he succeeded in fleeing via Sakhalin, Japan and America to London where he pushed his teacher, the gentle Herzen, against the wall. Michael Bakunin was a *hasardeur*, an adventurer, driven by a berserk demon of destruction. Madly talkative, he forced his entry into the Marxist International. In 1872 he was responsible for its disintegration. His credo was just as fiery as it was primitive: he was an anarchist of the first order. He wrote: "The smallest and most harmless state is criminal even in its dreams." He taught: Order is crime. Revolt is the good. And from these teachings he drew the consequences in his main work, *The Revolutionary Catechism*. "Hard on himself, the revolutionary also has to be hard on others. Every feeling of liking, of friendship, of love, of gratitude, every fraternal impulse has to be choked off by a single cold passion: the revolutionary work. For him there exists a single pleasure, a single consolation, a single remuneration, a single satisfaction: success as a revolutionary. Day and night he can have just one thought, one objective: uncompromising destruction. While pursuing this objective coldbloodedly and incessantly, he must be prepared to die himself, and just as prepared to kill, with his own hands, those who prevent him from reaching this objective."[7]

Bakunin did not write this alone. A spirit darker even than

his was at work here, that of his mysterious student Netchajev. We know little of the life of this Sergej Netchajev, and that little sounds like phantasmagoric journalism. In 1866 he appeared in St. Petersburg. Three years later he disappeared, claiming subsequently that the Czarist police had arrested and tossed him into the Peter-Paul Fortress. To his intimate friends he confided an extraordinary story. He said he had instigated an insurrection in the Fortress and fled during the ensuing confusion. That was his first mystification. In fact, he had left the country for Geneva to look up Bakunin, to whom he told another fairy tale: that Russia was ready for an uprising. He, Netchajev, commanded an armed organization that was preparing the coup. Bakunin got him some money, named him head of the Russian section of the International. In St. Petersburg Netchajev appeared with a piece of paper that lent him a magic aura. It said: "Alliance Révolutionnaire Européenne. Comité Général. Le 12 Mai 1869. No. 2771. Signé: Bakunin."

With this paper Netchajev bewitched everyone. He talked about a mysterious central committee whose inventor and sole member was he, himself, and in whose name he demanded unconditional obedience. He pulled a whole fictitious network of secret societies out of his hat. One of his followers, a student by the name of Ivanov, began to doubt the existence of this phantom conspiracy.

On November 21, 1869, in the circle of his Union of the Axe, Netchajev opened the trial against this "traitor." The same day Ivanov was garroted near the agricultural academy in Moscow. The medicine man of the revolution had become its first hangman.

His ideological contribution to revolutionary theory was the sentence: Everything is permitted in the name of the revolution. The revolutionary is justified, and indeed obliged to lie to his own people. He must do everything that increases the suffering of the oppressed, the bitterness and misery of the persecuted.

The third ideologist of revolutionary crime, a Bakunin student too, was Peter Tkatchev. He was the most obscure and also the most consistent terrorist on the battlefield of theory. He suggested the extermination of all Russians under the age of twenty-five because they were incapable of grasping the ideas of the revolution. He proclaimed the permanent terror as an end in itself; terror and revolution, according to him, do not stand in a means-and-ends relationship, they become one and the same thing. The leaders of the revolution are to enjoy unbridled power; their subjects are merely tools against whom one may use any means one chooses. When the Czar is killed, the Revolution raises its head: the head of a new Czar who will conduct a more horrible and absolute reign than the old.

Of these three logicians of the revolution, Bakunin was the only one at that time who directly influenced Russian events; Tkatchev and Netchajev were outsiders. All three came to a miserable end. Bakunin died completely isolated and ignored in his Swiss exile. After being imprisoned for twelve years, Netchajev ended in a penitentiary. Tkatchev disappeared in a madhouse. Their seed sprouted only forty, sixty, seventy years later. They did not have many readers, but among the few who studied their faded tracts were Lenin, Trotsky, and Stalin. Lenin called these teachings majestic, and Stalin made everyday practice of them.

Russia's youth had other plans. At the beginning of the 1870s it recognized how little had been accomplished with the dangerous and tireless propaganda work of the past decade. The innumerable tracts and pamphlets, demonstrations and calls to action had never reached more than a minority. Ninety percent of all Russians were illiterate. Their fate, their liberation, was at stake. All conspiracies to date had resembled a bourgeois monologue of the intellectuals. The most passionate articles from London and Zurich, the most troubled and troubling novels could not have the ear of the fifty million farmers who were the true Russia. At that moment of realization the revolution changed its setting, which had been the battlefield of theory, and set out on a crusade: it went "among the people."

Leave the universities, academies and schools! Turn away from a science which in its present form is only meant to shackle and choke you. Move among the people and liberate your brothers from criminal servitude.[8]

That was Bakunin's voice, which gave the signal for a turn-about that is without precedent in recent history. Thousands of aristocratic daughters and gymnasium students, young noblemen and optimistic sons of the bourgeoisie succumbed to a kind of intoxication and ventured forth on their mission "among the people." "Among the people"—this slogan of the young pilgrims of early Russian socialism gave them the name *Narodniki*.

Their socialism had acquired a peculiarly Russian coloring. The theorists of the revolution had realized at an early point that the West European teachings were not suited to Russian reality, which lacked a strong and self-confident bourgeoisie and an awakening industrial proletariat, which the teachings of Saint-Simon and Marx presupposed. The economic basis of Russian society continued to be the farmers. But how was this mute, huge, lethargic, ignorant, disenfranchised and backward class to be prodded to revolutionary action? How was one to preach socialism to a people who were firmly convinced that the earth stood on four whales?

The leading intellectuals among the revolutionaries discovered a startling solution to their dilemma as early as the first third of the century. Instead of bringing socialism to the village they found that it was at home there. All that mattered was to have it properly recognized.

This was a rather daring interpretation of the economic conditions in the village, and it was based on an arrangement that indeed had an ancient tradition and was spread throughout Russia: the communal ownership of the land. In former times the farmers in each village jointly owned the forest, the meadows, and the water; the farmland was raffled off every nine years among the members of the community. Serfdom had not much changed this system: the master left a part of his estate to the community. "We belong to the master, but the land belongs to us," said the farmers. "The earth comes from God and he has appointed the Czar so to make sure that everyone gets his share of God's earth."

From such shaky premises Bakunin drew the daring conclusion: "It will be an easy matter to get any village to revolt. The people are always ready to revolt and capable of organizing themselves after a revolution. All they lack is an awareness of their strength, hatred of their oppressors and the practice of revolution. The revolutionaries therefore have nothing to learn and nothing to teach the people. The people know their own suffering and its source. The revolutionaries should only stoke the hatred of the privileged classes, awaken the people's consciousness of their own power and train this power by means of attempted coups."[9]

On the basis of such words and assurances, according to a middle-class historian, "the Russian socialist broke all family ties, gave up his career, acquired a tan and a pair of coarse hands, stuck a forged passport in his boots, tossed a knapsack with books over his shoulder, took a rod in his hand, shook the dust of the rotten world off his feet and 'went on a trip without itinerary.'"[10]

This crusade among the people was not a genuine mass movement. But at its height, around 1874, it comprised roughly ten thousand members. A revolutionary action of such an extent was not possible without the tacit toleration of a large part of the bourgeoisie. It required considerable financial means and a minimum of organization. The Narodniki camouflaged themselves as shoemakers, traveling salesmen, teachers, and writers. They set up smithies, junk shops and drugstores. The girls, of whom an astonishing number participated, many of them wealthy and pretty, worked as midwives and medics. They had nothing to gain and everything to lose; every conversation, every trip, every meeting was a crime against the State, and the police pursued them to the most remote hideouts. The Narodniki took "conspiratorial apartments" and arranged telegram codes. They had their own messengers and illegal print shops. The editorials and analyses were now replaced by titles especially designed for the farmer: *Sketches from the Steppes, Little Demitrius, Strength Breaks Straw, They Have Caught the Denouncer, The Tale of Goworucha, The Tale of the Four Brothers, Live, The Deeds and the Execution of the Robber Stenjka Rasin, The Clever Mechanic, The Talk on Good Friday, The Golden Legend, How Our Land Came Not to Be Ours Anymore, Father Jegor.*

It was not entirely safe to distribute pamphlets of this kind because the farmers, who could not read, frequently took them to their priest to find out what they said. But the priests took the pamphlets directly to the police. That is why the agitators carried written instructions on how they had to conduct themselves in conversation with the farmers. Here are two examples:

> At one time God created all men equal and gave them the earth as a gift. But then came the noblemen and the officials and snapped up the best land for themselves. And you see, brother, now the farmers have to make high payments because they aren't supposed to get too fat. But the farmers forget that they are a hundred times stronger than their oppressors. They should take revenge now and . . . create a large state of the farmers which is ruled by a sense of brotherhood.[11]

Another typical argument:

> For this tankard of brandy you are now paying five kopeks. But the noblemen and the profiteers are putting four of these five kopeks into their own pockets; and if all the noblemen and profiteers were killed, all of us, and that also includes you, brother, could drink five tankards of brandy for five kopeks.[12]

Good will, glowing eagerness, passionate devotion: nothing could overcome the abyss separating the revolutionaries and the village. The crusade among the people was based on a grand illusion. Particularly the most decent among the Narodniki saw through this illusion the moment they stepped into their first farmer's hut. This is well illustrated by the report of a young girl by the name of Vera Figner, who was an exemplary figure among the intellectuals of the revolution: she came from a *haute bourgeois* family, she was one of the first women to gain access to a university, she left her career and her husband for the sake of the revolution, she lived in emigration, returned to Russia to "go among the people," and later joined the terrorist executive committee of the People's Will and spent twenty years as a prisoner in fortress Schlüsselburg.

For the first time in my life I came face to face with village life . . . I must admit, I feel lonely, weak, without energy among this sea of farmers . . . until now I had never had a close-up look at the poor farmer's existence. I knew the impoverishment of the people only from theory, from books, magazines, statistics. So as to escape the narrow track of family interests, the kitchen, the cards, the hunt for profit I seized science as a means for reaching the people . . . But where were the real people? Now, twenty-five years old, I stood before them as a child into whose hands something extraordinary, never-before-seen is pressed.

I began to fulfill my duties. Eighteen days each month I was traveling in villages and hamlets. Usually I stopped off at an inn. . . . In no time at all thirty to forty patients filled the room . . . It was impossible to remain diffident at the sight of so much sickness. Filthy, worn-out people, the illnesses all protracted, the adults mostly with headaches, rheumatism, headaches for fifteen years, almost all of them with skin diseases, incurable stomach and intestinal disorders, wheezing audible at a considerable distance, people of every age with syphilis, ulcers and boils everywhere. You touched yourself on the head: is this the life of men or animals? Where does this misery end? What hypocrisy all medicine was in the face of this horrifying condition? Can one even entertain the thought of protest under these circumstances? Isn't it merely ironical to speak to these people, who are pressed to the ground by physical want, of resistance and fighting? Isn't despair the only thing capable of breaking through this endless patience and passivity? Every day for three months I saw one and the same picture. These three months were a difficult test for me. The insights into the material existence of the people was deeply disturbing. I could not get any insight into its soul. I never opened my mouth to make propaganda.[13]

That was at the beginning of 1877. In October of the same year there began, in St. Petersburg, the monster trial of the 193. It was meant to be a reckoning with the activity of the Narodniki. Three thousand eight hundred people were involved, of which 770 were accused. But the minor trials were severed from the main proceeding, so that only 193 defendants remained, and it is to these that the show trial owes its name. It became a sensation. The defendants spoke as though they were the judges, as though they were reading the verdict—the verdict of the government of the Czar. They used the courtroom as a platform for their agitation, and the public either tacitly or vociferously agreed with them. Never before had such words been uttered publicly in Russia:

> This isn't a court but a silly comedy, possibly something worse than a whorehouse. There the girls do their business at least from necessity, at least with their own bodies; but here the senators, either out of venality or servility, out of cupidity or for promotion, do their business with the lives of others, petty brokers of truth and justice.[14]

These words, of the defendant Myshkin, provoked a tumult. It came to a clash between the police and the public. The hall had to be cleared by force. After this occurrence the defendants did not say another word. Mutely they listened to the verdict: 94 not guilty, 36 Narodniki to Siberia, the rest, Myshkin among them, sentenced to years of forced labor.

However, the political loser in the trial was the government. Public opinion decidedly took the side of the 193. In terms of propaganda the Narodniki had accomplished more in the dock than they had during their long crusade among the people. In the villages everything had remained the same. The agitation had collapsed in the face of the ignorance and misery of the farmers. Solovjev, one of the clearest heads of the movement, coldly drew the balance of the high-minded but hopeless endeavor and simultaneously gave the cue for the new and bloody turn of the conspiratorial fight:

> The activity of a revolutionary is completely useless on the flatland during the current political conditions. A change in these conditions must be achieved at any price. Therefore the reactionaries have to be destroyed, chiefly in the person of Alexander II.[15]

Once more the revolutionary movement changed the arena of its fight, once more it began a new chapter. It might carry the title: the protracted execution. This chapter begins on January 24, 1878, the day after the verdict on the 193, with a phantastic coup.

On this day the president of the police of St. Petersburg, General Trepov, held his weekly audience, which, as usual, was attended by numerous petitioners, among them a very carefully dressed lady by the name of Vera Sassulitch. The twenty-five-year-old visitor handed the president a written petition. The general, who was seated behind his desk, began to read it when his visitor calmly opened her handbag, took out a revolver and shot Trepov, wounding him severely but not mortally. Vera Sassulitch tossed away the revolver and was arrested without putting up any resistance. She explained her action with a single sentence: "This is the revenge for the maltreatment of the student Bogoljubov."

Everyone in Petersburg knew what this meant. Police president Trepov was notorious for his methods. It had become known that he had prisoners tossed into hot, airless holes from which the excrement was not removed. Several prisoners had been beaten to death. The student Bogoljubov had been whipped before the other prisoners, an incident that had become known through an indiscretion. It had even gotten into the Russian newspapers because of a jurisdictional dispute between the ministry of justice and the police authorities. The justice officials were liberal-minded and opposed any encroachment by the executive. Their *bête noire* was Trepov. The minister of justice talked the Czar into letting Vera Sassulitch have a jury trial.

This trial opened on April 1, 1878, and for the first time the pressure of public opinion was so strong that it came to demonstrations in front of the ministry of justice. The excitement was even greater than during the trial of the 193. Soon it transpired that Vera Sassulitch hadn't even known the maltreated student. She was the sole defendant and claimed to have no accomplices or accessories. The State's Attorney began his presentation in an unprecedented fashion by first justifying himself for accusing Vera Sassulitch instead of the wounded police president; he was convinced of the truthfulness of the defendant's motive and he openly presented the assassination attempt as "a praiseworthy protest of injured human dignity." The only thing punishable was the means of which she had availed herself. The verdict of the jury was just as sensational as this speech. The jury had to answer the question whether Vera Sassulitch was guilty of attempted murder. The verdict was a unanimous not guilty. The public in the courtroom cheered. High justice officials applauded. Sassulitch was carried to her coach on the shoulders of the crowd. The police provoked a riot. Three shots were fired in the crowd. The free Vera Sassulitch fled to Switzerland from the administrative justice of the secret police by whom she was liable to be deported. St. Petersburg society celebrated her unanimously as a *grande citoyenne*. The press openly expressed its approval of the verdict. Finally the censor prohibited any mention of the case. The minister of justice had to resign while the Czar paid sick calls to General Trepov.

Vera Sassulitch's shot acted as a signal. The next phase of the terror had begun. A brief chronicle of the events of the next few years provides the following picture:

February 1, 1878: Conspirators in Rostov shoot police spy Nikonov.

February 22, 1878: In Kiev State's Attorney Kotljerivsky is wounded by pistol shots on the open street. He had maltreated political prisoners.

February 25, 1878: Police Colonel Baron Heyking is knifed to death in broad daylight in one of the liveliest thoroughfares in Kiev.

March 24, 1878: A further assassination attempt on a police spy in Kiev fails. The intended victim wore an armored shirt. The assassin shoots himself.

June 14, 1878: Rosenzweig and Reinstein, two secret policemen who had infiltrated the organization of the conspirators, are found out and murdered.

August 4, 1878: After a hunger strike in the Peter-Paul Fortress the head of the Russian secret police, General Mesenzev, is "executed" on a St. Petersburg street. The assassins escape. One day later they publish a pamphlet entitled *A Death for a Death*, which contains a complete explanation for the verdict.

February 9, 1879: The governor of Charkov, Count Krapotkin, is shot in his carriage after returning from a ball. A note is found on his body stating the reasons for the verdict.

March 12, 1879: Mesenzev's successor, the new chief of the Russian secret police, General Drenteln, is assaulted and killed in St. Petersburg. There is no trace of the murderers. It becomes difficult to replace the general. His job is considered lethal.

This list is incomplete. The chronicle of the years 1878–1879 contains mutinies and student uprisings in all large Russian cities. When the police discovered a printing press or a meeting place of the conspirators the latter put up armed resistance. Prisoners were hardly ever released. The revolutionaries "confiscate" money transports. The first organized strikes occur in the cotton-manufacturing plants in St. Petersburg.

The inner logic of these events was perfectly apparent. Disappointed by the failure of its crusade among the people, the agitators had streamed back into the large cities and had formed new conspiratorial cadres. Self-defense against spies, denouncers, and traitors were the motive for the initial terrorist acts. Revenge against their persecutors, the Czarist officials, was a second one. But the higher the rank of the victim in the government hierarchy, the closer the conspirators came to their actual enemy, the nearer was the day of that execution that had been decided decades before.

"Thus it seemed odd to us to kill the servants who only fulfilled their ruler's will while leaving the ruler unshorn,"[16] wrote Vera Figner, the medic of the days of the great crusade; and her co-fighter Alexander Solovjov, around Eastertime 1879, reached the conclusion that: "I must do it. It is mine to do. Alexander II is mine and I refuse to yield him to anyone else."[17]

One week later, on April 2, 1879, Solovjev took five shots at the Czar, who was taking a walk in front of the Winter Palace. The Czar was not killed. Nor did the assassin succeed in committing suicide. The poison dose which Solovjev had in a capsule in his mouth was too weak. He was hanged after a summary trial and died without saying a word.

Finally the Czar had understood that it was his head that was at stake. The reaction of the government was immediate and draconic: a state of emergency was declared in large parts of European Russia; the six military governors were given dictatorial powers; all houses in the capital were kept under tabs by means of a regular, precisely arranged spy service; strict censorship of the news; radical tightening of passport control; and of control of poison and weapon trade; lifting of all academic freedom at the University of St. Petersburg; suspension of all regular courts; innumerable house searches; administrative arrests and deportations to which alone in the months of April and May twenty thousand people fell victim.

The more drastic the measures of the police, the greater the frequency and number of the posters that appeared on the walls of the houses of St. Petersburg with threats against the Czar. The illegal presses worked feverishly. The duel was approaching a climax.

On August 15, 1879 the executive committee of the People's Will constituted itself in the Russian capital. Earlier creations by this name had existed on paper only and had led a phantom existence. This time it was for real. The time of the amateurs was over. After decades of dilettantish piecework, planless individual actions, and naive expressions of outrage the revolutionary movement had finally provided itself with a central organ, which proceeded methodically and with the precision of a general staff. This collective of professional revolutionaries had grown out of the left wing of the old Narodniki movement. The executive committee, which was to become an execution committee, had drawn its conclusions from the failures of the sixties and seventies. It had perused the teachings of Netchajev and partially accepted them; the committee had learned just as much from its opponent, the secret police. These were its postulates:

A tightly centralized organization; dependence of the cadres on the central committee; strict discipline; collective leadership; organization according to the principle of the onion peel; development of the most modern technical means; division of labor and specialization; systematic distribution of the risk; long-term planning.

This model provided the executive committee with a decisive advantage over the secret police. It guaranteed the continuity of their work even when a few heads of the movement were arrested; it guaranteed a maximum of security and secretiveness within the organization itself; it heightened the effectiveness of all directives emanating from the central committee. One of its heads, Michailov, said of the central committee: "If the organization would order me to wash cups, I would do so with the same eagerness as I would the most interesting planning work."[18]

The committee finally recognized that agitation and terror, pamphlet and bomb, were merely two aspects of the same thing; in a certain sense it acted publicly: each terrorist action was preceded by a public announcement; each assassination was simultaneously an instrument of propaganda with far-ranging effects.

The printers therefore enjoyed a favored status among the specialized groups. They worked as a collective on the run. "The devices of the printing presses," it says in a contemporary report, "were the simplest in the world: a few boxes with type, a small cylinder with a sticky, glue-like substance; two bottles of printer's ink and a few brushes and sponges. Everything was so well ordered that it could be concealed in a quarter of an hour in a large closet."[19]

Their own passport office provided the conspirators with forged papers. They always had freshly cut stamps and seals on hand.

Dynamite once and for all replaced the axe. The organization had its own chemists who knew how to handle pyroxylin and nitroglycerin; mechanics who had a way with cables and detonators; and sappers to construct tunnels.

It was all over with the old carelessness of the nihilist years. The conspirators developed a system of safety signals and their apartments were selected and armed according to strategic principles. The old dress of the revolutionaries, which had become a joke, disappeared: instead of the obligatory plaids, high boots, and blue spectacles a certain luxury took over. The conspirators had recognized that wealth provides protection.

It is by no means superfluous to throw a glance at their origins and life-style. Most of the conspirators were outsiders within their own class, sons and daughters of the high nobility, the upper middle class and officers corps. Their fathers were generals, privy counselors, and estate owners. Surprisingly, many older people from their class tacitly approved of the conspiracy and even supported it: by means of donations or by providing illegal asylum or by forwarding messages. Petit bourgeois, farmers and workers appear in the ranks of the conspiracy only in the seventies. Surprisingly high too, from the beginning, was the percentage of women in the conspiracy: the police files prove that every fourth member was a woman. The legends which were disseminated in Western Europe about the so-called nihilists seem particularly silly. The State-supported yellow press spoke of orgies of free love, wild marriages, and all sorts of other philistine titillations. The truth was far different from such bourgeois phantasies: the typical revolutionary was rather a puritan than an epicurean; led an extremely strict life, was conscientious, scrupulous, and marvelously modest. No member of the executive committee was over thirty. They gave themselves the following statutes:

"Every committee member commits himself:
1. To exert all spiritual and mental energy in behalf of the revolutionary cause, to give up family ties, sympathies, love and friendship for its sake;
2. If necessary, to give up one's life without consideration for oneself and others;
3. To own nothing that is not also the property of the organization;
4. To negate one's individual will and subsume it under the majority decision of the organization."[20]

On August 25, 1879, the committee met in a formal court session and pronounced the death sentence on the Czar. It was published the following day. Simultaneously there began the systematic preparation for carrying out the verdict.

The Czar was on his estate Livadiya on Crimea at the time. He was supposed to return to St. Petersburg in November. Three railroad lines came under consideration for the trip. Three mine assassinations were prepared over a period of weeks. One of the conspirators got himself a job as a gatekeeper with the railroad. Along one of the other lines they acquired a house. Along the line Kursk–Moscow they succeeded in renting a hut in the vicinity of a suburban station. The three houses were occupied by one commando each. Only those living in the buildings were allowed to show themselves in public. Provisions, spades, pickaxes, hand drills, cables, electrodes, and detonators had to be delivered at night to avoid attracting attention. Eight sappers each dug a tunnel through the ice-cold groundwater toward the tracks. A small compass indicated the direction. On the table in the living room stood a bottle with nitroglycerin. The woman of the house kept watch, a revolver in hand, to shoot at the bottle and blow up the house in an emergency. After two months' work all three mines had been placed, one of them along the appropriate route.

"November 19, punctually at the appointed hour, two brightly lit trains drove through. Stepan Shirajev did not connect the electrodes upon the first signal, which Perovskaja gave, and the first train passed unharmed; upon the second signal the second train was blown into the air."[21] It was the royal baggage train. The Czar had escaped once more.

The committee had taken account of possible failures and was planning a second assassination. Already in fall the carpenter Stepan Chalturin had gotten a job at the Czar's winter residence. He made himself out to be a goodhearted fool and played his role so well that a member of the guard detail even wanted him to marry one of his daughters. He was quartered in the cellar where the artisans lived; exactly two floors above was the royal dining hall. Every day he smuggled in small amounts of explosive in a lunch-box type case. When he had carried in fifty kilos the specialists declared that that was sufficient.

On February 5, 1880, Chalturin put the box into the corner of the fire wall and lit the fuse. It was toward evening. He had enough time to leave the palace. The explosion could be heard all over town. The lights went out all over the Winter Palace. The Admiralty Plaza was blacked out. Ten guard soldiers were killed. The food had been served in the dining hall. The floor trembled, mortar fell from the ceiling, the china was broken. But the Czar was not harmed: he owed his life to the lateness of his guest, Count Alexander of Serbia. Chalturin was able to escape and continue his conspiratorial work. He was later arrested for other reasons and ended on the gallows on March 22, 1882. The police recognized the carpenter from the Winter Palace only as a corpse.

Vera Figner, who had played an important role in the executive committee of the People's Will, reports:

> The assassination attempts created such an atmosphere that if we had stopped our terrorist activity at that time, volunteers or even an entirely new organization would have appeared at once with the removal of the Czar as their task. New assassination attempts were inevitable and the executive committee undertook them.[22]

In December 1881 two terrorists moved into a house in Little Garden Street through which the Czar's carriage drove occasionally, and opened a store there under the appellation: "Mr. & Mrs. Kobosev, cheesemongers." They bought three hundred rubles' worth of cheese, but the kegs in their shop contained earth; a tunnel was being dug from the cellar of their house under the street. A dynamite charge was prepared. Simultaneously a chamber to be filled with explosives was being drilled into the foundations of the Stone Bridge.

The committee finally selected six particularly agile people from a crowd of volunteers; a remote training area was located in the outskirts of Moscow; and in week-long trials the six terrorists learned the use of the thrown bomb, a kind of primitive and heavy but highly volatile hand grenade.

On March 1, 1881, the Czar leaves the palace. Dozens of observers are distributed all over St. Petersburg. All imaginable roads have been taken into consideration. Six bomb throwers are ready, in addition, two mines are primed. The royal carriage does not pass through Little Garden Street. A message reaches the executive committee that the Czar will take the route across the Catherine Canal. It is Sunday, the streets are very quiet. Two terrorists signal the arrival of the carriage to the bomb throwers. They wave their veils. (This gesture is like a farewell to the nineteenth century.) Ryssakov, the first man, tosses his bomb and destroys the coach without harming the passengers. The Czar dismounts and has the assassin brought before him. At this moment Grinewitzki tosses the second bomb. It kills Alexander II on the spot. Grinewitzki dies from his wounds an hour later in the hospital. Asked for his name he replies: "I don't know." Those are his last words.

The protracted execution had ended. Those who performed it no longer feel like underlings. Ten days after Alexander II's death they send an open letter to the victim's son. This letter, which was disseminated by the thousands, talks to the new Czar as an equal. It is a unique document, deluded and prophetic, a great testament of a moral victory and of a political defeat.

The Executive Committee to Czar Alexander III:

Completely understanding the present mood of your Majesty, the Executive Committee, however, does not feel justified to make room for the feelings of natural delicacy which would otherwise have demanded a certain postponement of the following declaration . . .

The bloody tragedy that occurred on the Catherine Canal neither was chance fate nor should it have surprised anyone; rather, after all the events of the past years, it seems like inevitable necessity, and the one whom fate has put at the head of the state must be aware of the deep significance of this necessity. Only someone completely incapable of analyzing the life of nations can present such events as the crimes of individuals or of 'a gang'. . . .

Indeed, the government can continue to arrest and to hang as it pleases; it is still capable of destroying individual revolutionary organizations. We admit that it will even destroy the most important of them. But . . . the idea of the revolution will continue to spread. A horrible eruption, a bloody fight, a convulsive revolutionary shock will complete the destruction of the old order.

Where do we find the explanation for the horrible perspective which reveals itself herewith? Indeed, Sire, it *is* a horrible and melancholy perspective. Don't believe that all of this is mere talk. We perceive more strongly than anyone else the saddening loss of so much talent and so much energy . . . But why the necessity for this bloody fight?

It is, Sire, because a genuine government in the actual sense of the word does not exist here at the present time. According to its very principle, a government must be an expression of what the people want. . . . However with us—excuse the expression—the government has degenerated into a court clique and rather deserves the name gang of usurpers. . . . There are only two ways out from a situation such as this: either a revolution or—a voluntary appeal by the highest power to the people. In the interest of the fatherland . . . the Executive Committee turns to your Majesty with the suggestion to take the second path. Be assured that as soon as the highest authority ceases to act arbitrarily, as soon as it demonstrates decisively that it will listen to the demands of the people's conscience, it will then be able to pension off the spies that compromise your government, will be able to send your convoys back to your barracks and burn the gallows that demoralize the people. The Executive Committee will then cease its activity of its own accord . . .

We hope that feelings of personal bitterness will not deaden your sense of duty nor your willingness to hear the truth. You have lost your father—we have not only lost fathers, but also brothers, women and children and our best friends. But we are prepared not to voice our feelings where the well-being of Russia demands it, and we expect the same of you.

We promulgate no condition; we simply remind you of the standing conditions of which, in our opinion, there are two: (1) A general amnesty for all political criminals of recent times, since they did not commit any crimes but only fulfilled their duty as citizens. (2) A convocation of the representatives of all the people for the revision of the present form of state and social life and their transformation according to the wishes of the people. However, we consider it necessary to remark that a legalization of the highest authority by means of people's representatives can be achieved only when the elections are held in complete freedom . . .

This is the only path to lead Russia back into the path of peaceful and normal development. We solemnly declare before the whole world that our party, for its part, will submit completely to a national assembly of this kind and will not permit itself to start any kind of violent action against a government sanctioned by the national assembly. And now, Sire, make your decision! You have a choice of two ways. The decision is yours.[23]

The Czar replied to this letter as rulers at all times have replied to those who gave them their verdict:

> In our great sadness God's voice commands us to hold fast to the reins of government in the trust in the Godly destiny and in the belief in the power and the truth of the autocratic force which we have been appointed to strengthen and defend against any attack.[24]

For twenty years the Czar was right, as was the open letter of the terrorists: *Indeed, the government can continue to arrest and to hang as it pleases; it is still capable of destroying individual revolutionary organizations. We admit that it will even destroy the most important of them.*

The executive committee of the People's Will was decimated within two years, its adherents were cut to pieces. The protracted execution of Alexander II remained without visible results: there was no uprising and Russia remained quiet. In some regions the farmers even mourned. Only the prisons filled up and the ironical justice of history once again created that symmetry that is peculiar to such great duels: the crowning of Alexander III was postponed for one year out of fear of further assassinations, and the Czar lived heavily guarded in his palace for the rest of his life. Like his opponents, the surviving terrorists in fortress Schlüsselburg, he could not take a single step out into the open. The autocrat of all the Russians had become his prisoners' prisoner.

The terrorists owe their triumph and their defeat to one and the same circumstance: that they were individuals and acted on their own account. They did not represent any far-flung interest or ideology, but only their own cause, which was everyone's cause. That constitutes their dignity and their blindness, the attribute of prophets. Alienated from their own class they did not find another that could have understood them. They could not count on mass support, only on themselves and on a bloody future.

During Alexander III's reign only a single assassination attempt was made on him. It ended in complete fiasco. The five conspiring students were executed. One of them, Alexander Ilich Uljanov, had a brother who was taking his high school finals at that time in his hometown Simbirsk, a tiny provincial locality on the Volga. This brother's name was Vladimir Iljitch, and in the words of the Open Letter, he was to "complete the destruction of the old order." However, he did this under the name that was meant to conceal him and which is part of history today: the name of Lenin.

Translated by Michael Roloff

Dreamers of the Absolute

Part II: The Beautiful Souls of the Terror

The bomb which on March 1, 1881, killed Czar Alexander II, the autocrat of all the Russians, acted like a bugle call throughout Europe. Even during the second half of the 1870s the Russian terrorists had enjoyed a singular reputation in the West. Three years before his violent end the Czar had created the notorious Ochrana, a highly specialized secret police whose methods the GPU and NKVD could lay claim to even in our day: like so many features of Stalinism, the police terror of this regime, too, has its roots in the Czarist tradition. The paranoid features of the ruler are reflected in the secret police whose raison d'être is the ruler's mortal dread of being killed, which in turn becomes the real reason for the existence of the State. The response to this is the logic of the assassination: if the life of the State depends solely on the life of the ruler, killing him suffices to bring about a revolutionary change in the society. The ruler's idée fixe of being irreplaceable infects his opponents; they take him at his word, though this has only been a delusion on his part. Individual terror is based on the conviction that history is made by emperors, kings, and presidents; a conviction that is shared by emperors, kings, and presidents. No bomb thrower can change the great and anonymous social forces: the technical and industrial potential, the aggregate conditions of the classes, the relationship of wealth to the lack of it and the administrative apparatus. It is for this reason that no modern assassin has become truly famous; even the two gunmen of Sarajevo were only pawns in a larger game. The actions of bomb throwers remain anecdotal.

Anecdotes, however, if they have a fine point, can be more expressive than whole volumes. Assassination became an historical allegory in the desperate actions of the conspirators who appeared around the turn of the last century. One can detect social outlines even in the tendrils of their plans, in the artistic detail of their assassination attempts, which have not been completed to this day; the element of utopia is present even in their operatic attitude, and has not been disproved by all their failures.

The impression they made on their audience and on their victims was as immense as their immediate political effect was unreal. "Protection"—the sinister word *Ochrana* means just that in Russian. Alexander II looked for it with every means at his command and could not find it. The year he founded his personal security force the very thing it was supposed to protect him from had already begun to swamp the entire continent. In 1878 assassinations were attempted on three of his crowned cousins: on the German emperor, on Alfons XII of Spain, on Umberto I of Italy. After Alexander himself succumbed to his opponents the terror against the heads of State took on epidemic proportions.

1883: Attempt on the German Emperor.
1894: Murder of the President of the French Republic.
1898: Murder of Empress Elisabeth of Austria.
1900: Assassination attempt on the English successor, the Prince of Wales, and on the German Emperor. Murder of King Umberto of Italy.
1901: Attempt on the German Emperor.
     Murder of President McKinley of the United States.
1903: Murder of King Alexander I of Serbia.
1905: Attempt on the Spanish Royal couple in Paris.

In that decade those who were feared learned to fear and tremble themselves. In the middle of the peaceful, stable *haut bourgeois* belle époque, it became a mortally dangerous profession to stand at the head of a State. Of course most of these assassinations were not the work of a secret organization, party, or ideologically motivated group. Most often the motives of the perpetrators remained obscure; though toward the end of the 1880s the International of the Anarchists had organized the black terror and provoked unrest in France, Spain, and the United States; yet few if any of the attempts on the crowned heads of Europe could be charged to their account. These were mostly the work of amateurs, individual Herostrati and fanatics, including a number of madmen.

However, the wave of political crimes that swept Europe at that time cannot be simply put down to a number of private neuroses. What bubbled up was the bloody undercurrent of those good old times. The hatred of the bourgeoisie was so enormous that all it took was the example of a single excuse for it to discharge itself violently in the form of detonations of which kings and ministers were not the only victims: the bombs of the nameless terrorists who sought to tackle the big powers single-handedly exploded in theaters, luxury restaurants, and stock exchanges, in clubs and parliaments. In 1892 alone, there were registered in the United States 500 bombing attacks, and more than 1000 in Europe.

But in those particular years when the specter of anarchy haunted the countries of the West and the dreams of the bourgeoisie, during those years it was quiet in Russia. The growing industrial proletariat was gathering in new parties. There were strikes and unrest; but the individual terror seemed to have vanished. Since the Ochrana had destroyed the conspiracy of the People's Will no strong conspiratorial groups out for direct action were left in Russia. For twenty years the leading men of the regime could feel relatively secure. A second generation of terrorists does not appear on the scene until 1901. This circle of conspirators called itself "The Fighting Organization of Social Revolutionaries," and we are far better informed about its methods, mentality, and history than about the old Narodniki.

For this precise, even intimate, knowledge we are indebted

to a unique source: the memoirs of a terrorist by the name of Boris Sawinkov. Sawinkov was one of the heads of that fighting organization, and was a typical professional revolutionary —conspiracy had become his flesh and blood. He knew how to change his identity as easily as his shirt; could recognize a police spy at a hundred paces; he sparred with the Ochrana with the ease of a superior boxer. The mobility of this man, who stood on every wanted list of the Russian Empire, borders on the incredible. The itinerary of this illegal person contains the following way stations between the years 1903–1906: Archangelsk—Vardö—Oslo—Antwerp—Geneva—Cracow—Berlin—St. Petersburg—Geneva—Nizza—Berlin—Moscow—Riga—Warsaw—Geneva—Paris—St. Petersburg—Geneva—Charkov—Vilna—Helsinki—Stockholm—Geneva—Warsaw—Moscow—Sevastopol—Bucharest—Paris.

Sawinkov is nowhere and everywhere at home. He was a *dépaysé*; he was what was to be called "a displaced person" fifty years later. This very condition of not belonging seemed to provide him with the utmost incentive: unchallenged, without passport he fled from banishment and crossed the Russian-Norwegian border at Varanger-Fjord on a Murmansk-steamer; went from Poland to Germany on a smuggler sled with a horde of Jewish emigrants; reached Rumania from the Crimea on a fishing trawler after an adventurous crossing of the Black Sea.

This activist, this highly trained trapeze artist of conspiracy, now proves to be, in his memoirs, an introverted ruminator who seeks almost desperately to find insight into the deepest motives for his actions. In this respect he resembles his co-conspirators all of whom, so to speak, were metaphysicians of The Terror. They considered their work problematic and this problem pursued them. This distinguishes them from the old brand of terrorist who didn't know doubt and couldn't have been less interested in their souls. However, these men and women of 1905 were not only extraordinary personalities; they also were aware of it. They were determined not only to track down their opponents but also their own innermost secrets.

In the summer of 1903 Sawinkov encountered the two decisive figures of the Fighting Organization for the first time.

> In Geneva I made the acquaintance of Michail Rafailovitch Gotz. He was of small stature, emaciated, with black curly beard and a pale face. He captivated you with his feverish, lively, young eyes. He asked me: "You want to participate in the terror?"—"Yes."—
> "Only in the terror?"—"Yes."—"Why not in the general work of the party?"—"I consider the activity of the terrorist to be of decisive importance. But I am at the disposal of the central committee and am prepared to undertake any task it assigns to me."—"Fine. I can't give you an answer yet. Wait. Stay in Geneva for a while."
> One day in August a man came to my room, he was roughly thirty-five years old, very fullbodied, with a broad kindly face, as wide as though it was filled with stones, and large brown eyes. That was Jevgenij Filipovitch Asev.
> He shook my hand, sat down and said, lazily dropping his words: "I've been told that you want to work in the terror." I repeated what I'd told Gotz. I also mentioned that I regarded the assassination of Minister Plehve the most important task at the present time. Asev continued to listen to me with the same lazy air and made no reply. Finally he asked: "Do you have comrades?" I mentioned Kaljajev and two others and told him my life's story. Asev listened to it quietly and took his leave.
> He came a few times to us, didn't say much and listened carefully. Finally he said: "It's time to go to Russia. Go somewhere with your comrades from Geneva, settle in a small town and check whether you're being watched!"

Gotz was the ideologist, Asev the practical leader of the terror. Formally the Fighting Organization was an executive organ of the Social Revolutionary Party, which had been founded in 1900. Its program was not Marxist. The Socialist Revolutionaries believed in the direct transition from absolutism to socialism; in accord with the example of the traditional Russian village community, the masses of the farmers were to socialize their land directly. In Sawinkov's memoirs there isn't a single mention of this program; the Fighting Organization as a matter of fact rejected any control by the party. It was practically a party within the party, just as the Ochrana was a state within the State. This independence is very clearly expressed in the document that regulated the Fighting Organization's relationship to the Social Revolutionary Party:

> In accordance with the decision of the party, a special Fighting Organization has been formed which will assume exclusive control of the terrorist and disorganizational activity, and will do so on the basis of strict conspiracy and division of labor. This Fighting Organization receives from the Central Committee of the Party general directives as to the beginning and end of war activities and about the circle of persons against which it has to direct itself. In every other respect the Fighting Organization has the widest authority and is completely independent. Its only connection to the party is through the center, and it works completely independent of local cells. It has its own organization, own personnel, own account, and financial sources.

In practice this meant that the Fighting Organization was responsible only to itself. Its members were completely disinterested in questions of ideology, they undertook no agitation whatsoever, read no pamphlets and lived in a peculiar isolation interrupted only by the violence of the detonation of one of their bombs. Paradoxically, what the newspapers called politics was profoundly irrelevant to them. But in that case, what was their concern? What did they want? What did they believe?

> Pokotilov was walking excitedly, drops of blood on his forehead, pale, with feverishly wide pupils. He said: "I believe in the terror. For me the entire revolution consists of the terror. There are only a few of us now. You'll see there will be many. Tomorrow I won't be here any more perhaps. And this makes me happy. I am proud. Tomorrow Plehve will be dead."
> The quiet, modest, shy Dora Brilliant lived for only one cause: for her belief in the terror. She loved the revolution. She tortured herself about the slightest setback. She admitted that it

was necessary to kill Plehve but she was afraid of this murder. She couldn't make her peace with the shedding of blood. It was easier for her to die herself than to murder. Still, she kept asking us to entrust her with the bomb and permit her to participate in the assassination as one of the throwers. What she considered to be the most difficult task she did not want to leave to others to do: that would have meant a separation from her comrades. She considered it her duty to cross the threshold to direct participation: the terror was exemplified to her by the sacrifice which the terrorist makes of himself.

Kaljajev placed the terror at the center of the revolution. In Charkov he said to me: "You know, I'd like to live until I can see: here, you see, is Macedonia. There the mass terror exists, there every revolutionary is a terrorist. And with us? Five, six men—fini— . . . and the others are engaged in peaceful activities. But can a Social Revolutionary be so engaged? A Social Revolutionary without a bomb isn't a Social Revolutionary any more. And can one talk about the terror without taking part in it? . . . I know, a fire will sweep across all of Russia. Macedonia is everywhere, also here with us."

For the terrorists of 1905 the assassination of the mighty of this world was not merely a tactical means for achieving this or that party program: it became an act of liberation in and of itself. They did not deny that they became guilty but this guilt was immediately expiated by the highest possible risk: their act of murder is simultaneously an act of suicide. Every conspirator counted on his own death. "Give me a bomb," said Dora Brilliant, "I have to die." And Kaljajev, during a discussion, to Asev the planner of the assassination attempt:

"There is one method which won't miss."—"Which one?"— "Throwing yourself under the horses' hooves." Asev regarded him closely. "How do you figure that?" "The carriage comes. I throw myself with the bomb under the horses. Either the bomb explodes—in that case the carriage can't go on—or it doesn't and the horses shy. In any event, there is a delay. At this moment a second bomb thrower has to go into action."—"But at that moment you yourself explode."—"Of course."

What lent the twenty-seven-year-old Kaljajev the strength to hold such an attitude? We will never know, but much points to the fact that it was the conspirators' complete solidarity—it made these shattered ones, who had no ties outside their immediate circle, who had cut themselves off from family, from their friends, from class and interest group immeasurably stronger than they would ever have been by themselves. The fraternity of their conspiracy already fulfilled their anticipation of what a future society might be like.

The members of the Fighting Organization planned their assassinations with extreme care. Technically they were far superior to their predecessors, the Narodniki. They were artists of The Terror. Particularly Asev developed methods of great elegance. The conspirators met at masked balls, in public baths, and theaters. Some of their means even evince a certain black humor: thus, for example, they had the habit of depositing their bombs in a safe-deposit box they had rented at the Dshamgarovsh Bank. The house of Minister Plehve, who was to be their first victim, was watched with incredible precision for weeks on end. One of the conspirators therefore turned street vendor. Sawinkov has recorded the ruses he used to divert the police away from himself:

I am standing on the Chain Bridge, waiting. When I see a cop eyeing me, I pull down my cap, make a deep bow and say: "Your Highness, allow me to ask who lives in these palatial rooms. Is it by chance the Czar himself, there are so many superior-looking people at the doors?" The cop looks me up and down and grins. "Idiot," he said. "Clodhopper. You don't understand anything. That's a minister who lives there." "A minister?" I said, "that means someone who's the head general?" "Idiot. Minister means minister . . . got it?" "Yes, Sir," I said, "now I understand. But," I say, "in that case it must be a very wealthy minister? He probably makes a hundred thousand a year?" The cop grins again and says, "You dope . . . the crap you spew out . . . hundred thousand . . . higher: say, a million . . ." Then I notice that the spies are beginning to move out, the carriage in other words is ready to go, Plehve is about to leave.

The cop says: "Take off. You s.o.b.'s have no business hanging around here . . ." I go behind the bridge, stand there as if I want to tighten my belt and see: Plehve is driving . . .

And then another instance: somehow or other a mounted cop had noticed me. "What are you doing around here, you s.o.b.?" he said. "Scram!" he says. "Beg your pardon, your Highness," I say, "because business is so good here . . ." Whereupon he proceeds to shout: "Nonsense! . . . Guard, take him to the station." A guard leaps down from his post and says: "Come, let's go." We turn the corner and I take out a ruble and say: "Here, Mr. Guard, be so kind and take it, as a sign of admiration, and let me go for Christ's sake. I am just a little man. That's what makes it so easy to do something to me." The guard looks at the ruble, then at me. He takes the ruble and says: "All right, you s.o.b., disappear but watch out, you're gonna end up at the station anyhow . . ."

Kaljajev, who was nicknamed "the poet," was particularly outstanding at this systematic observation work that preceded every assassination.

He lived in a little hideaway on the outskirts of the city in a room with five other men, and he led the life of a traveling salesman—in every detail. He did not permit himself the slightest deviation. He got up at six and was out on the street from eight in the morning until late at night. The innkeepers soon began to consider him a devout, sober and capable fellow. It wouldn't have occurred to them in their wildest dreams that he might be a revolutionary . . . He had his own theory about Plehve's excursions. Kaljajev could deduce from the slightest sign on the street—the number of Ochrana people about, the way the cops looked, the demeanor of the lieutenants and guards—whether Plehve had already driven through this particular street or whether he was still on his way. He not only knew the height and width of the carriage, its color, the color of the wheels but also described the carriage step, the doorhandle, the harness, the lantern, the coachbox, the axles, the windows . . . He knew all the minister's spies and could spot them unfailingly in the crowd.

As camouflage for the conspirators' headquarters, Asev created a very different environment from the one to which the terrorists had been accustomed. He pretended to be the agent for a British bicycle firm, rented a magnificent apartment in one of the best sections of St. Petersburg. Dora Brilliant had to assume the role of his wife; Sasonov, who was to throw the bomb at Plehve, played their servant.

The evening before the assassination Sawinkov and Sasonov had a conversation in a park: "Now you are going to go and probably never come back . . . Tell me, what do you think you will feel afterwards . . . after the murder?"—"Pride and Joy." —"Nothing but pride and joy?"—"Naturally."

After he was sentenced, Sasonov wrote to his friend from prison: "I have never lost my awareness of sinning."

And Sawinkov comments in this connection: "Another feeling, still unknown to us at that point, mingled with the pride and joy."

On July 15, between eight and nine in the morning, I met Sasonov at the Nikolai Railroad Station and Kaljajev at the Warsaw Station. Sasonov was wearing a railroad worker's uniform, Kaljajev was camouflaged as a porter. Borishansky and Sikorsky also arrived at the Warsaw station with the next train from Dünaburg. The comrade who worked as our cabbie hitched up the horses and drove to the North-Hotel where Schweizer, the explosives technician, lived. Schweizer sat down in the cab and distributed the bombs around ten o'clock at the previously arranged spots. The biggest bomb, which weighed twelve pounds, was for Sasonov. Its form was cylindrical, it was wrapped in paper and tied with a string. Kaljajev and Sasonov did not hide their bombs but carried them openly in their hands. Borishansky and Sikorsky hid their bombs underneath their capes.

The distribution was handled in exemplary fashion. The bomb throwers were to walk in a previously arranged sequence along the English Prospect toward the canal and along the canal toward Plehve's carriage. They walked forty paces apart. Sasonov was to toss the first bomb. It was a clear, sunny day. I saw Kaljajev at the church gate. He had taken off his hat and crossed himself before the picture of the saint.

I called to him: "Janek?" He turned around and crossed himself again. "Is it time already?" "Of course. Ten minutes after nine. Get going!"

He kissed me and with his easy gait hurriedly fell into step behind Sasonov. Sasonov's uniform buttons glinted in the sun. He was carrying his bomb in his right hand, wrapped under his arm. One could see that it was difficult to carry.

I was walking on the Ismailov Prospect. Just looking at the street allowed me to infer that Plehve would pass by at any moment. The police lieutenants and guards made an excited impression. Ministerial spies stood at the street corners. At that moment I saw Sasonov on the bridge and right behind me I heard the sharp clapping of a rapidly moving carriage. The minister's carriage with its black horses was rushing past. A few seconds elapsed. Sasonov disappeared in the crowd. These few seconds seemed infinitely long. Suddenly a heavy and impressive and odd sound penetrated the monotonous street noises, as though someone had struck a cast-iron plate with a cast-iron hammer. At that same moment the windows rattled. I saw a small swirling column of greyish–yellow smoke, black at the edges, rise from the ground. This column spread out more and more and by the time it reached the fifth-floor level it over-whelmed the entire street.

Kaljajev could see the explosion from the street, and he saw the carriage explode. But it was not clear whether the minister was dead or not, whether a second bomb was needed. When he stood on the bridge like that the blood-spattered horses galloped past him, dragging the remnants of the wheels. When Kaljajev saw that that was all that was left of the carriage he understood that Plehve was dead.

Gravely wounded, Sasonov was seized and taken to a hospital where he was operated on in the presence of the Minister of Justice. He refused to give his name and said nothing. From prison he sent a coded message to his friends:

Dear Brothers! I don't know whether I played my role as I should have to the end. I thank you with my whole heart for your trust. You gave me the opportunity to know a moral satisfaction which is not comparable to anything in the world. This satisfaction has eased the pain I felt after the explosion. I had scarcely come to after the operation when I breathed a sigh of relief. Finally it is over! I was ready to sing and scream with joy!

Police Minister Plehve, with the pogroms against the Jews on his conscience, had been removed from the world. The assassination not only made a profound impression on public opinion but also on the Russian government. The quasi-liberal policies of Plehve's successor, Witte (even if they were only tactical, that is, in the final analysis, were meant to deceive), provided a certain playing room for the opposition.

The terrorist Fighting Organization of course had no intentions of resting on these laurels. From all parts of Russia it received money, many thousands of rubles. The group met in Paris and immediately began to prepare its next assassination. Grand Duke Sergius, a son of the murdered Czar Alexander II was to be its next victim. He was one of the most influential —and reactionary—advisers of the present ruler.

The planning of the assassination, in which Asev was deeply involved, took several months. In February 1905 the time had come. This once Kaljajev, the poet, was to throw the first bomb. Sawinkov reports:

Kaljajev was the same in Moscow as in Petersburg (during the Plehve assassination). But he already felt that his end was near. The last time I saw him was toward the end of January when the assassination was decided on. He was emaciated, wore a large beard, and his glowing eyes seemed to have sunk into his head. He was wearing the blue uniform of a coachman and a red cotton shawl around his neck. He said: "You know, I've become very tired . . . the nerves . . . I believe I can't go on any more. . . . but what luck if we win . . . I won't relax until Sergius is dead. If only we had Sasonov with us! What do you think they'll get out of him in prison? If we succeed, the revolution will have come. I am sorry that I won't see it any more. But if we don't succeed . . . you know what? In that case I think we have to do it the Japanese way . . ." "What do you mean with Japanese?"—"The Japanese didn't surrender during the war."—"Well, so what"—"They committed harakiri."

That was Kaljajev's mood before the murder of Grand Duke Sergius.

On the evening of February 2, 1905, there was a bitter frost in Moscow. Kaljajev stood in the shadow of the gate at the city hall, on the lonely and dark plaza. The Grand Duke's carriage appeared at the Nikolai gate toward nine o'clock. In the darkness it seemed to Kaljajev as though he recognized the coachman, Rudinkin, who usually drove the Grand Duke. He had already raised his arm to toss the bomb when he saw sitting in the carriage with the Grand Duke his wife Elizabeth and two of his brother's children, Maria and Dmitri. He let down his arm and went away.

He met me in the Alexander Garden and said: "I believe I acted correctly. Can one murder children?" He couldn't go on speaking he was so excited. He understood what was at stake when he let such a unique opportunity slip by: not only his life but that of the whole organization. If he had been arrested with the bomb in his hand, the assassination would have been impossible for a long time to come. I said to him: "I find your decision correct. I admire it greatly."—"But the question whether the organization has the right to kill also his wife and his nephews—this question must be clarified. I insist on it. If you decide to kill the whole family I'll go to the theater and throw the bomb, no matter who sits in the carriage." I told him that I considered such a murder impossible.

The assassins unanimously endorsed Kaljajev's behavior, and nothing characterizes their moral caliber more than this. They have not found their equals in the bloody events of the twentieth century. Albert Camus has made the most precise formulation of what distinguishes them from all terrorists who came after them: "Two different kinds of men. One of them kills and pays with it for his life. The other justifies thousands of crimes and accepts honors in payment."

Sawinkov and those like him not only brought the technique of assassination to a state of utmost perfection. Their conscience too was a precision instrument. Familiarity with death did not dull but sharpened it. The conspirators of 1881 already had made their executioner office difficult for themselves. Their declaration to the American People on the occasion of the assassination of President Garfield in July 1881 demonstrates the precision of their thinking:

In the name of the Russian Revolutionary Party we protest acts of violence. In a country where the people's freedom permits them the free expression of their ideas, where the people's will not only makes the laws but also nominates the person who enforces them political murder is the expression of a despotic tendency which we want to eliminate in Russia. Despotism is always damnable and violence is only justified when it opposes violence.

The members of the Fighting Organization made as sure as they could that their actions did not harm innocent people, a conscientiousness that manifested itself in the smallest detail. When two Englishmen were fined one hundred pounds each in London for having provided the conspirators with English passports the Fighting Organization offered to reimburse them at once. Later, when the plan to kill Admiral Dubassov in the Moscow–St. Petersburg Express was broached Sawinkov turned it down: "The explosion might have killed innocent persons if there had been the slightest element of sloppiness."

When Sawinkov was arrested in 1906 in Sevastopol he made a plan to flee the fortress: he decided to shoot at the guard officers if necessary, but preferred to commit suicide rather than endanger the life of the common soldiers.

Grand Duke Sergius did not elude his pursuers.

When I reached the Cast-iron Gate I heard a distant muffled sound. I paid no attention to it because it scarcely resembled the sound of an explosion. In the restaurant I met Dora Brilliant. We walked toward the Kremlin. At the Iberian Madonna a street boy came running towards us, screaming: "They've got the Grand Duke. His head is off!"

The people were running toward the Kremlin. Dora and I stopped. Dora bent towards me and began to weep. She was in no condition to restrain her tears. Her entire body was shaken by this deep sobbing. I tried to calm her down. She kept repeating over and over: "We killed him. I killed him."—"Whom?" I asked because I thought she meant Kaljajev.—"The Grand Duke."

A letter by Kaljajev to his friends, dated March 20, 1905:

I remained alive entirely against my will. I threw the bomb from four feet away, no more than that, on the run. I was seized by the whirlpool effect of the explosion, saw how the carriage burst. I can still remember the smoke and splinters shooting directly into my face, my cap being torn off. Five feet away I saw the Grand Duke's torn clothes and his bare body. My jacket was burnt. I turned around. There was no one close by. I left. At this moment I heard voices from behind: "Stop him! Catch him!" The sled with the spies almost ran over me. I put up no resistance. "Look whether he has a revolver," the Ochrana person said tremulously "Thank God, thank God it didn't get us." I felt sorry that I didn't have a bullet for this glorious coward. "Why are you holding on to me?" I said. "I'm not going to run away. I've done my job." We drove in a cab through the Kremlin and I felt like screaming: *Down with the goddamn Czar, long live liberty, down with the goddamned government!*

A few days later there occurred an encounter which seems particularly incredible. The Grand Duchess Jelisavjeta Fedorovna, the murdered man's wife, paid his murderer a visit in the tower of the Butyrki Prison where Kaljajev was confined in solitary.

Kaljajev wrote from prison:

I assure you, we looked into each other's eyes with a secret feeling, like two survivors: I thanks to chance, she because the organization, because I wanted it that way; because we had spared her life.

And that was what I read in the face of the Grand Duchess— gratitude, if not to me then to the fate that had spared her. "I beg of you," she said, "take this picture as a keepsake from me. I want to pray for you." And I took the picture. For me it was a symbol of her contrition over the crimes the Grand Duke had committed.

"My conscience is clear," I said. "I am sorry to have saddened your life. But if I had a thousand lives to give, I would give every one of them. Farewell, I have done my duty and I will do it to the end. Take care, we will never see each other again."

On April 5, 1905, Kaljajev stood before his judges. These are his last words: "I am not a defendant before you. I am your prisoner. We are two warring powers. We are separated by mountains of corpses. You have declared war on the people, we have accepted the challenge. You are in no position to judge me as a person. This trial is as incapable of setting me free as it is of condemning me. Take a look around: everywhere there is blood and groaning. It is you who are on trial, in the court of history. It will pronounce your verdict."

Sentence was passed at three o'clock. Kaljajev was condemned to death by hanging. He said: "I am glad about the verdict. I consider my death the highest protest against a world of tears and of blood." At dawn on May 10 Kaljajev, without a coat, dressed completely in black, wearing a felt hat, mounted the scaffold. Standing motionless on the structure he listened to the reading of the verdict. The priest offered him the crucifix to kiss. Kaljajev refused. He said: "I have already told you that I have done with my life. I need no consolation. I am ready to die." The hangman Filipov threw the noose around Kaljajev's neck and kicked the stool out from under his feet. Kaljajev lies buried behind the fortress wall of Schlüsselburg, between the rampart that surrounds the fortress on the seaside and the Kings Tower.

The assassintion of Grand Duke Sergius assumes a special place among the numerous actions the Fighting Organization undertook. It was simultaneously its high and its turning point. On March 17, 1905, with seventeen mysterious arrests, there began an ominous chapter in its ominous history. The clamp-down of the police was inexplicable. Neither Kaljajev nor any of the other assassins had divulged the names of their comrades. Nonetheless an invisible net began to close in around the conspirators. In June of the same year there were further arrests. By summer only Gotz, Asev, Sawinkov, and Dora Brilliant were left of the heart of the group. These four immediately began soliciting new members and preparing new assassinations.

Asev returned to Nishni Novgorod at the beginning of August. His first words were: "We are being spied on." I hadn't noticed and therefore didn't believe him at first. A few days later Asev and Silberberg noticed a spy behind them on the street. When I returned to the inn I could detect a certain, scarcely perceptible change in the innkeeper's demeanor towards me. Immediate and decisive measures had to be taken to insure our safety. If we went on working in Novgorod we had to count on our entire organization soon being surrounded by spies.

With every means of their arrant conspiratorial technique Sawinkov and the other members of the circle tried to shake off their pursuers. They succeeded for a while but then the Ochrana people reappeared. To elude them, Sawinkov retreated to an out-of-the-way estate in the Klin district.

The day I arrived the woman of the house came excitedly into my room and said: "You're being spied upon."—"Impossible."—"The gardener was just here. He said two spies followed you from the railroad station. They asked for you."

Thrice Sawinkov barely escaped arrest. Finally only one explanation is left for the continuous arrests and the activity of the spies: betrayal. The police were in the know about the every movement of the conspirators. The police had to have an informer among the conspirators or in the Social Revolutionary Party. In August 1905 Gotz and Sawinkov received an anonymous letter:

Comrades! The party is threatened by a pogrom. It is being betrayed by two exceedingly dangerous spies. One of them is a certain Tatarov, the other an engineer by the name of Asev . . . Destroy this letter at once, make no copies or excerpts. Act quickly without lifting the secret!

The accusation against Asev was grotesque. Every member of the group knew that Asev had planned, organized and led

even the most frightful acts against the government. The case
of Tatarov was somewhat less clear-cut. This man was a member of the party's central committee. He knew more about the
Fighting Organization than it did about him. Quite a few
matters in his life, especially his profession (he owned a publishing firm) were obscure. The Organization discussed the
case outside the country.

> In Geneva I found Gotz sick and in bed. He asked me what I
> thought of the anonymous letter. "Nothing," I said.—"And
> Tatarov?"—"I can't imagine that he's the provocateur."—"I
> think the letter was written by the police itself. Some kind of
> intrigue is behind that. But it certainly looks as if there's a
> traitor in the party. That's the only explanation for our being
> spied on in Nishni. One has to investigate the matter. The
> situation is very serious. We have to arrive at a revolutionary
> position: that is, neither names nor authorities can count for us.
> Not one individual but the whole party is in danger. Therefore
> we must go on the assumption that each one of us is suspect. I
> don't except myself. You know my life. Who has something to
> say against me?"
>
> Everyone who was present was questioned in this manner.
> Then Gotz said: "Tatarov is suspect. As best as I can count, he
> has spent five thousand rubles on business matters in the last six
> weeks. Where does he get his money? Besides, his publishing
> venture looks uncertain; or rather: much too certain. He never
> has any trouble with the censor. How is that possible?"

The conspirators began to investigate the case very conscientiously and with the same moral precision that characterized their assassinations. First they formed their own investigating committee; Tatarov was not shot in the back, he
was asked to appear. At his hearing, which was held in Geneva,
he became embroiled in contradictions.

> We also sought to clear up Tatarov's role outside the meet-
> ings. I visited him privately at his inn. When I entered he was
> sitting in an armchair, his face in his hands. We didn't greet
> each other. He turned around towards me.

"I've known you for so long," I said, "that I can't believe that you would betray us. I'll gladly defend you before the committee. But you have to explain your behavior. I don't understand it. You have to be completely open with me. That is the only thing that can save you."

Tatarov remained silent and did not take his hands from his face. From his trembling shoulders I could see that he was crying. He said: "When I speak with you I feel like a bastard. When I am alone my conscience is quiet."

That was all. I couldn't get more out of him.

Driven into a corner, Tatarov tried to save himself by pointing the finger at Asev. He claimed to have information from a reliable source. Asked what source he had in mind, he had to admit to a connection with the secret police if only a remote one.

Finally I was completely convinced of Tatarov's guilt. Of course I was aware that legal proof was lacking. A jury would have had to acquit him. However, the revolutionaries in the defense of their party against infiltration by the police unfortunately have no other choice but to resort to the methods of their opponents. They have to judge the police agents in their ranks by standards which don't meet the strict norm of an orderly proceeding.

The investigating committee reached the unanimous conclusion that Tatarov was guilty. With that he was condemned to death.

I turned to the central committee and declared myself prepared to organize the execution. The central committee agreed to this proposal and gave me the financial means to carry it out.

Newspaper report from Warsaw:

On March 22 an unknown person entered the apartment of the priest Juri Tatarov and killed his son with a revolver shot. The police has no clue as to the murderer's motive. The unknown perpetrator left no traces.

One year later Minister/President Stolypin declared publically before the Third Duma that Tatarov had in fact worked for the secret police. The terrorists' investigating committee had been right.

The Fighting Organization went immediately back to work after the liquidation of Tatarov. The danger inside the party seemed to have been eliminated. Eight new assassinations were being prepared. The most important of them was to be that of Minister of the Interior Durnovo. Gotz suggested an open assault for once.

Without entering into the technical details of the plan, Asev said: "I can only agree if I head the operation."—"That is not permitted. The organization cannot sacrifice its chief, not even for this operation. You have to withdraw this condition."—"But what we are considering is a public assault, in a case like this the leader has to lead. I have to do it."

Before this plan could be realized, the police moved in again. Gotz was arrested in the summer. Other unexplained arrests followed. Sawinkov, too, was finally cornered in Sevastopol. For two months he was in investigative detention in the fortress. But already on July 19 there appeared the following notice on the wall of the fortress: IN THE NIGHT OF JULY 16 BORIS SAWINKOV, UPON THE DECISION OF THE FIGHTING ORGANIZATION, WAS FREED FROM THE FORTRESS OF SEVASTOPOL. LONG LIVE THE SOCIAL REVOLUTIONARY PARTY!

Sawinkov escaped to Paris by way of Rumania. It would be impossible for him to be active in Russia for the foreseeable future. The Fighting Organization had been decimated by the continuous bloodletting. The majority of their members had been shot, hanged or banished. Those who remained were about to undergo their most profound disappointment.

In Fall 1907 Sawinkov received another letter from Russia accusing Asev of working for the police.

> We didn't pay any attention to these reports. We considered them police intrigue. Of course, it was advantageous to the Ochrana to besmirch the leader of the revolution and to incapacitate him in this way. I had seen Asev work. I knew his silent consistency in revolutionary activity, his faithfulness and his terrorist courage. I did not doubt his honesty. No rumor could shake my love and respect for Asev.

However the rumor did not die out. A journalist by the name of Burtzev kept spreading it, and the central committee decided to place Burtzev before a court of honor so as to squelch once and for all the slandering of Asev, which was exceedingly damaging to the reputation of the party. Sawinkov did not agree to this procedure.

> I did what I could to prevent it. To subpoena Burtzev, so I thought, would not silence the rumor but only lend it further dissemination. Otherwise it is extremely difficult to squelch a rumor, particularly one originating with the police. And then, a court proceeding struck me as incommensurable with the dignity of the Fighting Organization. The suspicion cast on Asev not only insulted him but all terrorists. Such an insult could not be answered with mere words.

Asev, however, insisted on the investigation.

> A court of arbitration is absolutely essential. The senselessness of these rumors can only be cleared up by such a court.

In October 1908 a formal court was established at Rue Lhomond 50 in Paris. Two grand old figures of the revolutionary movement were among the six judges: Count Kropotkin and Vera Figner, who had managed to leave Russia after being imprisoned for twenty years in the Schlüsselburg fortress. Burtzev kept insisting on the truth of his accusations. He produced circumstantial evidence that badly implicated Asev. Sawinkov tried to disprove it.

> I could not convince the court with my reasons. Figner retained her old trust in Asev but Kropotkin was wavering. He thought Asev capable of a double game; that is, he considered it possible that the head of the Fighting Organization was simultaneously betraying his own group to the government. One of the judges said to me: "You kill someone on the basis of evidence like this."
>
> In November Asev came to Paris. He was restless, tired and downright beat. "So you say that Kropotkin suspects a double game?"—"Yes."—Asev said nothing. Then he suddenly laughed. "Yes, you aren't particularly clever. You could be deceived, all right.—Besides, I've heard that there's some new material about me. Where did you get it? From the police?"—"That I can't tell you. Listen Asev, I don't quite understand your behavior. I suggested to you not to go before the court and to return to Russia. Our terrorist work would refute all rumors. You didn't want that. You wanted to face the court and now you are trying to affect the conclusion of the procedure through me. But who is the accused here? Burtzev or you? In any case, now you have to appear before the court yourself, refute Burtzev and defend your honor. No one can do that for you."—"I thought you would defend me as a comrade."—"We have done what we could."—"So you think it is better if I appear before the court?" —"Yes, it is better." He didn't reply for a long time. Then he said: "No, I can't. I don't have the energy for it."
>
> He seemed completely beaten. After a while he stood up without saying a word. He kissed me before going.
>
> This conversation awakened the first, fog-like suspicion in me.

In January 1909 the court of honor judged Burtzev to be not guilty. With that Asev was condemned. He escaped to Russia. The Czarist police did not arrest but protected him. In February 1909 an interpolation in the case of Asev was broached in the Duma. Minister President Stolypin replied to the request of the Social Democratic and Liberal factions with the following words:

Asev began to work for the police in 1892. At first he acted as a liaison man between the Ministry of Police and illegal circles. Then he was assigned to the Moscow Ochrana section. He also performed valuable service for us outside of Russia. Until 1905 he worked for the director of the St. Petersburg department of the secret police. Of course Asev was not continuously active in our behalf. Every time he came under suspicion, every time there was a large wave of arrests he was given several months' leave.

A leading Ochrana man testified that Asev was the biggest agent provocateur the Ochrana ever employed. The government paid him a yearly salary of 14,000 rubles for his spy activity.

The Fighting Organization was wrecked by this man. He not only decimated it physically, he also broke its moral backbone. Just as a man like Kaljajev cannot be measured by the ordinary standards of political justice so Asev was not your run-of-the-mill denouncer. The mystery surrounding him will never completely disappear. It is of satanic stature. The slightest of Asev's moves is of dizzying ambiguity. He not only betrayed the revolutionaries to the government, he also betrayed the regime to the revolutionaries. He was not only a member of the Social Revolutionary Party. He was doubtlessly one of the most talented and radical terrorists of all time. He planned and organized an endless series of assassinations and terrorist acts that were directed against the following persons: Duke Obliensky, the Governor of Charkov; the Governor of Ufa; Minister of the Interior Plehve (his highest superior, that is!); Grand Duke Sergej Aleksandrovich; Governor General of St. Petersburg, General Trepov; the Governor General of Kiev, Kleigels; the Governor of Nishni-Novgorod; the Governor General of Moscow, Admiral Dubassow; the Governor of Saratow; the City Chief of St. Petersburg, General von Launitz; the Military Attorney General Pavlov; Grand Duke Nikolay; Governor General of Moscow Herschelmann; General Min; Colonel Riemann; Ratchokovsky, the head of the political section of the Ochrana (another of Asev's superiors!); Gapon, a revolutionary and police agent; Admiral Tshuchinin; Minister President Stolypin; and finally, the Czar himself.

This list proves that Asev was by no means a mere instrument in the hands of the secret police. He was no one's tool. He was a man who did not let himself be used, not even by his comrades. It was he who used everyone else. But to what purpose? That is something we can only speculate about. However, we know from the testimony of the Russian conspirators the incomparable feeling that overcame them in that moment of utter solitude when they reared back to throw the bomb. With the bomb they simultaneously took their own fate, that of their victim and that of their entire cause into their hand. This moment lifted them outside themselves and above everyone else. Asev must have felt an extreme augmentation of this feeling, which all the terrorists tried to describe, but in vain: the feeling to stand above all imaginable parties in the struggle in which he participated, which he led, and from which he withdrew. No ruler in this world could be haughtier than this. The sovereignty which became his was boundless, and it was void.

The Fighting Organization offered an ideal arena for the realization of the horrifying freedom Asev had chosen. Its tendency to make terror an absolute, the artistic trait in its work, doubtlessly proved a challenge to someone like him. But the secret police obliged him in just the same way. The two roles that Asev played demanded precisely the same training, the same life-style, the same methods: a climate of camouflage, of mistrust, of guardedness, prevailed on both sides; on both sides did the job demand the same decisiveness, the same coldness, the same work in unchartered and trackless areas. Basically each conspiracy becomes infected by its opponent and vice versa. Asev's double game obeyed the same rules on both sides. The advantage he had over everyone else was the ability to switch from one system of reference to the other at a moment's notice and not to think a single sentence without covering himself.

Perhaps Asev even helped create the most sophisticated calculation where the secret police itself becomes an instrument for the revolution. One can imagine a point of view where the conspiracy and its opponents, the police, appear as accomplices. This thought seems fantastic. Maurice Laport, the historian of the Ochrana, calls provocation the foundation of its activity. The unlimited authority that the government afforded the police became dangerous to the regime itself, for its interests by no means coincided entirely with those of the secret police, which primarily wanted to secure its own existence—which, however, depended on that of a revolutionary movement. The Ochrana would become superfluous unless there were a conspiracy to combat. The revolutionary terror did not abate with the founding of the Ochrana. On the contrary, an organized and continuous illegal movement did not exist until the founding of the Ochrana. The secret agents of the Czarist regime play such a role in it that their provocations have become part and parcel of Russian revolutionary history. Provocation is an extremely ambiguous means. Although it delivers the conspirators to the courts and justifies the continued existence of the police, it also makes certain of an uninterrupted chain of revolutionary acts.

"The tradition of the Russian Revolution of 1917 is, to a by no means insignificant extent, the product of the Russian secret police," says Hannah Arendt. What is certain is that Asev's work, this impenetrable work which is distorted by a macabre dialectic, provided the Czarist regime with some of its most horrible wounds and the revolution with some of its most secret and complicated victories. We have no definite information of the end of this infernal man; but it is said that he hanged himself.

Boris Sawinkov reached the age of forty-five, which, for a man of his metier, is considerable. In August 1924 he was seized by the Soviet police. Four weeks later a military tribunal condemned him to death. The central committee pardoned him to ten years imprisonment. A few weeks later Sawinkov threw himself into the stairwell of his prison. He was instantly dead. The Communists always heaped scorn and derision on Sawinkov and his friends. The preface to the Russian edition of his memoirs, written by a certain Felix Kon, characterizes the conspirators of 1905 with the words: "Hysterical . . . foaming at the mouth . . . slanderers . . . ruthless petit bourgeois . . . decadent ruminators." That is the traditional vocabulary of Communist polemics, which has always been marked by a peculiarly ornery and quarrelsome tone. The political exceptions taken to the terrorist conceptions are more serious. It is indeed remarkable that Sawinkov mentions the major events in 1905 in Russia only in asides: the unrest in St. Petersburg, Bloody Sunday, the demonstrations, the huge series of strikes in the fall of that year, the entire first Russian Revolution, which failed but won decisive concessions from the Czarist government—all that lies outside the field of vision of the "individual terrorist." With good reason and complete decisiveness Lenin turned against the Social Revolutionaries from the beginning, criticizing their anarchic tendencies and laying bare their social prerequisites. They never understood the historic role of the proletariat. Lenin's political analysis proves the political ignorance of the conspirators but it does not disprove their actions; indeed, like every purely political argument, it misses the essence of the actions.

The Communists never understood what was at stake for this unforgettable band of just murderers. Vera Sassulitch and Jegor Sasonov were not interested in party lines or political recipes, nor in a social doctrine. What was at stake for them was their and everyone else's weal and salvation: a salvation that was of this world and which could be achieved only at the price of their life. In that second of truth when they tossed the bomb they realized their salvation and anticipated that of the others.

And like their salvation so their damnation. Kaljajev on the one hand, Asev on the other; they embodied the two most extreme possibilities, the most extreme models of existence of their historic moment. It is comprehensible that their example must be unbearable for the Communists. For it reminds them of an unknown greatness that is beyond all calculation. In the execrations that Lenin and his students heaped on the murderers of the Czar, there mingles with the rational arguments a premonition of the limits of their power, a touch of fear, a trace of secret concern. The example of Kaljajev is a threat to every future rule that is founded on the suffering of its subjects. Fifty years before Kaljajev stepped on the scaffold, Marx, who saw deeper than his successors, fashioned a phrase that does justice to Kaljajev and all those like him. Marx called them: *the dreamers of the absolute.* One such dreamer, an anonymous one in the crowd, suffices to instill dread into all those who hold power on this earth.

Translated by Michael Roloff

Portrait of a Party

*Prehistory, Structure and Ideology of
the Partido Comunista de Cuba*

At first glance it does not look at all extravagant; it resembles an old acquaintance from the sullen, somewhat strong-smelling family of Communist parties. The office of the local chairman somewhere in the Cuban provinces with its pain-stakingly clean ashtray, with the fading posters on the wall ("We salute the irresistible growth of the Party!"), with the green janitor's armchairs and the brown sofa, the pamphlets, courses and placards, which go forever unread: homely as well as utterly depressing at one and the same time, and familiar from Olmütz, Zeulenroda and Jegorjesk. Only the olive green uniform and the fat pistol holster speak a different dialect.

Like this dusty outpost in Oriente Province the top of the Communist party of Cuba, too, appears to lack nothing of the permanent inventory of such institutions: Politburo, and Secretariat, Central Committee and Commissions for this and that, central organs and schools for cadres: all of this can be found in the Government House in Havana. The familiar mildew isn't missing either, this peculiar, unmistakable blight on the words that the party uses and makes unusable.

So it might appear as if things in the Cuban party were going—if not always to the satisfaction of the CPSU—pretty much as they do everywhere, as if the party were as reliable as usual, at least in the way it functioned, in its mechanism; so that each and everyone who felt like it would find his way easily around in its domicile, as easily as the tired Catholic knows how to find his confessional and font when he is abroad. "Unshakable," "wise," "imperturbable," but primarily powerful, narrow-minded, mediocre, blessed with an unscrupulous good conscience and with an immense stomach, as is their wont, an obscure historical logic has yet had its effect on such parties: handmaidens of a cunning greater than their own, it was in their banal offices that the decisions—wherever socialism or what was considered as such was to be constructed—were reached.

Yet not in Cuba. The *Partido Comunista de Cuba* (PCC) has no more in common with the other governing CPs than their façade. And this façade is deceptive. This party is one of the youngest in the world. It exists in its present form and with its present name only since 1965. That means it was founded seven years after a victorious revolution that came to power without its cooperation. This fact alone makes it a unique phenomenon, even a scandal. For a Communist party's self-image is primarily that of an avant-garde of the revolutionary struggle and not as an administrative shell imposed on the revolution *post festum*. The founding fathers of Communism always had more in mind with their concept of the party than a mere instrument of power. The famous "leading role" does not simply fall into the party's lap. It must be earned in the long and patient preparation of the revolution and in the decisive fight for power. A party that constitutes itself only after the victory—after a victory that was not of its making—will suffer all its life from this birth defect. It lacks historical legitimacy. Its authority will always rest on insecure bases.

So as to understand the PCC and the role it plays today one must know its prehistory. With its name it tries to assume inheritance of the old CP. This lineage is however—as will be shown—a rather makeshift construct.

The first CP of Cuba was founded in 1925. It is no easy matter to give a résumé of its course, its detours, its devious games and tactical name changes over the next thirty-five years of its existence, especially because the sources are obscure and no one ever wrote a reliable party history. All in all, however, its physiognomy offers a familiar picture: it was a typical CP. Its strategic somersaults, too, have less to do with Cuban affairs than with the interests of the Soviet Union; it would remain incomprehensible without reference to the Stalinist Central Committee. The PCC began its work under modest circumstances, which nonetheless earned it a rapidly growing status of illegality despite its small membership (after five years the party numbered 2000 members), and was hindered by internal strife (its cofounder Mella, who enjoys a considerable reputation in Cuba today, was expelled in 1929 and murdered under mysterious circumstances). Its operations were confined primarily to the cities and the rural proletariat, especially in the sugar, tobacco, and textile unions, but also had a basis, from the beginning, among intellectuals, chiefly at the University of Havana.

After the world economic crisis of the 1920s imperialism sought to salvage its Cuban positions by means of a police dictatorship; president Machado Gerardo was the dummy for this maneuver. In 1933 his regime was overthrown by a revolutionary mass movement. Workers and student united on the streets of Havana; a general strike was called, which was extraordinarily successful despite poor organizational preparation. The spontaneous, violent mass actions of that time are in many ways reminiscent of the revolt in Paris in May 1968. A radical student government was formed after the dictatorship had been chased; however, it disintegrated soon after. The new candidate of the Americans, a sergeant by the name of Batista, put an end to this first Cuban revolution with a military coup; that happened in 1935.

The CP's role in these events was ambiguous to say the least. The attitude of the basis was revolutionary: in the countryside there occurred occupation of the estates, the formation of Red

Guards and of local Soviets, very similar to the Asturian uprising of 1934. At the same time, however, the party leadership
negotiated with Machado, who promised concessions. Thereupon the Communists asked the striking masses in Havana to
return to work.[1] The PCC demands met with as little success
as did those of the CPF in 1968 in Paris.

It is hardly worth trying to follow the party's political con-
volutions between 1935 and 1945. They followed, schematically, the line of the Comintern. By concentrating its attacks
on "social fascism" after the successful uprising, the PCC actually played directly into Batista's hand. And in the process
even its anti-imperialist position went to pot: "The CP must
do everything to prevent the intervention by the USA, and
therefore it must make certain concessions to the Americans . . .
Therefore it directs its attacks first of all against the ruling
class in Cuba itself."[2] What the PCC had in mind was to
negotiate with the Americans so as to buy up US enterprises
and to manage them as concessions or as monopolies instead of
nationalizing them.

The party, under the leadership of its general secretary Blas
Roca, followed the Popular Front line just as schematically
after 1935. Under Cuban conditions this meant direct
support of Batista. The Communists were able for the first
time to appear in public with the front group, the *Partido
Unión Revolucionaria* (PUR); and one year later Batista
announced that the party would be allowed to operate freely
from now on since it had foresworn its violent road to socialism and had decided on peaceful and constitutional methods.
In 1939 the party was formally legalized; it amalgamated itself
with its predecessor PUR into the *Partido Unión Revolucionaria Comunista* (PURC).

There now arose regular cooperation between the Communists and Batista whom they praised as a "great democrat"
and "leading exponent of our national policies, the embodiment of the holiest ideals of Cuba."[3] Two leading Communists entered Batista's government as ministers without port-
folios: Juan Marinello and Carlos Rafael Rodríguez. It was

the first time that a Latin American CP acquired and accepted cabinet posts.

It would be unfair to conceal the fact that the Batista regime of that time differed considerably from the military dictatorship of the late fifties. In 1940 it was a reformistic government strongly influenced by the American New Deal and regarded itself as a form of social democracy. The constitution of the same year enlarged the sphere in which the unions could operate and even promised land reform. "The Cuban people can thank our cooperation with President Batista for the fabulous constitution of 1940,"[4] said the Party.

The Communists managed to secure for themselves most of the key positions in the newly founded Cuban Union Congress (CTC). The bureaucratic representatives of the workers' aristocracy, which became more and more powerful in the 1940s, were under its complete control. The party membership, too, increased from 5000 (1940) to 37,000 (1946).[5] After the dissolution of the Comintern the party rechristened itself once more, into *Partido Socialista Popular* (PSP). That is what it was called since 1944 and anyone in Cuba who speaks about the old CP calls it by this name. It enjoyed its best year in 1946: the party paper *Hoy* had one of the highest newspaper circulations in Havana, and the Communists managed to get ten percent of the popular vote.

But a few years later the PSP had lost its place in the sun. The coup of 1952 brought a sudden end to its politics of alliance. Batista's second dictatorship of course paid less heed to the wishes of Cuban capital than it did to the international strategy of imperialism. It was no more than a local reflection of the sharpening of the cold war. The beautiful constitution turned out to be just a scrap of paper. In 1953 the party was prohibited; Batista created a bureau for the suppression of Communist activities; the leading functionaries had to emigrate or were arrested. Still, the PSP was not the chief target of the suppression; for years it was able to send its formally prohibited publications through the mails, and leading Communists like Blas Roca, Juan Marinello and Carlos Rafael

Rodríguez could live undisturbed in Havana until the late fifties. Numerous old CP people appeared in the administration of the dictatorship; two of them became undersecretaries of State. This entry into the ministries should probably not be regarded as evidence of opportunism on the part of certain individuals but put down to a party mission. Nonetheless, one can't simply talk about a mutual hands-off policy between Batista and the Communists. The dictatorship's plan was rather to keep the Communists in reserve in case one needed them to blackmail the Americans. Batista's colleague in the Dominican Republic, Rafael Trujillo, engaged in similar though less successful maneuvers of this kind.

The PSP also maintained this ambiguous attitude during the phase of the armed struggle against the dictatorship. If one wants to grasp the internal political situation in revolutionary Cuba, one must study the events of 1953–1958 from this viewpoint; for the policies of the Communists during that period poisoned the atmosphere for such a long time that the consequences can be felt to this day.

The PSP made the following public declaration after Fidel Castro's first armed attack on the Moncado Barracks and on a military object in Oriente Province:

> We oppose the actions of Santiago de Cuba and Bayamo. The putschist methods which were used are characteristic of bourgeois groups. This is an adventurous attempt to conquer military bases. The heroism manifested by the participants is wrong and unproductive; at its root are mistaken bourgeois conceptions . . .
>
> The whole country knows who has organized, directed and led the action against the barracks. The line of the PSP and the mass movement has been and is: Fight against the Batista tyranny and then unmask the putschists and adventurers of the bourgeois opposition which act against the interest of the people! The PSP considers it necessary to bring the masses together in a united front against the government so as to find a democratic way out of the Cuban situation, to resurrect the constitution of 1940, to secure civil liberties, hold general elec-

tions and form a government of the national democratic front . . .

In its fight the PSP bases its support on the masses and condemns the putschist adventurism which is directed against the fight of the masses and against the democratic solutions which the people desire.[6]

This is the position the Communists maintained for the next five years. Castro did not accept these attacks lying down. In 1956 when a Cuban magazine accused him of being a Communist he replied:

What right does Señor Batista have to speak of Communism? After all, in the elections of 1940 he was the candidate of the Communist Party; his jokers hide behind hammer and sickle; his portrait hung next to Blas Roca's and Lázaro Peña's; and half a dozen ministers and confidants of his are leading members of the CP.[7]

The Communists were not invited to the first negotiations about forming a united front against Batista in 1957, and when such an agreement was reached the following year, five months before the overthrow of the dictator, the CP still wasn't there. Its role in the general strike of April 9, 1958—which the Castro movement had called and from which it had expected a decisive turn of events—is also in doubt. The leadership of the party did not openly turn against the undertaking; however, it predicted its failure and distanced itself from it once it had been defeated. Carlos Rafael Rodríguez declared to a French journalist that he hoped these futile actions would teach Castro a lesson: he would realize now that he didn't have a chance by himself; he would have to enter into a broad coalition with the liberals too and tone down his anti-American propaganda. In a letter to the same journalist Rafael Rodríguez explained that the Communists did not feel that "there were sufficient forces in Cuba to bring down Batista and create a progressive anti-imperialist government."[8] Still, the Daily Worker, which at that time was also the voice of the Cuban CP, greeted the objective of the general strike at least insofar as it meant "one step toward the organization of the masses and away from the excessive preference for the heroic but not decisive guerrilla war, the senseless throwing of bombs and sabotage."[9]

The first negotiations between Fidel Castro and the PSP, in the Sierra, did not occur until late in the summer of 1958 after the defeat of Batista's counteroffensive, during the height of the guerrilla. Not much is known about the negotiations. Neither of the two sides has published any documentary material about it. The only thing certain is that Rafael Rodríguez went into the mountains in July and that further emissaries followed him in the fall. However, according to the testimony of the Communists themselves, no binding arrangement was reached before Castro's victory.[10] So the Cuban revolution owes nothing to the PSP for its position at that time. Some of the guerrilleros of 1957–1958 still speak with bitterness of the "treasonable" policies of the old CP—however, only in private; for the public this subject is of course taboo.

Easy to say, treasonable policies. The other side of the balance can be reckoned with equal ease. The attack on the Moncado Barracks was indeed a dilettantishly planned, militarily hopeless adventure; the Communist assessment was technically absolutely correct. It left out only one factor: the psychological effect that Castro achieved with his speech before the court. And in order to understand the PSP leadership's skepticism one must look at the power relationships in Cuba in 1958, which Castro himself has admitted. According to Castro the revolutionary army in summer consisted of 180, in fall of 500 and December 1958 of 800 to 1000 men.[11] Anyone who claims that he always knew should probably be charged with forgetfulness rather than prophetic powers. The political calculations of the Communists in 1958 betray just as much common sense and just as little trust in the incredible as those of the Americans.

Those who today pretend to have known better at the time also like to suppress the fact that Castro indeed led military actions but that his programatic declarations were scarcely more than a reformist mishmash. Even as unself-sufficient, pat and doctrinaire a book as Blas Roca's *Fundamentos del socialismo en Cuba* (the first of numerous editions—each of them being made to conform to the changing party line— appeared in 1943) is far superior to Castro's speeches in analytic power if not in revolutionary fervor. And the party unquestionably played a considerable role in the politization of the Cubans with its tenacious, boring piecemeal work over a thirty-five-year period. But its politics, however mistaken it may have been, also gained the PSP one thing: it is the only party that managed to bring its organization intact through all the changes. The very first year of the revolutionary government demonstrated that this fact was of central significance for the future of Cuba.

Volumes upon volumes have been written about the first two years of the revolution. When, on what day was the decision for socialism reached, and who is responsible for it? The opponents of the revolution, in their scholastic eagerness, have developed a conspiracy theory according to which it was a diabolically directed process. Their speculations are filled with secret agreements, ulterior motives, wire pullers. In fact, the contradictions that became apparent in the years 1959–1960 and their socialist solution cannot be explained by some kind of "world conspiracy"; the inner logic of Castro's decisions can be gleaned, rather, from objective national and international necessities of this struggle. Fidel did not choose these necessities; he did not even provoke them. Only two reactions were thinkable to the increasing pressure of imperialism from the outside and the sharpening of the class conflict inside: capitalism or the turn to socialism. The problematical development of the party shows the enormous difficulties with which the path was paved.

After January 2, 1959, there existed in Cuba only one of the old parties that could operate legally and officially. That was the PSP. Nonetheless the Communists found themselves in something less than a pleasant position. They were not represented in the newly formed government; Fidel Castro and his people mistrusted them and were bitter about them. In the first months of the year it looked as if a public rupture was in the immediate offing.[12] On May 21 the leader of the Cuban revolution still held an openly anti-Communist speech:

> Our revolution is neither capitalist nor communist! . . . What matters to us, who are attached to a humanist doctrine, are the people, and we mobilize all our energies for the good of the majority. We want to free mankind of every dogma; we want to make the economy and society free without terrorizing or forcing anyone. Today's world situation confronts us with the choice between capitalism which starves people and communism which solves their economic problems but suppresses their freedoms which are dear to them . . . Capitalism sacrifices the human being, communism with its totalitarian conceptions sacrifices human rights. We agree neither with the one nor the other . . . Our revolution is not red but olive green. It bears the color of the rebel army from the Sierra Maestra.[13]

The Communists did not let such speeches go unanswered. Aníbal Escalante, a leading functionary of the PSP, accused Fidel, and not altogether unjustly, of "ideological confusion." The subsequent polemics, which were conducted in the pages of *Hoy*, the CP paper, and Castro's organ, *Revolución* dragged on into the summer. And at the plenary session of its central committee on May 25 the PSP was openly critical of the politics of the revolution:

> We are a small country that lies in the immediate vicinity of the U.S. The imperialist influence has deformed our economy; we are therefore dependent on imports even when it comes to feeding our people. In view of these circumstances, all leftist-extremist tendencies and all excessive measures on the part of the revolution, all attempts to ignore the realities and the concrete difficulties facing Cuba have to be sharply opposed.[14]

Those were the initial opposing positions in Spring 1959, which formed the basis for a complicated power play that oscillated for several years between animosity and partnership. In this struggle the Communists primarily had to contend with Castro's political organization, the Movement of the Twenty-sixth of July; and secondly with the remnant of another grouping from the time of the fight against Batista, the Directorio Revolucionario.

The Movement of the Twenty-sixth of July was a kind of radical social democracy that has no parallel in Europe. It was ultra Left with respect to its strategy and tactics, but with respect to its basis and its program it bore the imprint of the national bourgeoisie. It never had a firm ideology. Its name testifies to its origin and to whom it is indebted for its coherence: to the actions of a decisive group that had found its ideal leader in Fidel Castro. It lacked a theory and was heterogeneous. Its founding document is Castro's speech *History Will Acquit Me* before the court in Santiago de Cuba. The text manifests Castro's revolutionary élan and rhetorical brio yet its programatic content is paltry and not self-sufficient. Its most important demands are return to bourgeois democracy; moderate agrarian reform; favorable treatment of the small farmers, founding of cooperatives, indemnification of the large estate owners; reduction of rents, public-housing programs; fight against corruption in the State apparatus; school reform; nationalization of the utilities. These ideas had been the common property of the reformistic opposition in Cuba since the 1930s and had found their clearest formulation around 1950 by the Partido del Pueblo Cubano (ortodoxo) under Eduardo Chibás.

Ex post facto: there was no lack of speculation about secret far-reaching intentions of Fidel Castro. He himself has hinted that he didn't always announce his true objective openly, and has tried to make himself retroactively into a Marxist. Numbers of counterrevolutionary authors, especially the American Theodor Draper, have tried to infer a carefully planned deception from the contradictions that became evident later on. These naive bookkeepers of history speak of a "betrayed revolution." In this fable the role of the betrayed of course devolves on the bourgeoisie, which allegedly was cheated of its just rewards for cooperating in the fight against Batista. It is of no great concern to us what transpired in Castro's soul, but what is certain is that the program of 1953 contains no Marxist intentions whatever. It contains nationalistic, populist and anti-imperialist elements. There is no trace of Leninist features.

This has had a lasting effect on the organizational form of the movement. Structurally it never existed as an organized party. It has no firm leader cadres. There never could be any exclusions from the movement since there was no formal membership. The movement has never held a congress, neither openly nor illegally; there is no elected leadership. Inasmuch as one can speak of a program it has been thrust on the movement from the top. The possibility of discussion and of the formation of a political will existed only informally through the personal influence of individuals on Castro. The movement had no institutional character whatsoever. It was a creature of its founder and of his closest confidants (and even these few as became quickly apparent after the victory of the revolution were entirely replaceable and interchangeable); and their line too was dependent on the leader's insights and his learning process; it never formed itself by means of theoretical insights but resulted immediately from the practice of forced actions and reactions.

On one occasion, at the union congress of October 1959, Castro openly proclaimed the personalistic character of his grouping: *If the movement is to be used to attack its founder, it will stop being the movement of the 26th of July.* That is consistent. It never was more than the instrument of its charismatic leader who alone could guarantee its cohesion. For like every radical reformistic formation this movement was heterogeneous in the extreme: an amorphous coalition whose cracks became apparent immediately after the victory. There was no clear-cut class basis; the decisive integrating factors were the person of the leader and the mutual enemy. Internally the greatest tension within the movement existed between the worker aristocracy and the bourgeois elements, between proponents of a purely formal bourgeois democracy and decisive social reformers; between pro- and anti-Communists; between adherents of cooperation with the USA and decisive opponents of American imperialism. During the fight against Batista there had been the additional growing tension between *llano* and *sierra*, urban opposition and guerrilla in the mountains. Among the people in the lowlands a certain opposition spread against the caudillo whom they feared in Fidel, and against the "militarist" faction—by which they meant the fighters in the mountains.[15]

Besides his own movement and the PSP there existed a third political organization that Castro accepted. That was the Directorio Revolucionario. Though it was numerically even smaller than the Movement of the Twenty-sixth of July and though it had an even narrower basis, limited primarily to the radical wing of the student movement, this group however had acquired tremendous fame for itself through one daredevil action: the assault on the palace of Batista on March 13, 1957, which had produced fifty dead. After several ill-fated commando undertakings in the East of the island the directorio had concentrated its activities on the city guerrilla and had participated in the operations in the interior only in 1958, on the so-called second front in the Escambray mountains. The ideological differences between it and the July movement were few and the initial rivalry had long ago been decided in Fidel's favor. After the victory the directorio ceased to play a role as an independent factor.

On January 2, 1959, Castro found himself in a curious situation. Although he commanded undivided power, he had no structured political organization. His only active apparatus was a numerically small and politically inexperienced rebel army. Instead of a real party he only held a formless movement in his hand in which the centrifugal forces were rapidly beginning to dominate. The diverging class interests manifested themselves more and more. Bourgeois, petit bourgeois and worker-aristocratic forces began to slow down the revolutionary process. Fidel saw himself confronted with a growing opposition within his own ranks. His reaction was simple and sweeping: he poured the child out with the bath and liquidated the Movement of July 26 as an independent political power. Retrospectively he described this event to Simone de Beauvoir in March 1960:

> Why, we asked, doesn't the revolution have cadres, no apparatus? Allowing for all differences, the replies coincided in the essential points: the Movement of July 26, which had carried the revolution, did have an apparatus but it was a petit bourgeois apparatus which could not keep up with the continuation of the revolution, with its radicalization and particularly with the progressing agrarian reform. That is why the Movement was dropped.[16]

Its end—half destruction, half disintegration—can be dated fall of 1959. At that time July 26 lost its control over the two most important mass organizations in Havana: the union congress CTC and the student organization FEU. In both instances Castro personally intervened, both times he ensured the defeat of the candidate proposed by the grass roots. Within a few months the university as well as the union movement had lost its independence.

At the same time more and more socialists assumed key positions in the government. Osvaldo Dorticós assumed the presidency in July 1959, Núñez Jiménez took over the agrarian reform bureau INRA; Raúl Roa became foreign minister, Raúl Castro minister of defense. All four were close to the PSP.

The last reformistic illusions ended in 1960. The increasing sharpening of the conflict with the USA, the de facto engagement to the socialist camp, the agrarian reform, which had been brought to a radical end and the nationalization of all large undertakings of the banks and transport businesses no longer permitted any doubt that Cuba, if not in name, in actuality had entered the path to socialism. But this socialism still had no party, no clear-cut program and no firm ideological platform.

This situation became unbearable in the long run. A country, even if it is small and basically manageable like Cuba, cannot do without a political organization. The destruction of the old State apparatus and of all political groupings except for the PSP produced a vacuum, particularly on the middle and lower level, a vacuum that threatened to lead to utter disorganization. Redress could be imagined coming from two diametrically opposed quarters: it could be created through the self-organization of the grass roots or through an arrangement at the top, the constitution of a party from the top down. Castro selected the second alternative.

The first trial balloon was launched by the Communists. At the eighth party congress, Blas Roca declared that it was desirable to unite and amalgamate all revolutionary forces in one movement. That was in August 1960. The problem was raised and decided internally during the following months. On December 2, 1960, behind closed doors, party schools were formed that were supposed to train cadres for a future unity party. Fidel Castro personally conducted the meeting.[17]

The difficulties of creating a party from the top down were obvious. Since the Movement of July 26 and the Directorio Revolucionario existed only on paper at this point, the PSP in fact controlled the only working political apparatus in Cuba. Castro had nothing to put up against it except his enormous authority with the masses. A particular psychological obstacle was the taintedness and reservations about the CP that Fidel sought to remove in an interview with *Unita*, the newspaper of the Italian CP. Asked what he thought of the PSP, he said:

> It is the only Cuban party which has always insisted on the necessity of radical structural changes in our society. However,

it is true that the Communists mistrusted me and my comrades at the beginning. But this mistrust was justified, and the party's attitude was politically and ideologically correct. Although we had read Marx we guerrilla leaders in the Sierra were at that time full of petit bourgeois prejudice and errors.[18]

In May 1961, after the invasion of Playa Girón and the declaration of Havana that proclaimed the socialist character of the Cuban revolution, the first hints of the imminent founding of the party became public. In June Ché Guevara declared before the students of the University of Havana that the party already existed de facto in the unity of all revolutionary party organizations even if it hadn't constituted itself. All that was left to do was actually found it and name Fidel its General Secretary. Shortly afterward an open communique appeared according to which the party was to be built up in two phases. A preparatory organization called ORI (Organizaciónes Revolucionares Integradas) was supposed to be the preliminary step of a United Party of the Socialist Revolution (Partido Unido de la Revolución Socialista, PURS), which was to be founded later on. No founding congress took place; it remained obscure who actually led ORI; it filtered through only with time that Aníbal Escalante had been declared organizational secretary and that Blas Roca belonged to the inner circle of leaders. No party program was ever proclaimed. A speaker for ORI merely announced in August that the party would be built according to Marxist–Leninist principles.

The convoluted name ORI already manifested the inherently problematical nature of this founding. The "integration" that it announced in practice amounted to a mere adding of party indexes: insofar as they had not removed themselves to Florida, the followers of July 26 and Directorio Revolucionario were simply thrown into the same pot with the old CP. This collection process produced a total strength of 15,000 members. No one apparently thought of recruiting new members from the population. The methods with which the party was built up and led of course were a pure derision of those Marxist–Leninist principles that it invoked.

The declaration that Castro made in his famous speech about the future role of the party and about his relationship to it on December 2, 1961, is therefore difficult to accept at face value. He began with the correct assessment that he had exercised power alone and undivided until now. But this situation supposedly had never corresponded to his wishes, it would have to end; from now on the power belonged in the hands of the party.

> A Leninist Party is the best, the only effective guarantee for the continuity of the exercise of power and the general revolutionary line. I am convinced that a form of government which rests on the administration of the state by a revolutionary organized party with collective leadership is the best political system that humanity has developed in the course of history. The party must take over the leadership.[19]

Did such a party exist or didn't it? And where was its collective leadership? It took nine months for the Cubans to find out anything authentic about it. On March 9, 1962, a lapidary announcement appeared in the press from which one could gather that a national directorate of ORI had been formed. It consisted of twenty-five persons and had been willy-nilly appointed by Castro himself. Thirteen members had come from July 26, two from the old Directorio Revolucionario and ten from the PSP.

This new "integrated" party apparatus lasted for exactly eight days. On March 17 and 26 as well as on April 10 Fidel broke the recently created truce and with unexampled vehemence initiated a grave party crisis, which almost led to the suicide of the leader of the just-founded ORI:

> The party secretaries have erected an arbitrary dictatorship over the whole country. Everywhere it has come to despotic measures, to individual acts of violence. Honest revolutionaries have been delivered up to the terror . . . These gentlemen, who want to force their ideas on others, can scarcely be distinguished from Batista and his hangmen![20]

[The organizational secretary of the party] Aníbal Escalante has called a sect of privileged people into life. The provincial secretaries have behaved like Gauleiters. Nepotism and terrorism are spreading. We have founded ORI but excluded the revolutionary masses. We don't have an apparatus but a yoke, a straightjacket . . . What does that mean, Integrated Revolutionary Organizations? The only ones who have organized themselves here were the people of the PSP . . . It's the same in every province: who became the party secretary of ORI? The former provincial secretary of the PSP. It is the same thing in every local chapter: who became local secretary of ORI? The former local secretary of the PSP! . . . If we look at the results we are forced to conclude: that is a pile of shit.[21]

In fact, this result had been inevitable: the superior organization of the structure of the old CP had so to speak naturally come out on top. The ORI secretariat had become a kind of second government; a power basis that was relatively independent of Fidel had been formed. Aníbal Escalante was considered the culprit: Fidel attacked him as a sectarian (because he preferred his comrades), as an opportunist (because he did not attack the old Batista adherents sharply enough), and as overly ambitious (because he sought to create his own power base). The ORI secretariat was reformed at once in March 1962. Aníbal Escalante went into exile in Moscow and was not allowed to return to Cuba until 1964.

At the same time there began a general housecleaning under the leadership of special commissions that were personally appointed by Fidel Castro, Ernesto Ché Guevara and Raúl Castro. The membership fluctuated by roughly fifty percent during this year. There was no general exclusion of the old Communists, but the autonomous power basis of the party was destroyed. In his speech against the "sectarians" Fidel had promised a reconciliation:

Comrades, from this moment on, every difference between the old and the new, between *sierra* and *llano*, between those who threw bombs and those who didn't, between those who have a Marxist training and those who don't must stop once and for all. From this moment on we must be united and stand together.[22]

Of course the desired integration was not to be achieved with imprecations of this kind. However, Castro's daring and ruthless measures put a stop to the tendencies of the party bureaucracy to become independent. To this day there exists no wide-spread materially privileged class of party functionaries, no homogeneous "new class" that considers itself beyond attack or held together by an esprit de corps or of well-defined material interests that might be capable of taking independent political action. To prevent its coming into existence is Fidel's conscious policy. But this policy has been bought at a costly price: that of weakening the political power of the party, which persists to this day.

A further result of the sectarianism crisis of 1962 was the testing of new, highly original methods of membership recruitment, which were without precedent in the socialist camp. The process that was first introduced in the summer of 1962, provides for the election of candidates for the party by non-members. Shop meetings are called regularly in all factories, agricultural cooperatives and offices of the country; the workers together suggest new party candidates. The following criteria are decisive for election: (1) only shop members with excellent work records are taken into consideration; (2) the candidate must accept the two declarations of Havana; (3) he or she must pledge to keep party discipline and pay his or her membership fee; (4) Batista collaborators and participants in the fake elections of 1958 are excluded; (5) the candidate's private life must be "spotless"; (6) he or she must fulfill his or her duties during land distribution; (7) he or she must be able to prove that the voluntary contribution of labor to the agricultural effort has been made. After the nomination there follows critical and thorough public discussion of the candidate. Only then comes the vote.

Of course a party commission always has the last word about a suggested shop candidate. A favorite vote in the *asamblea* does not guarantee membership. What is required is the confirmation by the party which frequently exercises its right to vetoing so-called "sectarian" and "tolerant majorities." Besides, the party can also accept members by itself, that is without this election process.[23]

Since that time the party has been growing uninterruptedly. In the last years the membership even increased rapidly, and today the PCC seems to be in the process of becoming a mass instead of a cadre party. The membership figure of 100,000 had already been far exceeded by 1968. One can only guess what effect this has had on the qualification of the members. The party secretaries keep emphasizing the necessity to raise the educational level; in 1964, for example, seventy-eight percent of the party members in Matanzas province had less than six years of schooling. The party sought to correct this lack with special courses.[24] Four out of five members still have to go back to school. Women constituted fifteen percent of the membership in 1963 and even today are heavily underrepresented in the party.

The long-announced PRUS (Partido Unido de la Revolución Socialista) finally constituted itself in February 1963. There was no founding congress this time either; the old ORI directorate, which had been appointed by Fidel, simply went on officiating (inasmuch as it made itself noticed at all). Basically it remained a question of one of the numerous rechristenings that make the study of Cuban party history into a kind of scrabble. The building up of the party was further protracted by a chain of leadership crises, in-fights and affairs. The restlessness at the top in 1964 reached a new high point in 1964. At least five leading old-time Communists were downgraded in the reshuffling process: Manuel Luzardo, minister for internal trade and member of the party directorate, was sharply reprimanded by Fidel in May; minister of trade Rigino Botí was dismissed in July; vice-minister for defense, Joaquín Ordoqui, heavily implicated in a scandal and the ensuing trial, was demoted in November and put under house arrest. He too had belonged to the directorate of PURS as had

Carlos Rafael Rodríguez, who had to give up the leadership of the agrarian reform bureau INRA to Fidel. Finally Juan Marinello lost his position as rector of the University of Havana at about the same time.

With that the leadership conflicts were, if not eliminated, at least controlled. The party existed, attracted little notice and reverted into a semi-torporous state. In October 1965 Fidel reached back and resorted to the tried and true method of rechristening, so as to reactivate the party: the old Communists had been outplayed. Fidel's control was complete. The internal political situation had developed to a point where he could assume the name Partido Comunista de Cuba (PCC) for his party. With that the usual organizational structure of a Communist party was also taken over. The party leadership since then consists of a Politburo (eight members), a central committee (one hundred members); and six party commissions (for the armed forces and for internal security; for economic questions; for education; for foreign affairs; for ideology and propaganda; and for constitutional questions; there is no control commission). The personal configuration manifests a strong concentration of offices in the hands of a few people. An analysis of the membership of the central committee provides the following picture (comparative figures in parenthesis: earlier ORI directorate):

Share of old-time Communists from the PSP: 18% (40%)
Share of officers: 69% (55%; in the Soviet Union: 15%); of these: active officers: 39% and officers of the security organs: 12%[25]

However, the study of organizational structures and functionary lists is, under Cuban conditions, of symbolic value at most; for the central committee owes its very existence to another stroke of Fidel's pen: it was simply foisted on top of the party without any discussion whatsoever. Besides, it happens to be the case with the Cuban CC that it has nothing to say. It plays a purely decorative role in Cuba. Its first meeting took place one-and-one-half years after it was formed. Its agenda consisted of a reply to the Venezuelan attack on Cuba in the Organization of American States. The second meeting was held on the occasion of Ché Guevara's death; the third and fourth and so far last occurred in January 1968—the question on the agenda was the trial of the so-called microfaction. It is obvious that the CC serves as nothing but a façade and reaches no decisions whatsoever. Nor does the politburo hold regular meetings or the secretariat. The organization of the party leadership exists on paper only. Fidel does not even take the trouble to conceal this state of affairs. Thus, in 1965 he called all officiating cabinet members into the CC of the PCC; they are still there today, although many of them have since been relieved and replaced by new ministers, who don't belong to the CC. Their appointment has been forgotten likewise.

A party convention of the PCC has never been convened. To the question whether the party has been completely organized, Fidel replied in summer 1965 to the American correspondent Lee Lockwood:

> The organization is practically complete at the roots. The leadership cadres are being organized at the moment. We will hold the first party congress sometime before the end of 1967. Delegations elected by members from all over Cuba will participate.[26]

The organizational secretary of the PCC Armando Hart confirmed this prediction to the correspondent Herbert Matthews in May 1966.[27] The party convention still has not occurred, there is no mention of elected delegations and no one in Cuba seriously believes that this will change.

The ideological state of the party corresponds to its desolate organizational condition. It is the question of the two sides of one and the same coin. The PCC has no program. Anyone inquiring of its ideology is invariably referred to Fidel's speeches whose contradictions are notorious; anyone who actually refers to them does well to take recourse to the most recent of them; for, to repeat what Fidel said a few years ago can have the most unpleasant consequences. (For this reason there is no collection of Fidel's speeches in book form.)

The ideological commission of the party (Comisión de Orientación Revolucionaria, COR) is exclusively occupied with agitational questions. It limits itself to proclaiming slogans of the day and propagating actual production goals. The party schools have to fulfill similar ideological tasks. The Escuelas de Instrucción Revolucionaria, founded in 1961, control the central institute in Havana and twelve provincial schools. The courses take three to six months. Like the intricate obscure course of the party itself, they too have been reorganized repeatedly. They can accommodate up to 30,000 participants per year. But their political significance has receded within the last year, weakened as they have been by the sectarianism crisis and sharp attacks by anti-doctrinaire scientists who particularly criticize the schematically adopted teaching manuals of Soviet origin, as well as occasional acerbic verbal slaps by Fidel himself. With respect to the commission's ideological work in the press and the mass media: it limits itself to undemanding vulgarization of the catch words that Fidel hands out and to opportunistic and eclectic commentaries.

The dominant ideological condition is probably best demonstrated with an example. The following quote is from a pamphlet that the ideological commission of the party published as "study material" under the title *Observations about Ideological Work*. The text of course does not contain the entire ideological repertoire of the party. Lacking in particular are the anti-imperialist and internationalistic elements that play an important role in Cuba. The following, however, can be considered complete and representative with respect to internal politics:

> While working out their plan for their ideological tasks the party should not use the crutch of general or supposedly "theo-

retical" theses. Of course it is important that the basic features of Communist morality should be outlined. But in this respect the speeches of Fidel, Raúl and Ché afford sufficient directions. An anthology of this kind throws more light on these questions than any theoretical speculation from our side . . . We also can determine more precisely what concrete questions concern each individual sector of the population and which the people as a whole. Our ideological task consists of deepening consciousness in this respect. This permits us to fix the relationship between social obligations and social striving. Among these obligations are primarily the following: the revolutionary discipline in general; work discipline; school discipline; the sense for the heroic; the obligation to work more and better; the obligation to continue to educate oneself; punctuality; responsibility; moderation; modesty; the spirit of scientific inquiry; firmness; preparedness to fight; the spirit of revolutionary solidarity; the organization of work and the proper use of all available production factors; the fight against sloppiness; the application of technology; the revolutionary wakefulness; a spirit of sacrifice; devotion to work; and the capacity to perform deep and objective analyses. The nature of our ideological work will consist of explaining the significance of each of these aspects and of showing which possibilities of work they open up. Only on this basis can the ideological work achieve a concrete category and liberate itself from any kind of intellectualism, from any kind of theorizing and metaphysics . . .

The ideological fight consists of transmitting explanations, information and instructions about those duties which the advance of the revolution imposes on each fighter. This task necessarily bears an eminently educational, didactic and instructional character. The ideological fight must essentially be conducted by means of explanation and convincing.

This daily fight consists essentially of transmitting to the people explanations, information and direction about what tasks the revolution gives each worker and the people in their entirety.[28]

It is apparent that this document avoids any kind of analysis of Cuban society. Class struggle does not appear in it, the production relationships play no role. The "spirit of scientific inquiry" is invoked but refuses to manifest itself; the "capacity to perform deep and objective analyses," which the text hopes for, is what it lacks. In this respect the text is scarcely unique. Its simultaneously primitive and bloated language shows the degree to which Marxist thinking in Cuba has gone to the dogs. Words like *concrete, category, analysis* are used completely out of context, as fetishes pure and simple. Every socioeconomic argument is carefully avoided. Cuban society consists of "the people," "the workers," and "different sectors." The revolution manifests itself to them as an alien, demanding and authoritative subject that can only express itself in Old Testament-like tautologies: "No hay argumento más fuerte que la obra misma de la revolución." There is no stronger argument than the work of the revolution itself. This sounds much like I am the one I am.

But who is "the revolution?" An allegorical figure? A hypostatic historical process? Or something that is only comprehensible through the embodiment in the *Jefe máximo*? This metaphysics, which the school text pretends to oppose, is one of its essential features. We can find information about what the revolution is "from the speeches of our leaders." But in Fidel's linguistic usage his own thinking and acting merges with that of the revolution. The leader's ad hoc speeches replace an ensemble of fundamental principles.

What is also characteristic is the naive moralizing tone of the ideological utterances that the party produces. Texts of this kind interest themselves primarily not for what is but for what should be. Its sentences are of purely hortatory nature. They form an endless series of exhortations. A system of virtues is postulated that, were it less confused, would remind one of medieval models. The magical repetition of the word consciousness is supposed to introduce the same into people's heads. But this consciousness is without concept, it understands nothing and exhausts itself in moralizing attacks. Certain elements from Ché's thinking return here, flattened and coarsened to the point of unrecognizability: an extreme voluntarism, vulgarized, results in the interchangeability of subjective and objective conditions, as if Marx could be stood on his head. The consciousness of the individual worker, once set aright, is supposed to determine the economic basis. This moralizing effort is supposed to drag society out of the bog of underdevelopment: everyone, like Münchhausen, by his own braid.

This idealism appears that much more obnoxious since it apparently couldn't care less about insight. It almost seems as if it wants to confirm its own ignorance. In that case it would be ideology in the most reactionary sense of the word, consciousness as façade, as an authoritarian element instead of a rational basis of historical necessity. Finally, one cannot help notice the text's furious animosity to theory. It can be found in all significant party pronouncements and doubtlessly can be traced directly to Fidel: "Let's have done with the theoreticians of the revolution! Let's have done with the Marxist theoreticians! The Marxist–Leninist who keeps developing theories is only a leech on the public's pocketbook!"[29] Fidel's speeches reek with such eruptions. Of course they frequently occur in less abrasive fashion, as in the anecdote from 1954/55 that Raúl Castro recounted to an American guest. At that time, imprisoned on the Isla de Pinos, Fidel gave his brother a few books by Marx and Lenin. "We read three chapters of *Das Kapital*," Raúl repeated laughing, "Then we tossed it aside. I'm sure Fidel hasn't looked at it since."[30] This has a certain charm; there probably is no Communist politician who has read beyond the third chapter; but there certainly isn't one beside Fidel who takes pride in this.

This however goes only a short way toward explaining the party and its leadership's nearly blind hatred of theory. It is completely un-Marxist and its roots cannot be found in Cuban revolutionary practice either. They are to be found, rather, in the intellectual tradition of the country. Except for the old CP the traditional theoretical substance is rather scarce; there never was a wide-spread reception of the Marxist classics. Ideological remnants from the Spanish colonial period occasionally manifested themselves as late as the 1940s; the American influence only barely concealed the general ignorance and the political underdevelopment in the capital, but inculcated a permanent sense for practicism. Hidden remnants from the anti-Communist periods of the Twenty-sixth of July Movement also play a role. The mistrust of the traditional Communist turn of mind became particularly prominent in the polemic against the "courses" of Soviet origin; in this instance, however, with justification. However, the Cuban party made the quarrel a pretext for suspecting everyone of being a dogmatist who argued at all theoretically. The confusion of dogma and theory belongs to Fidel's permanent repertoire. Yet it isn't immediately apparent what is supposedly undogmatic in the PCC's school texts and in what respects if any they are superior to their Soviet models and counterparts: in any event, they quite measure up to their narrow-mindedness and phrase mongering.

Besides, a threadbare or false theory cannot be simply countered by dismissing theorizing altogether. A consciousness that closes itself off from all conceptual work must inevitably atrophy. Moralizing rhetoric and simpleminded muddling on is all that is left. The ideology becomes an arbitrarily kneadable plastic. A kind of permanent obsolescence takes effect. Slogans are created to be discarded. Consistency as a criterion no longer plays a role.

With respect to Fidel himself, a further motive must be added, which, however, is more of psychological interest. He evidently has need to counter the prevailing ideologies with his own Cuban teaching. This claim however he cannot redeem by himself because his capacities as a theoretician do not suffice for this. That is obvious to anyone who takes the trouble of reading his speeches over a longer period of time.

Of course Fidel can corroborate his suspicion of pure theory with bitter experiences from the years of the struggle against Batista. His hatred of people where the revolution only takes place in the head is not only comprehensible but also completely justified: he lacks the necessary correlative to this suspicion that would be the rejection of a pragmatism that scrambles theoryless from one situation into the other and that reduces political action to the learning process of *trial and error*. A theory that is truly related to practice is an indispensable productive power. It demands criticism and makes it possible. It does not cover up social contradictions but makes them visible, allows their articulation and shows the possibility or impossibility of their solutions.

However, each theory also means holding fast to a fixed point of view. It makes it possible to check a decision rationally, and to that extent it limits the political sphere of action of someone who makes the theory his own. This goes to the heart of the matter. For Fidel has an infernal dislike of any power that might limit his absolute freedom of movement. He turns away every obligation, every control and every attempt to justify himself, even if it is a case where he would have to check his actions against his own insights. That is the real reason for his dislike of theory.

Such an unlimited sovereignty, however, can turn into arbitrariness. Under such conditions there exists only a single guarantee for the consistent and continuing policy of the revolution, and this guarantee is of a purely subjective nature. It lies in the integrity of the revolutionary Fidel Castro. The trust in him, who is someone without any checks, thus becomes the heart of the ideology. That is too little for a Communist party. It means that the PCC not only lacks historical but also ideological legitimacy.

What is the Cuban party and how does it function?

> First of all it is the revolutionary avant-garde, the political organization of the workers in which the power of the State manifests itself and which mobilizes the masses, the accomplishment of their tasks and the functions of the revolution. It brings up the masses, organizes them, leads and controls the administration, creates the work plans and watches over their execution. The party in one word is the political power. There is no dualism, no division of powers and of functions. After the first party convention we will be in a position to determine the

role of the party even more clearly. We will know even better then what has to be done and how it has to be done. (Fidel Castro, *dixit* 1965)[31]

Much time has passed since then, but nothing has changed. The party is supposed to govern but it does nothing of the kind. That does not mean that it is superfluous or without functions. On the local level it performs good administrative work in many places. Particularly in the small towns, villages and *bateys* of the island there are numerous effective party secretaries who perform tireless piecemeal work. They mobilize people for volunteer work in agriculture, act as peacemakers in the shop disputes, bring some sanity into the planification chaos, fight against disorganization and sloppiness, and act as girl fridays for all and everything during the solution of a thousand everyday problems in the Cuban provinces. They do this without clearly defined roles, usually on their own initiative, and accept many tasks that devolve on mass organizations such as unions or local government offices in other socialist countries. Sociologically the party also plays a real part in the fields of recruitment and advancement. However one thing it is not, under any circumstance: a political power.

Political power in Cuba is exclusively in the hands of a tiny number of persons who huddle around Fidel, and who are under no party discipline whatever. The only thing that counts is their loyalty to the Comandante-en-jefe. Therefore, it is quite irrelevant what party office they hold or whether they even belong to the PCC. (Some of Castro's most influential confidants haven't joined to this day.)

Fidel needs the party and can't stand it. It is burdensome. He scarcely ever attends its meetings. He can't do without its apparatus and fears it as a millstone around his neck. He runs with great endurance from the avant-garde, which he calls to arms. It will never catch up with him. He wants it and doesn't want it. Fidel's dilemma, therefore, is also the PCC's dilemma, an institution that has been simultaneously built and destroyed for many years. That is why the Cuban CP is a party without elected commissions, without party congresses, without statutes, without a program, without assigned responsibilities, without a clear self-understanding; a party without historical roots, without theoretical substance; a party without power; the shadow of a party that will perhaps never exist.

Translated by Michael Roloff

Tourists of the Revolution

The European Left manifests an arbitrary and ideological relationship to the socialistically governed countries with its discussions about revisionism and anti-revisionism, accomplishments' and 'deformations'; and anyone who pays close attention to these discussions often finds it difficult to localize the voices he hears—as though the speakers were ventriloquists from whom issued something like a socialist *Weltgeist*. When such a dislocation occurs, the fabric of the conversation is deprived of something that requires foremost consideration: the role of the observer that devolves on the Western Left with respect to those countries where socialism has found—if not its realization—at least serious attempts in that direction.

No matter what attitude or position one takes toward these countries—and they run the gamut from blind identification to vitriolic dislike—the verdicts are invariably reached *from the outside*. No one who returns from a sojourn in socialism is a genuine part of the process he tries to describe. Neither voluntary commitment, nor the degree of solidarity with which one behaves, no propaganda action, no walk through the cane fields and schools, factories and mines, not to mention a few moments at the lectern or a quick handshake with the leader of the revolution, can deceive about that fact.

The less the traveler understands this and the less he questions his own position, the greater and more justified will be the animosity that the voyager into socialism encounters from the very onset—from both sides. Such as in these lines:

THE TRAVELLERS

They come in the clothes of the affluent society,
a thorn in whose side they are, whose "unreliable elements,"
fitted out with academic titles,
writing books for the departments of sociology
of the best universities
(which underwrite the cost).
They get their visas in a jiffy,
are informed about anti-war campaigns,
about protests against the Vietnam war, in short:
they are treading the righteous path of history.
While they lounge in the shiny seats
of the international airports,
each flight they take an illegal act,
they feel pleasantly subversive,
their conscience is clean.
They are the comfortable travelers of the wave of the future,
with Rolleiflex cameras, perfectly suited
for the tropical light,
for underdevelopment;
with information charts for objective interviews,
if, however (of course), something less than impartial,
for they love the struggle,
the guerillas,
the zafras,
the hardships of life,
the vulgar Spanish of the natives.

After two or three weeks
(that's the maximum)
they write books about guerillas
or the Cuban national character,
about the hardships of life or
the vulgar Spanish of the natives.

Provided with systems, with methods,
they are obviously frustrated
by the missing sexual freedom in Cuba,
by the unfortunate puritanism of the revolution,

and they define that state of affairs
with honest melancholy
as the abyss between theory and practice.
In private (not in their book or at the round table)
they admit that they cut more cane
than the best machetero (those guys made fiesta all day).
These fourteen-day heroes declare
that the people in the inns want to dance,
that the intellectuals (completely depoliticized)
are still able to write poetry;
the night before their flight back, lying next to their women,
they believe
they have developed supernatural muscles.
They go at it like blacks, as though they were depraved.
The girls, pregnant every five years,
are delirious with these unaccustomed husbands,
now insatiable.
At home they look at slides
that show the family hero
surrounded by natives, fraternally embraced (...)

Herberto Padilla[1]

The travelers whom Padilla describes bear the distinctive features of the sixties; and perhaps the only ones who can judge how accurate and appropriate his observations and arguments are are those whom they are aimed at. But the mistrust that manifests itself in his text is not of today's vintage, nor of yesterday's. It exists since the existence of two established social systems and it is encountered by anyone who moves more or less freely between the two. This mistrust has hardened in the course of the last fifty years. It contains layers upon layers of past experiences, the recollection of misjudgments that have long since become a tradition with the Left in the capitalist societies.

However, the phenomenon cannot be gotten rid of by rhetoric alone. (Padilla's text, too, contains its hidden ambivalence.) What makes a more precise investigation necessary are the objective effects that these journeys into socialism have had over the years. These effects, of course, have nothing to do with the significance of the individual travelers who were not up to the role they were asked to play, nor with the import of their (mostly superficial) observations and their (frequently threadbare) arguments. What lends these reports significance and why they continue to play a certain, though diminishing, role has to do with the isolation of the socialist countries from the outside world. This exclusion is one element in international class warfare and, depending on how that conflict has gone since 1917, it has assumed the forms of blockade, ostracism, military cordon sanitaire, "iron curtain," The Wall, and so on. This condition finds its administrative equivalent in travel restrictions, different forms of censorship, anti-emigration edicts and complicated permission procedures of all kinds. The extent to which these measures were made necessary by socialist transformations, how far they have become bureaucratically institutionalized and are politically superfluous are questions that cannot be investigated here; nor can they be resolved in principle or once and for all time.

In any event, the consequences are serious. The flow of communication between the socialistically governed countries and the outside world is disrupted. Socialism becomes an internal and secretive affair, only accessible to those who have the opportunity to peek behind the mystifying façade. Ignorance and manipulation become the rule. These consequences don't necessarily devolve primarily to the disadvantage of the class enemy. On the contrary: the governments and monopolies of the capitalist world have news and spy services that are in a position to make up the information deficit. On the other hand, the Left is thrown back on anachronistic forms of communication if it is dissatisfied with the information and deformation provided by the bourgeois media. Among these surrogates the trip, the visit, the eye-witness report play an important role. The sources of error of this kind of information nexus are self-evident, and we shall try to name them. Considered as a whole, it is paradoxical that the social-socialist movements in the West have been generally dependent on individual views when it came to finding out something about collective life and production procedures; that is, for information about huge industrialization processes they have had to rely on a pre-industrial messenger service. No wonder the wanderers frequently cut a ridiculous figure. The puny flow of information is scarcely their fault. It has objective causes.

Now that the old difficulties have not disappeared but have become surpassable, and every one of us can travel to the USSR almost at will, to Bulgaria, the DDR, and Czechoslovakia, the criticism of the travelers also turns against those who stay at home. A lack of curiosity is spreading among the West European Left that, at first glance, is astonishing and that requires an explanation. Year after year, many of the comrades go to Sardinia, to Greece, or to Amsterdam; however, they assiduously shun contact with the Hungarian or Ukrainian reality. These avoidance strategies, too, have their pre-history. Even during the thirties and forties many Communists preferred, if possible, to avoid the USSR, which they praised in their writings as the true home of the working class—even when this country was open to them at all times. For this, however, they had more concrete reasons than present travelers. Brecht, for example, stayed only a few weeks in the USSR during his trip from Finland to California, avoiding contact with Soviet reality as much as possible—evidently so as not to endanger himself. Today many comrades fear contact for other reasons. And sheer disinterest on the part of the politically active is probably not one of them. What those who remain behind are afraid of, rather, are their own illbodings. They don't even let it get as far as contact with the reality of the socialist countries so as not to endanger their own fragile convictions. That is not to say that the others leave their fears behind when they journey into socialism. On the contrary: the same concern that keeps some at home others drag around with them. It's part of their moral handbaggage. The inquisitive ones, too, have developed their defense mechanisms in the last fifty years—to soften the shock when a purely imagined reality encounters an historical one. The first to characterize this operation was Lev Trotzky:

"Today the book market of all civilized countries overflows with books on the Soviet Union. . . . The literature which is dictated by blind hatred assumes an increasingly smaller proportion; a considerable part of the new works on the Soviet Union on the other hand, are acquiring an increasingly benign if not enchanted air. . . . The publications of the 'Friends of the Soviet Union' fall into three main categories. Dilettantistic journalism of a descriptive genre, more or less 'leftist' reports constitute the great majority of articles and books. Then we find publications of humanitarian, pacifistic and lyrical communism which, if anything, are even more pretentious. In third place stands the economic schematization in the spirit of the old-German lectern–socialism. . . .

"What unites these three categories despite their differences is their obeisance to the fait accompli and their preference for soporific generalizations. They are incapable of rebelling against their own capitalism, and are therefore that much more eager to support themselves with a revolution that is already subsiding. Before the October Revolution not one of these people or their spiritual ancestors seriously asked themselves in what manner or form socialism would realize itself. Therefore, it comes that much easier to them to acknowledge what they find in the USSR as socialism. This not only provides them with a progressive appearance, but also with a certain moral fiber which, however, does not commit them to anything. This kind of contemplative, optimistic, anything but destructive literature, which presumes that all troubles are over, has a very calming effect on the readers' nerves and therefore is readily accepted. In this way an international school, which might be called *Bolshevism for the enlightened Bourgeoisie,* or in a strict sense *Socialism for radical tourists,* is imperceptively coming into existence." [2]

Trotzky's analysis, however, leaves untouched one centrally important aspect of the matter: *the institutional side* without which the Tourism of the Revolution remains incomprehensible. Whoever overlooks this side sooner or later arrives at a moralizing attitude that fixes on the character of a single individual. All one finds out this way is that X is naive, Y corrupt, and Z a hypocrite. But this explains nothing and nothing is won by it.

The institutional basis of "radical" or "revolutionary" tourism is the *delegacija* system. *Delegacija* actually means nothing but delegation, but the word has acquired a special meaning in Russian and designates official travelers of all kinds, even if they appear by themselves or in small groups; and it is by no means necessary for these people to have been delegated by anyone.

The following elements—inasmuch as they affect travelers from outside the country—are what make up the system:

1) The *delegate* is not undertaking the trip on his own account. He is invited. Normally he does not pay his own expenses. He is a guest and is therefore under the aegis of the unwritten laws of hospitality. From a material viewpoint this arrangement can lead to corruption; from a moral viewpoint to a defusing of criticism.

2) The *delegate* has to deal with hosts who occupy a monopolistic position. Paid-for trips also exist in capitalist countries; governments, organizations and firms particularly like to invite journalists, a procedure, which is considered a normal aspect of public relations. But usually the traveler is not dependent on such invitations, he can also travel without them. In contrast, the invitation as a *delegate* was (in every) and is (in some) countries the only possibility of acquiring a visa, the local currency, a room and transportation.

3) Compared to the general population, the *delegate* is in every respect a privileged person. When there is a shortage he enjoys precedence over the natives; hotel rooms, seats in public transportation, cars and chauffeurs are reserved for him; during longer stays he is permitted to buy at special shops; admission to special events normally off-limits to others and considerable sums are often made available to him.

4) The *delegate* is always cared for by an organization. He isn't supposed to—no, he isn't allowed to—worry about anything. Usually he receives a personal guide who functions as translator, nanny, and watchdog. Almost all contact with the host country is mediated through this companion, which makes distinct the *delegate's* segregation from the social reality surrounding him. The companion is responsible for the traveler's *program*. There is no traveling without a program. The guest may express his wishes in this respect; however, he remains dependent on the organization that invited him. In this respect he is treated as though he were still under-age.

The combination of being spoiled and impotent is reminiscent of infantile situations. Such visitors' lack of self-sufficiency can reach utter helplessness; it seems as though this state of affairs meets with the approval of the responsible organizations. The socialist countries have institutions that specialize in this kind of work; they are usually called "Society for the Friendship with the People" or something on that order. But all other organizations—from State apparatus and party apparatus to the women's organizations—have sections that take care of official guests.

The *delegacija* system is a Russian invention. It has its beginnings in the early twenties, and one can't assume that it was the intention from the start to pull the wool over the foreigners' eyes and to put them in a position that would lead to an inevitable loss of contact with reality. Anyone who assumes this kind of conspiracy demonizes a complicated relationship by inventing a theory which doesn't even completely apply today when it has become difficult to distinguish between cynicism and experience. For even now a delegate who, say, goes to Hungary, Cuba, or the Georgian Republic, will encounter completely genuine expressions of hospitality, and the trouble people take on his behalf not only serves to shield him from reality but also to protect him from situations that he might be unable to handle by himself. This was even more the case during the Russian civil war; that is, during the periods when the system was being created and when it was nearly impossible for a foreigner to travel to Russia without running the danger of dying from hunger, freezing to death, or being shot.

But that is just one side of the coin. Also, one should not forget that no cheaper or more effective means for influencing the outside world has ever been devised than the *delegacija* system. That is certainly one reason why it has spread from Russia over half the world. A few early examples give proof of its effectiveness. The first report is from Victor Serge and refers to the year 1920.

"The II. Congress of the Communist International continued its work in Moscow. Foreign colleagues and delegates lived in a hotel in the center of the city, the Djelovoi Dvor, which is situated at the end of a long boulevard whose one side consists of the white battlement-crowned wall of the Kitai-Gorod. Medieval portals beneath one nearby old tower lead to the Warvarka where the legendary house of the Romanovs stands. From there we went to the Kremlin, a city within the city, all of whose entrances have guards that control the passes. The twin-power of the revolution, the Soviet Government and the International, were meeting there in the palaces of the autocracy, amidst the Byzantine churches. The only city that the foreign delegates did not get to know —and their lack of interest in this respect confused me— was the living Moscow with its hunger rations, its arrests, its filthy prison stories, its black-market façades. Luxuriously fed amidst the general misery (although, in fact, one served them too many rotten eggs), led through museums to exemplary kindergartens, the delegates of world socialism gave the impression of being on vacation or traveling as tourists through our wasted, besieged republic. I discovered a new form of unawareness, Marxist unawareness. A German party leader, athletic and full of optimism, said to me quite simply that 'the internal contradictions of the Russian revolution contain nothing surprising' for a Marxist, and in that he was undoubtedly right, but he used that general truth as an umbrella to avoid the immediate appearance of reality—which has its importance despite everything. The majority of the bolshevized left Marxists assumed this complacent attitude. For them the words 'Dictatorship of the Proletariat' magically explained everything without their ever thinking of asking where the dictatorial proletariat was and what it was thinking, feeling and doing. . . .

"All in all, the foreign delegates were actually a disappointing crowd that delighted in valuable privileges in a famished country; they were quick to be enthusiastic but mentally lazy. One saw among them few workers and many politicians. 'How happy they are,' Jacques Mesnil said to me, 'that they can finally watch parades from the official rostrum.' " [3]

Franz Jung's following observations fall into the same period: "Hunger also left its mark at the headquarters of the International, the Hotel Lux. Almost the entire intellectual and political elite of Europe and the world that stood close to socialism was presented to the Kremlin via the Hotel Lux —invited guests of honor of the government, sympathizers who had been advised to make the trip to Moscow and leading members of various Communist parties who had been ordered to Moscow.

"In May 1920, the food supply system of Hotel Lux had broken down. The distinguished hotel guests sat at long tables in the spacious dining room but could get nothing except tea with which everyone could provide himself from the samovars, which stood about everywhere. Several times a day, at irregular intervals, large bowls with caviar were placed on the tables together with plates of lox, but no bread and no kasa. Anyone who took the time to wait with his tea was bound to get caviar and lox at some point during the day.

"The prominent guests were very indignant at that time, most of them because they had upset stomachs due to the caviar and lox. They mentioned among themselves that if they were at the head of the government of the victorious revolution the food supply would be better organized, especially in the quarters of the government guests such as the Hotel Lux—they would see to that. They talked about this from early in the morning till late at night, at tea before the steaming samovar, while waiting for the next bowls full of caviar and plates with lox." [4]

Seven years later the contradictions within Soviet society had become even more acute and the blindness of certain visitors assumed grotesque proportions: "All opponents of 1927 went to the end of their terrible road, each in his own way no matter whether they let themselves be constantly humiliated out of loyalty to the party or put up constant resistance out of loyalty for socialism . . .

"What a crass contrast to these men were the foreigners, famous writers, Communist delegates, liberal guests of high rank who celebrated the tenth anniversary of the revolution in Moscow at that time! And they gave us lectures on how to be clever! Paul Marion (the future undersecretary of state in Pétain's government), member of the central committee of the Communist Party of France, was scattering boulevard bon mots about Moscow, knew how to appreciate the young Russian women and tried to explain to me that we were utopian; he himself saw the mistakes of the Communist movement very clearly, but continued to support it because 'despite everything, it was the only force . . .' He was just an average Frenchman—without intelligence—who was primarily interested in always coming out smelling like roses. All in all: buyable. . . .

"I met Barbusse, with whom I was corresponding, in the Hotel Metropole, guarded by an interpreter–secretary (from the GPU) and supported by a very pretty secretary doll . . . I was coming from the overcrowded rooms of the suburbs, from which comrades disappeared every night. I saw their women whose eyes were much too red and clouded with fear for me to feel very indulgent toward the great official foreign guests who were coming on tour; besides, I knew who had been chased from the hotel to accommodate the great writer . . . Barbusse had a large emaciated and supple body topped by a small, waxen, hollow-cheeked face with suffering lips. Right away I had a very different impression of him, primarily concerned not to be pinned down to anything, not to see anything that might have pinned him down against his will, concerned to conceal thoughts that he wasn't allowed to express, evading every direct question, always elusive, with uncertain glances, describing curves in the air with his slim hands while uttering words such as 'depths,' 'breadth,' 'augmentation,' and all this so as to make himself in fact the accomplice of the stronger side. But since one didn't know yet whether the struggle had really been decided, he had just dedicated one of his books to Trotzky, but didn't dare visit him so as not to compromise himself. When I mentioned the repression he acted as though he had a headache, as though he didn't understand, as though he were rising to wondrous heights of thought: 'Tragic fate of the revolution, breadth, depths, yes yes . . . oh my friend!' With a kind of cramp in my jaw I noticed that I was facing the human incarnation of hypocrisy." (Victor Serge)[5]

Examples such as these would probably enable one to develop a comparative psychology of such "Friends of the Soviet Union" and other countries, as well as of their trusting listeners at home; however, so as to become politically relevant such an analysis would have to go beyond individual idiosyncrasies and search out the historically determined elements of the wishful thinking and their blindness to reality and their corruption. The point is not to discover that "man is evil," but why professed socialists let themselves be politically blackmailed, morally bribed, and theoretically blinded, and not just a few individuals, but in droves. Such a reckoning of course cannot confine itself to an investigation of the "Tourism of the Revolutionaries"; this phenomenon, after all, is only one of the symptoms.

Let us return to the objective, institutional side of the *delegacija* business. The last example contains a suggestion how the system developed between 1920 and 1927; that is, from its crude beginnings to a far-flung, highly differentiated apparatus. Henri Barbusse, after all, was not a comrade, no central committee ever sent him to Moscow to the Comintern. Although he scarcely represented more than himself, he was received like a State guest. Yes, it is questionable in what sense, if any, he even belonged to the Left; his social position, his habits, his actions, and thinking characterize him rather as a typical bourgeois intellectual. And this was what constituted his political usefulness to the Soviet leadership at that time. The greater the precision with which the socialist bureaucracies learned to calculate such tactical victories, the more far-reaching their attempts to utilize the "Tourism of the Revolutionaries" as part of their political purposes. Under such circumstances it was inevitable that the *delegacija* system becomes differentiated. Varying categories of visitors, running the gamut from reactionary journalists to deserving party members and ultra-leftist sectarians, were assigned to different organizations, fitted out with carefully graded privileges and then sluiced through the country. A renegade who is an expert in these matters describes how the system functions in practice:

"A free-lance writer ranked somewhere near the bottom of the hierarchy. However, I was not a simple free-lance; I had an "organisation"—the MORP—which, being affiliated to the Comintern, was situated somewhere in the middle range of the pyramid. Moreover, I was a Party member, which improved my grading; but only a member of the German, not the Russian Party, which lowered it. I also carried on me a letter from *Agitprop Ekki* (Department of Agitation and Propaganda of the Executive Committee of the Communist International) which again considerably improved my grading.

"Such 'to whom it may concern' letters serve as a kind of passport in the Soviet Union. It is on their strength that the citizen obtains his permits, his accommodation, ration card, and so on. Accordingly, these letters are very carefully worded and graded, to convey the exact degree of priority to which the bearer is entitled. Mine was a "strong" letter, signed by the head of *Agitprop Ekki,* Comrade Gopner, in person. It said that I was a delegate of the Revolutionary Writers' League of Germany, and that I was travelling under the sponsorship of the Comintern.

"On the other hand, I was also a bourgeois foreign correspondent, working for several important newspapers, and duly accredited as such with the Press department of *Narkomindyel,* the Ministry of Foreign Affairs. This placed me in one of the top grades on another side of the pyramid, as it were. It entitled me to accommodation in *Intourist* Hotels where such existed; to travel in the "soft class" on trains; and to buy my food at *Insnab,* the co-operative stores reserved for the diplomatic corps, the foreign Press and foreign technical advisers. I disliked availing myself of these bourgeois privileges, but as I was travelling alone through remote and famine-stricken regions of the country, it was often the only way of obtaining food and shelter.

"I was careful never to show my bourgeois, *Narkomindyel,* documentation at the Party offices and factories that I visited, nor to travelling companions, for the immediate result would have been to arouse distrust and suspicion. On the other hand, I never showed my Comintern letter to hotel managers, railway officials and co-operative store managers—it would have deprived me of the preferential treatment for bourgeois tourists who have to be humoured for reasons of propaganda. Such a double existence was not regarded as dishonourable. On the contrary, it reflected the basic dualism of "*Narkomindyel* line" and "Comintern line"—the two aspects of the Soviet Union as a respectable international power, and as a clandestine centre of the world revolution. To bear this duality constantly in mind was one of the first lessons taught to every Party member.

"Thus I travelled symbolically in two different guises, and literally with one set of documents in my right-hand pocket, another in my left-hand pocket. I never mixed them up, thanks to the simple memorising device that the Comintern was "on the left."

"Even so, it would have been impossible for me to travel alone without falling back on the help of the only organisation that functioned efficiently everywhere throughout the country: the GPU. In every railway station in the Soviet Union there was a GPU Commissariat which maintained a minimum of order in the chaos. The function of the "Station GPU" was not political surveillance, but to act as railway officials, travel agents and information centres for official travellers. When I got out of the train in a new town, I went straight to the Station GPU, presented my papers, and was provided, as a matter of routine, with those basic necessities which no individual traveller can obtain without the "organisation" behind him: a room or bed, ration-card, means of transportation. My sponsors were the Comintern and the Foreign Ministry, neither of which had branch offices in small places; so the Station GPU took me under its wing until it was able to hand me over to the care of the slow-moving local Party Committee or Government Guest House. In short, the Station GPU had none of the sinister associations of that notorious body, of which it formed a kind of administrative public-service branch. It was, as I have said, the only efficient institution throughout the country, the steel framework which held the pyramid together . . ." 6

Between 1925 and 1939 a great number of European intellectuals went, like Koestler, on a search for the coming time. The enormous dissemination that the literature produced by these "Friends of the Soviet Union" enjoyed was due to a massive need for concrete utopias—which the Soviet Union seemed to embody at that time. These books were by no means solely designed for the proletariat inasmuch as it was organized within the Communist parties, but also, and even primarily, for the petit-bourgeois intellectuals and the new "middle class" of employees who felt that capitalism endangered their existence. What secured a broad public for the "Tourism of the Revolution," therefore, was its bourgeois traits. The more euphoric, the more welcome this literature was: its illusions, which seem defects to us, were perhaps the basis of its success.

Of course, this literature never dominated the field. Since we are dealing with the Left or "leftist" tourism we will disregard the flood of anti-Soviet hate literature that the West produced after the October Revolution. It goes almost without saying that the wars of intervention and the economic and political pressures found their ideological complement in the press, in books and in film, that capitalism did not forego a propagandistic counter-offensive. Yet the Left too, produced documents of disillusion and vehement criticism of Soviet conditions alongside the literature of illusion. Such testimony begins to appear occasionally as early as the twenties. Particularly the anarchists published early reports of their experiences that shed a critical light on developments in the USSR. Examples of this are the books by Rudolf Rocker (*My Disillusionment in Russia*, New York 1923), Alexander Berkman (*The Bolshevik Myth. Diary 1920–24*, New York 1925), and Emma Goldman (*Living My Life*, New York 1934). Of course, these reports were written at a time when the *delegacija* system was still unknown, and only a small minority of people took any notice of them.

The French–Romanian writer Panait Istrati was presumably the first apostate among the "radical tourists." As Honorary President of the Society of Friends of the USSR, he had been invited to attend the tenth anniversary of the October Revolution in Moscow and had been received like a State guest. He aired his disappointment in a report *Après seize mois en URSS*, which was published in 1929 in Paris. This report manifests the radical turn-about from one extreme to the other that is characteristic of the anti-Communist utterances of many former pilgrims. Not a single argument muddies the flow of Istrati's confessions; the newly found disgust is only the reverse of the former blind belief. It is just as helplessly emotional and politically ignorant: "History," Istrati states very calmly, "confronts the workers with the question not whether they want socialism in fifteen years but whether they want their freedom at once." [7]

Istrati's piece, however, was only a bumbling predecessor of an entire wave of critical reports and analyses that began to appear in the thirties against the idolization of Stalinist USSR. The most sensational of these nay-sayings was by André Gide.

This famous man joined the Communist party at the age of sixty-three and then participated actively in the fight that helped the United Front to a short-lived victory in 1936. That same year he traveled to Moscow as guest of the Soviet Writers' Union and from there through large parts of the Union. The two books, which he published after his return, *Retour de l'URSS* and *Retouches à mon retour de l'URSS* (both Paris, 1936 and 1937 respectively) had a bomblike effect. Within one year more than 100,000 copies were sold and there were translations into fifteen languages.

What happened to André Gide in Russia? Nothing but the same treatment that his predecessors had enjoyed and taken little notice of; except that Gide was not Barbusse— on the contrary: for the first time the *delegacija* system revenged itself on its inventors.

"And indeed what disturbed me most when I got there, was not so much to find imperfections, as to meet once again with the advantages I had wanted to escape from, the privileges I had hoped were abolished. Certainly I thought it natural that a guest should be received as well as possible and everywhere shown the best. But what astonished me was that there was such a gap between this best and the common lot; such excessive privilege beside so mediocre or so bad an ordinary. . . .

"And of course I see that without any actual attempt at corruption it may very well be advantageous for the Soviet Government to make the way smooth for artists and writers and for all who will sing its praises; but I also see only too well how advantageous it may be for the writer to approve a government and a constitution which favour him to such an extent. This at once puts me on my guard. I am afraid of letting myself be seduced. The excessive advantages

I am offered over there frighten me. I did not go to the USSR to meet with privileges over again. Those that awaited me were flagrant.

"And why should I not say so?

"I had learnt from the Moscow newspapers that in a few months, more than 400,000 copies of my books had been sold. I leave you to calculate the percentage of author's rights. And the articles so richly paid for! If I had written dithyrambs on the USSR and Stalin, what a fortune! . . .

"These considerations would not have restrained my praise; neither will they prevent my criticisms. But I confess that the extraordinarily privileged position (more so than in any other country in Europe) granted to anyone who holds a pen—provided he writes in the proper spirit—contributed not a little to open my eyes. Of all the workers and artisans in the USSR writers are much the most favoured. Two of my travelling companions (each of them had the translation of one of his books in the press) searched the shops for antiques, curiosities, bric-a-brac—something on which to spend the thousands or so roubles they had cashed and knew they would not be able to take away with them. As for me, I could hardly make any impression on an enormous balance, for everything was offered me gratis. Yes, everything; from the journey itself to my packets of cigarettes. And every time I took out my note-case to settle a hotel or restaurant bill, to pay an account, to buy stamps or a newspaper, the delightful smile and authorative gesture of our guide stopped me. 'You're joking! You are our guest, and your five companions too.'

"No, I had nothing to complain of during the whole course of my tour in the USSR, and of all the spiteful explanations that have been invented to invalidate my criticisms, that which tried to put them down to the score of personal dissatisfaction is certainly the most absurd. I had never before travelled in such sumptuous style. In special railway carriages or the best cars, always the best rooms in the best hotels, the most abundant and the choicest food. And what a welcome! What attentions! What solicitude! Everywhere acclaimed, flattered, made much of, feasted. Nothing seemed too good, too exquisite to offer me. I should have been ungracious indeed to repulse such advances; I could not do so; and I keep a marvellous remembrance of it all, the liveliest gratitude. But these very favours constantly brought to mind privileges, differences where I had hoped to find equality.

"When, after escaping with great difficulty from official receptions and official supervision, I managed to get into contact with labourers whose wages were only four or five roubles a day, what could I think of the banquet in my honour which I could not avoid attending? An almost daily banquet at which the abundance of the hors-d'œuvre alone was such that one had already eaten three times too much before beginning the actual meal; a feast of six courses which used to last two hours and left you completely stupefied. The expense! Never having seen a bill, I cannot exactly estimate it, but one of my companions who was well up in the prices of things calculates that each banquet, with wines and liqueurs, must have come to more than three hundred roubles a head. Now there were six of us—seven with our guide; and often as many hosts as guests, sometimes many more." [8]

Gide's criticism of Soviet society is based in many respects on thoroughly bourgeois premises, most distinctly where he laments the country's "uniformity" and its inhabitants lack the "personal touch." For example, when he notices that Soviet citizens "own little private property" and when this outrages him he strikes an involuntary comic note. Brecht made some comments on this subject at the time, comments which should give "radical tourism" something to think about—above and beyond the case of Gide.

"The French writer André Gide has enriched the great book of his confessions with a further chapter. A tireless Odysseus, he has provided us with the report of a new venture, however without being able to divulge on board which ship this report was composed and where this ship is traveling to.

"Everyone who watched what he was writing at the time when he was preparing his last mistake had to look forward with considerable apprehension to his departure for the new continent. He greeted it as an individualist, primarily as an individualist.

"He set out like someone who is looking for a new country, tired of the old one, doubtlessly eager to hear his own yelp of joy, but what he was really looking for was *his* new country; not an unknown but a known country, not one that others but one that he himself had built, and in his head at that. He did not find this country. It apparently does not exist on this planet.

"He set out far too unprepared. But he did not travel untouched. He did not only bring the dust on his shoes. Now he is disappointed, not about the fact that the country does not exist but about the fact that this is not his country. One must understand this: After his trip he was in a position to say: This land is like so and so, its people do this and that, I don't quite understand. He expected a verdict of himself, he was one of the crowd that looked expectantly at him. He probably lacked the intention from the very beginning to communicate what this land is like, but what he is like, and that didn't take much time, this booklet was written quickly. He sat down and wrote . . . 'Everyone's happiness evidently consists only in de-personalization. The happiness of everyone is only achieved at the price of the individual. To be happy you must be uniform.'

"Here he broaches the question about the well-being of the people, and he is right: there probably never was a regime which so calmly admitted as the criterium of its effect the question whether the people were happy, and that means the many. Gide recognizes their happiness, he describes it in many places in his book, but immediately doubts whether what looks like happiness to him is happiness; that is, what he himself always calls happiness. He saw happy persons, in great numbers, but they were 'de-personalized.' They were happy but they were uniform. They lacked nothing to be happy, but Gide lacked something. Thus he reaches no new insight about happiness except perhaps that it is a scarce commodity. The reality he saw did not warp his measuring rod which he brought and took back with him. He did not come back happy, but as a personality. Also, what he called personality he will go on calling personality; he saw one country which lacked it: one sixth of the earth.

"Well, he is a skeptic like so many great clerics. His skepticism of course is not very general, not directed to all sides, it is a particular kind of skepticism, namely that of his class, the bourgeois class.

"It is skeptical toward other classes. Toward the concept of personality, toward his own, thoroughly bourgeois, concept of personality he is not skeptical. Here people are living under completely new, unheard-of conditions, for the first time the masses are in control of the means of production, making it impossible for individuals to use their talents to exploit others. Perhaps those personalities decay which were formed under other conditions and new kinds of personalities begin to form, which are meant for other kinds of social work, with other differentiations? Such personalities he would not call personalities." [9]

Brecht's critique of Gide is marked by rationality and equanimity, something one cannot claim for the reaction of the Communist parties. From now until the end of his life they were to call Gide a hyena, a perverse purveyor of filth, and mixer of poisons. Rereading his books today one must admit, however reluctantly, that they have outlasted much of what his Marxist opponents put on paper at that time. Probably only the crassest fanatic would disagree with some of his observations about bureaucracy and repression, official mendacity, and the privilege business. Gide was certainly wrong in considering himself a Communist, certainly he was unschooled in theory and politically naive and his taking sides was sentimental. Still, his idealism did not keep him from publishing the following table in which the approved representatives of the Diamat simply couldn't develop any interest at all:

	MINIMUM & MAXIMUM INCOME	USUAL INCOME
Workers	from 70–400 rubles	125–200 rubles
Small employees	80–250 rubles	130–180 rubles
Domestics	50–60 rubles (of course including room and board)	
Middle-rank officials and technicians, specialists, and those in "very responsible positions"	300–800 rubles	
High officials, certain professors, artists, and writers	1500–10,000 rubles and more; some, it is indicated, receive between 20,000 to 30,000 rubles per month.[10]	

There is a very simple reason why Gide's yellowed critique
is not only acceptable but still readable today: it is his complete solidarity. This solidarity with the Russian workers and
farmers is colored by Protestant moralism and is not devoid
of idealistic mist; yes, at times is so simple as to be awkward.
Still, it provides the decisive criterium. It is this solidarity
that distinguishes Gide's report from the tirades of the other
disillusioned ones, that separates him once and for all from
the anti-Communist filth of the cold war, as well as from the
arrogant know-it-all attitude and the malicious gleefulness
that survives in some writers of the Left to this day.

Of course, one cannot compare today's attitude quite that
simply with those of yesterday. Much has changed since Gide's
days also with respect to traveling in countries like the Soviet
Union. The infrastructure has improved, tourism has become a firmly established social institution—above and beyond caring for State guests of the revolution. The Intourist
Bureau, the football club, the Ministry of Foreign Trade, the
Writers' Union—every organization today has its specialists
who take care of the *delegacija* unobtrusively and routinely.
The GPU no longer exists and to mention its successor is
considered bad form as much on the part of the hosts as the
guests.

The USSR also is no longer the favorite travel objective of
"radical" or "revolutionary tourists." The interest of this
peculiar and ambiguous group has fallen on younger revolutions, on the non-European transitional societies.

The goals have changed, but the objective as well as subjective mechanism has remained the same. What Gide wrote
before his trip to the Soviet Union is still valid:

"The stupidity and insidiousness of the attacks on the USSR is
largely responsible for our conducting its defense with a certain wil-
fulness. These yapping dogs will begin to praise the way things are
going in Russia at the very moment when we will stop doing so, because their praise will only be for the compromises and slander, for
the deviations from the original objective which abet the gleeful
exclamation: 'There, you see!' " [11]

The objections which are meant to prevent any criticism of the socialist transitional societies have scarcely changed since Gide enumerated them in 1937:

"1) that the malpractices which I have pointed out are exceptions to the rule from which one shouldn't draw any conclusions (because one cannot deny them);

2) that in order to admire the present state of affairs one needs only to compare it to the previous one, the condition before the conquest (mean to say: before the revolution);

3) that everything I complain about has profound ontological reasons which I have been unable to fathom: passing temporary evils in view of an imminent and that much greater state of well being." [12]

The sterile debate between the admirers and defenders is being continued at any price, even at that of solidarity with the peoples who are being discussed, inasmuch as there is any room left for them between arrogance and loss of a sense of reality. Trotzky's dictum is still valid: "What really hides behind the 'official friends'' animosity to criticism is not so much concern for the fragility of socialism as the fragility of their own sympathy for socialism." Here, then, a recent example of this state of affairs:

"*China after the Cultural Revolution* is what Maria Antonietta Macciocchi calls her reports; a more fitting title would be *Marie Antoinette in Wonderland*. For this book by an Italian Communist Party delegate tells us less about China (where the author traveled together with her husband, the foreign political editor of *Unita*) than it does about the petit bourgeois mentality characteristic of so many party intellectuals. Her blindness toward the situation at her place of work, her incomprehension of production relationships and of human and social costs entailed by them, and her typical admiration of the colorful and sensuous aspect of goods becomes evident from the description which the author gives of a silk weaving plant in Hangchow which produces 'fifteen color' Mao pictures in large series: 'The thousand machines are spinning briskly always in the same rhythm, and from the looms pour the great beards of Marx and Engels, the pointed muttonchops of Lenin, the face of Mao with his forage cap. Then the gobelins showing historical events: Mao at the proclamation of the 20th of May; Mao in a bathrobe before the famous crossing of the Yangtze. . . . The poems of Mao too are printed in black and white. . . . The factory has 1700 workers who work three shifts, day and night, to satisfy the demand.'

"We too have visited this factory. But we didn't only see the 'glowing colors' of the large and small Mao pictures. The workers are standing in dark places where one ruins one's eyes and are exposed to incredible noise. The day shift lasts 8½ hours, the night shift 6½ hours. Seven days of vacation per year. Fifty-six days maternity leave including delivery time. Staggered wages, premiums as work incentives, preferential treatment for the drafting teams as compared with the producers. The Communist delegate has heard and seen nothing of this. She doesn't lose a word over it. When we met her recently and asked her about this discrepancy she said vehemently: 'Perhaps you don't know Italian factories?' 'Of course,' we replied, we know them as well as American and Soviet factories; but it never occurred to us to claim that Italy, the USA or the USSR are socialist countries.

"For Macciocchi, on the other hand, China is an ideal socialist country which 'manifests an entirely new model of industrialization.' This is due to the fact that she spent less time in the factories than in the company of functionaries who took her to the best restaurants in Peking." [14]

It is no accident but the political consequence of such an attitude that the great majority of "radical tourists" assiduously ignore the true situation of the working class in the socialistically governed countries. This striking disinterest is only barely concealed by means of declamatory slogans. The usual visits to factories and kolchozes tend to meet the indifference of these visitors at least halfway. They cannot and are not set up to break through the social segregation of the guests, whose contact is limited to designated individuals from the functionary class and to foreigners who live in the same hotels. This umbrella is so effective that most of the political tourists don't have the slightest idea of the working conditions even after weeks or months in the host country. Ask them about wages and working hours, protection against unlawful dismissal, housing assignments, the number of shifts worked and the premium system, living standards and rationalization and usually they have no answer. (In Havana I kept meeting Communists in the hotels for foreigners who had no idea that the energy and water supply in the working quarters had broken down during the afternoon, that bread was rationed, and that the population had to stand two hours in line for a slice of pizza; meanwhile the tourists in their hotel rooms were arguing about Lukács.)

In any event, there are indications that the Western traveler's awareness of problems is increasing. More and more reporters try to dispense with the ideological veil their status foists on them. Of course, one is more easily blinded when it is a question of one's own privileges. Even where the political intent of these privileges goes undetected one senses them more and more as a moral scandal, and they become problematical at least in this respect, as in the following reflections by Susan Sontag who visited Hanoi in Spring 1968:

". . . Hence, the store to which we were taken the third day to get tire sandals and have us each fitted for a pair of Vietnamese trousers. Hieu and Phan told us, with an almost proprietary pride, that this was a special store, reserved for foreigners (diplomatic personnel, guests) and important government people. I thought they should recognize that the existence of such facilities is 'un-Communist.' But maybe I'm showing here how 'American' I am.

I'm troubled, too by the meals at the Thong Nhat. While every lunch and dinner consists of several delicious meat and fish courses (we're eating only Vietnamese food) and whenever we eat everything in one of the large serving bowls a waitress instantly appears to put another one on our table, ninety-nine percent of the Vietnamese will have rice and bean curd for dinner tonight and are lucky to eat meat or fish once a month. Of course I haven't said anything. They'd probably be mystified, even insulted, if I suggested that we shouldn't be eating so much more than the average citizen's rations. It's well known that lavish and (what would be to us) self-sacrificing hospitality to guests is a staple of Oriental culture. Do I really expect them to violate their own sense of decorum? Still, it bothers me. . . . It also exasperates me that we're driven even very short distances; the Peace Committee has rented two cars, in fact—Volgas— that wait with their drivers in front of the hotel whenever we're due to go anywhere. The office of the NLF delegation in Hanoi, which we visited the other day, was all of two blocks from the hotel. And some of our other destinations proved to be no more than fifteen or twenty blocks away. Why don't they let us walk, as Bob, Andy, and I have agreed among ourselves we'd feel more comfortable doing? Do they have a rule: only the best for the guests? But that kind of politeness, it seems to me, could well be abolished in a Communist society. Or must we go by car because they think we're weak, effete foreigners (Westerners? Americans?) who also need to be reminded to get out of the sun? It disquiets me to think the Vietnamese might regard walking as beneath our dignity (as official guests, celebrities, or something). Whatever their reason, there's no budging them on this. We roll through the crowded streets in our big ugly black cars—the chauffeurs blasting away on their horns to make people on foot and on bicycles watch out, give way. . . . Best, of course, would be if they would lend us, or let us rent, bicycles. But though we've dropped hints to Oanh more than once, it's clear they don't or won't take the request seriously. When we broach it, are they at least amused? Or do they just think we're being silly or impolite or dumb?" [15]

The only traveler I know who has thought the problem of "radical tourism" through to the end is the Swede Jan Myrdal. With a conscientiousness that makes a veritably puritanical impression compared to the usual sloppiness in these matters, he gave an account (in his book *Report from a Chinese Village,* written in 1962 and published the following year) of the circumstances of his trip and his own situation. His reflections, therefore, and their exemplary character justify a longer quote.

"We financed our journey to China and our travels in China with our own resources. We probably could have become 'invitees'; the Chinese suggested this to us on several occasions, when we spoke of reducing our expenses, and that we did not do so was less because we thought that we would be corrupted—I have never believed myself to be easily corruptible and I don't think that I change my opinions because of small economic gains—but I intensely dislike the international junkets, the pleasure trips at public expense. The big powers, the Soviet Union, the United States, China, France, Great

Britain, are all subjecting the writers of small countries like Sweden (and of each other) to well-intentioned economic pressure through different forms of free travel 'with all expenses paid.' Even if I don't think I would be corrupted, I'm against the whole tendency. It has a perverting influence on the intellectual morals of the writer, it runs counter to the free expression of ideas. I can't stop this tendency, but I can at least say no for myself. I distrust free-loaders whether they are capitalists, communists, liberals, conservatives, anarchists or just plain sellers of words. I have never liked being grateful to anybody. And I can't understand how the public—that after all pays for it—can put up with this spectacle of politicians, writers and sundry 'public figures' banqueting their way around the world on a spree of phrases.

"But as my funds were by no means unlimited and as there were, and are, few facilities in China today for the tourist with a slim pocketbook, this led to certain conflicts. . . . I'm not criticizing the Chinese; in every country in which I have lived I have had to take up a discussion with the bureaucracy in order to be left in peace to do my work. The Chinese officials were reasonable and it took rather less time to convince them than it has taken in many other countries; also there was no question of corruption. They followed their regulations and I wanted to have these regulations changed.

"One of the prerequisite conditions for travelling in China today is that you accept interpreters and guides. We were given ours by the Chinese People's Association for Cultural Relations with Foreign Countries. I will come back to the question of interpreters, but I just want to point out that you either accept this condition or you don't travel outside Peking, Canton, Shanghai—and more often than not, not even there. I don't like this. But it is a tendency that is spreading from country to country. Even in Sweden we are starting to take in 'invitees,' give them guides and see to it that they keep looking at what we want to show them. I'm disturbed by this tendency. It gives strength to my fears that we, all over the world, are moving towards a more 'supervised' form of existence. But in this case I could not just say no, find a third way out or shift the emphasis. Either I have my travel supervised—or I stay at home, quite probably supervised in one way or another even there. However much I dislike it, I have to accept this condition. . . .

"Our chief interpreter was Pei Kwang-li. She had come with us from Peking. She was the most flexible, the best linguist and the most hard-working of the interpreters I had come across in China. I had tried several interpreters before getting hold of her, and we had been working together for about two weeks when we arrived at the village. She was supposed to go back to Peking from Yenan and it was only after some quite hard discussion that I managed to take her with me to Liu Ling. She was of great help to me in the village. She was friendly and cheerful and interested in the work. I gathered that she was afterwards criticized for her work with me. When we came back to Peking, she went away on vacation and after that she was not so friendly, natural and relaxed as she had been during the month in Liu Ling. She later on—when the book was finished—interpreted for us during our trip to Yunnan and during that trip she was cold, formal, dogmatic and even (which in China says much) quarrelled violently with us on the grounds that we showed 'anti-Chinese' opinions. As our 'anti-Chineseness' was our opinions about toil and sweat and peasant hunger that she had understood so well in Liu Ling, I cannot explain this change in her behaviour otherwise than that she had through 'criticism and self-criticism' come to evaluate us and our work in a different way and change her opinions about our way of working. Because of this I got rather less information in Yunnan than I had hoped for.

"The authorities in Yenan were very eager that we should not sleep in the village. They promised to arrange for us to be ferried there and back every day. We wanted, of course, to live in the village, we even demanded to be allowed to do so. The 'Old Secretary' of the village strongly supported us. To him it was a point of honour. After some discussion the Yenan authorities were (with some reluctance) convinced of our point of view. (The reluctance can be interpreted in many ways, one of them is that the Yenan authorities wanted us to be as comfortable as possible. They probably wanted to be kind. It is not their fault that their kindness would have made this book impossible.) We then lived in a stone cave (normally the party secretary's office) and I worked in another (the brigade's conference-room). Since we lived in a cave in a village of caves and ate the village food and the whole time associated with the villagers, it would be easy to say that we lived as one of the people. But that would be a romantic and thus mendacious description of reality. We were the first foreigners to have lived in the village, and the village honour required that our cave should be whitewashed and that we should eat well. We lived considerably better than the villagers. . . . As a guest in a village you eat well, you also eat with a certain reverence, because you know that you are eating the fruits of the toil and sweat of the people around you. But you never say so to your hosts. There is pride in toil. There is nothing 'objective' about food in a poor peasant village. It does not come out of a tin, neither is it something you carry with you from the city. But I was not one of the villagers. And I was not living like a Chinese peasant. . . .

"The decision to have an upper limit to the interviews, i.e., not to continue far up in the bureaucratic structure above the village, was contained in the idea of the book itself. But first I had thought of including at least some representative from Yenan, who could give the slightly larger picture of the village in its setting. I even tried to make that interview and spent one morning in Yenan interviewing the local party secretary, a young man. Unfortunately he was too dogmatic, too official to be of any value. (And this is a typical problem all over Asia: the middle echelon of bureaucracy is mostly young and dogmatic and narrow-mindedly inexperienced. The old experienced peasants are illiterate, the bright young administrators are already high up and the old intellectual generation of revolutionaries or 'national figures' are slowly fading away.) I don't blame the young bureaucrat from Yenan. He ran true to type, but when he flatly stated: 'We have here in our part never had any difficulty, never committed a mistake, never made a fault and we have no problems today,' I broke off the interview with a few nice, pleasant phrases, and decided that he was not to be included in the book and that I had better go back to the village and talk with the peasants."

Despite the careful thoughts Myrdal has addressed to the problems that the "observation" of a transitional society creates, and as convincing as his report seems, he cannot provide us with a general solution to these difficulties. Such a solution not only presumes a different attitude on the traveler's part but also a change in the objective conditions. The *delegacija* system will not disappear until the isolation of the socialistically governed countries is overcome and until the foreigner's as well as the indigenous worker's freedom of movement has been guaranteed. When everyone is free to choose his own companion—or decide to dispense with him; when the infrastructure is sufficiently developed to insure lodging, transportation, and food for everyone who is underway, when the total dependence on guides and controlling institutions has vanished—then the *delegacija* business will not necessarily cease of its own accord, but dependency, bribery, segregation from the working population, reality loss, and uncritical ingratiation as well as the privileges that are its material substratum will become straitjackets that everyone who does not feel comfortable can discard.

Such a development is foreseeable, that is, as an unplanned and perhaps unwished-for but necessary complement of a policy of global co-existence—whose questionable sides, incidentally, are no secret. But to ascertain its positive aspects does not mean to capitulate to the two-dimensional theories of convergence so much in favor with bourgeois observers. However, it is thinkable that the Left in the West will not use the opportunities that are becoming manifest here. Little speaks for the fact that those who adhere to socialism in the West will take up the confrontation with the attempt to realize it. Now that the objective difficulties are decreasing and it is becoming less and less a question, in many countries, of endangering anyone by talking with them, now that traveling is ceasing to be an individual privilege, it should be possible to launch a massive attack on this overdue task which no one has performed as yet: the analysis of socialist societies or those that go by that name. Individual messengers cannot undertake such an investigation. We have tried to detect the reason for their failure. But whoever curses the "radical tourism" of the last fifty years in order to conceal his own disinterest will find it difficult to reply to the question that is put to him when he is having his beer, or at streetcorner meetings or at demonstrations, the question: "Why don't you go live in the East?"

Translated by Michael Roloff

A Critique of Political Ecology

As a scientific discipline, ecology is almost exactly a hundred years old. The concept emerged for the first time in 1868 when the German biologist, Ernst Haeckel, in his *Natural History of Creation*, proposed giving this name to a subdiscipline of zoology—one which would investigate the totality of relationships between an animal species and its inorganic and organic environment. Compared with the present state of ecology, such a proposal suggests a comparatively modest program. Yet none of the restrictions contained in it proved to be tenable: neither the preference given to animal species over plant species, nor to macro- as opposed to micro-organisms. With the discovery of whole ecosystems, the perspective which Haeckel had had in mind became redundant. Instead there emerged the concept of mutual dependence and of a balance between all the inhabitants of an ecosystem, and in the course of this development the range and complexity of the new discipline have grown rapidly. Ecology became as controversial as it is today only when it decided to include a very particular species of animal in its researches—man. While this step brought ecology unheard of publicity it also precipitated it into a crisis about its validity and methodology, the end of which is not yet in sight.

Human ecology is, first of all, a hybrid discipline. In it categories and methods drawn from the natural and social sciences have to be used together without this in any way theoretically resolving the resulting complications. Human ecology tends to suck in more and more new disciplines and to subsume them under its own research aims. This tendency is justified not on scientific grounds but because of the urgency of ecology's aims. Under the pressure of public debate ecology's statements in recent years became more and more markedly prognostic. This "futurological deformation" was totally alien to ecology so long as it considered itself to be merely a particular area of biology. It must be clearly understood that this science has now come to lay claim to a total validity—a claim which it cannot make good. The more far-reaching its conclusions, the less reliable it is. Since no one can vouch for the accuracy of the enormous volume of material from every conceivable science on which its hypotheses are constructed, it must—precisely to the degree that it wishes to make global statements—confine itself to working syntheses. One of the best know ecological handbooks—*Population, Resources, Environment* by Paul and Anne Ehrlich—deploys evidence from the following branches of sciences either implicitly or explicitly: statistics, systems theory, cybernetics, games theory and prediction theory; thermodynamics, biochemistry, biology, oceanography, mineralogy, meterology, genetics; physiology, medicine, epidemology, toxicology; agricultural science, urban studies, demography; technologies of all kinds; theories of society, sociology and economics (the latter admittedly in a most elementary form). The list is not complete. It is hard to describe the methodological confusion that results from the attempt at a synthesis of this sort. If one starts from this theoretical position there can, obviously, be no question of producing a group of people who are competent to deal with it. From now on ecology is marginally relevant to everyone; and this, incidentally, is what makes the statements in this article possible.

1. THE CENTRAL HYPOTHESIS

What till recently was a marginal science has within a few years become the center of bitter controversies. This cannot be explained merely by the snowballing effect of the mass media. It is connected with the central statement made by human ecology—a statement that refers to the future and is therefore at one and the same time prognostic and hypothetical. On the one hand, everyone is affected by the statement, since it relates to the existence of the species; on the other, no one can form a clear and final judgment on it because, in the last resort, it can only be verified or proved wrong in the future. This hypothesis can be formulated as follows: the industrial societies of this earth are producing ecological contradictions, which must in the foreseeable future lead to their collapse.

In contradistinction to other earlier theories of catastrophe this prognosis does not rest on linear, monocausal arguments. On the contrary, it introduces several synergetic factors. A very simplified list of the different strains of causality would look something like this:

1. Industrialization leads to an uncontrolled growth in world population. Simultaneously the material needs of that population increase. Even given an enormous expansion in industrial production, the chances of satisfying human needs deteriorate *per capita*.

2. The industrial process has up to now been nourished from sources of energy which are not in the main self-renewing; among these are fossil fuels as well as supplies of fissile material like uranium. In a determinable space of time these supplies will be exhausted; their replacement through what are basically new sources of energy (such as atomic fusion) is theoretically conceivable, but not yet practically realizable.

3. The industrial process is also dependent on the employment of mineral raw materials—above all of metals—which are not self-renewing either; their exploitation is advancing so rapidly that the exhaustion of deposits can be foreseen.

4. The water requirements of the industrial process have reached a point where they can no longer be satisfied by the natural circulation of water. As a result, the reserves of water in the ground are being attacked; this must lead to distur-

bances in the present cycle of evaporation and precipitation and to climatic changes. The only possible solution is the desalination of sea-water; but this is so energy-intensive that it would accelerate the process described in 2 above.

5. A further limiting factor is the production of foodstuffs. Neither the area of land suitable for cultivation nor the yield per acre can be arbitrarily increased. Attempts to increase the productivity of farming lead, beyond a certain point, to new ecological imbalances, e.g. erosion, pollution through poisonous substances, reductions in genetic variability. The production of food from the sea comes up against ecological limits of another kind.

6. A further factor—but only one factor among a number of others—is the notorious "pollution" of the earth. This category is misleading in so far as it presupposes a "clean" world. This has naturally never existed and is moreover ecologically neither conceivable nor desirable. What is actually meant are disequilibriums and dysfunctionings of all kinds in the metabolism between nature and human society occurring as the unintentional side effects of the industrial process. The polycausal linking of these effects is of unimaginable complexity. Poisoning caused by harmful substances—physiological damage from pesticides, radioactive isotopes, detergents, pharmaceutical preparations, food additives, artificial manures, trace quantities of lead and mercury, fluoride, carcinogens, gene mutants, and a vast quantity of other substances are only one facet of the problem. The problem of irreversible waste is only another facet of the same question. The changes in the atmosphere and in the resources of land and water traceable to metabolic causes such as production of smog, changes in climate, irreversible changes to rivers and lakes, oceanographic changes must also be taken into account.

7. Scientific research into yet another factor does not appear to have got beyond the preliminary stages. There are no established critical quantifications of what is called "psychic pollution." Under this heading come: increasing exposure to excessive noise and other irritants, the psychical effects of

overpopulation, as well as other stress factors which are difficult to isolate.

8. A final critical limit is presented by "thermal pollution." The laws of thermodynamics show that, even in principle, this limit cannot be crossed. Heat is emitted by all processes involving the conversion of energy. The consequences for the global supply of heat have not been made sufficiently clear.

A basic difficulty in the construction—or refutation—of ecological hypotheses is that the processes invoked do not take place serially but in close interdependence. That is also true of all attempts to find solutions to ecological crises. It often, if not always, emerges that measures to control one critical factor lead to another getting out of control. One is dealing with a series of closed circuits, or rather of interference circuits, which are in many ways linked. Any discussion that attempted to deal with the alleged "causes" piecemeal and to disprove them singly would miss the core of the ecological debate and would fall below the level which the debate has meantime reached.[1]

Yet even if there exists a certain, but no by means complete, consensus that the present process of industrialization must lead *ceteris paribus* to a breakdown, three important questions connected with the prognosis are still open to debate. The first concerns the time-scale involved. Estimations of the point in time at which a galloping deterioration of the ecological situation may be expected differ by a magnitude of several centuries. They range from the end of the 1980s to the 22nd century. In view of the innumerable variables involved in the calculations, such divergencies are not to be wondered at. (For example the critics of the MIT report, *The Limits of Growth*, have objected to the results given there on the grounds that the mathematical model on which it is based is much too simple and the number of variables too limited.) A second controversial point is closely related to the first; namely that the relative weighting to be given to the individual factors which are blamed for the catastrophe is not made clear. This is a point at issue, for example, in the debate between Barry

Commoner and Paul Ehrlich. While the latter considers population growth to be the "critical factor," the former believes that the decisive factor is modern industrial technology. An exact analysis of the factors involved comes up against immense methodological difficulties. The scientific debate between the two schools therefore remains undecided.

Thirdly, it is obviously not clear what qualifies as an environmental catastrophe. In this connection one can distinguish a number of different perspectives dictated by expectation or fear. There are ecologists who concern themselves only with mounting dangers and the corresponding physiological, climatic, social and political "disturbances"; others, like the Swedish ecologist, Gösta Ehrensvärd, contemplate the end of social structures based on industrialization; some prognoses go further—those of what in the United States are called "doomsters" talk of the dying out of the human species or the disappearance from the planet of a whole series of species—primates, mammals and vertebrates. The tone in which the respective ecological hypotheses are presented ranges correspondingly from the mildest reformist warnings to deepest resignation. What is decisive for the differences between them is naturally the question of how far the process of ecological destruction and uncontrolled exploitation is to be regarded as irreversible. In the literature, the answer to this question is made to depend on the one hand on an analysis of the factors involved; on the other, on temporal parameters. The uncertainty which is admitted to prevail on these two points means that there is no prospect of a firm answer. Authors like Ehrensvärd, who start from the premise that the end of industrial societies is at hand, and are already busy with preparations for a post-industrial society—one which, it should be added, contains a number of idyllic traits—are still in the minority. Most ecologists imply that they consider that the damage done so far is reversible, if only by tacking on to their analyses proposals to avert the catastrophe of which they are the prophets. These proposals will need to be critically examined.

2. THE ECOLOGICAL "MOVEMENT"

Ecology's hypotheses about the future of industrialization have been disseminated, at least in industrialized capitalist countries, through the mass media. The debate on the subject has itself to some extent acquired a mass character, particularly in the Anglo-Saxon and Scandinavian countries. It has led to the rise of a wide, although loosely organized, movement whose political potential is hard to estimate. At the same time the problem under discussion is peculiarly ill-defined. Even the statements of the ecologists themselves alternate between the construction of theories and broad statements of Weltanschauung, between precise research and totalizing theories linked to the philosophy of history. The thinking of the ecological groups therefore gives the impression of being at once obscure and confused. The very fact that it is disseminated by the mass media means that the debate generally loses a great deal of its stringency and content. Subordinate questions such as that of recycling refuse or "pollution" are treated in isolation; hypotheses are presented as unequivocal truths; spectacular cases of poisoning are sensationally exploited; isolated results of research are given absolute validity and so on. Processing through the sewage system of industrialized publicity has therefore, to some extent, led to further pollution of a cluster of problems which from the start cannot be presented in a "pure" way. This lack of clarity is propagated in the groups which are at present actively occupied with the subject of ecology, or rather with its *disjecta membra*, with what is left of it. The most powerful of these groups is that of the technocrats who, at all levels of the state apparatus and also of industry, are busy finding the speediest solutions to particular problems —"quick technological fixes"—and implementing them. This they do whenever there is a considerable potential for economic or political conflict—and only then. These people consider themselves to be entirely pragmatic—that is to say, they are servants of the ruling class at present in power—and cannot be assumed to have a proper awareness of the problem. They can be included in the ecological movement only in so far as they belong—as will be demonstrated—to its manipulators and in so far as they benefit from it. The political motives and interests in these cases are either obvious—as with the Club of Rome, a consortium of top managers and bureaucrats —or can easily and unequivocally be established.

What is less unequivocal is the political character of a second form of ecological awareness and the practice that corresponds to it. Here it is a matter of smaller groups of "concerned and responsible citizens," as they say in the United States. The expression points, as does its German parallel, "citizens' initiative," to the class background of those involved in it. They are overwhelmingly members of the middle class, and of the new petty bourgeoisie. Their activities have generally modest goals. They are concerned with preserving open spaces or trees. Classes of school-children are encouraged to clean up litter on beaches or recreation grounds. A boycott of non-biodegradable packaging is organized, etc. The harmless impression made by projects of this kind can easily blind us to the reserves of militancy which they conceal. There only needs to be a tiny alteration in the definition of goals and these groups spontaneously begin to increase in size and power. They are then able to prevent the carrying through of large-scale projects like the siting of an airport or an oil refinery, to force high-tension cables to be laid underground or a highway to be diverted. But even achievements of this magnitude only represent the limits of their effectiveness for a time. If the hypotheses of the ecologists should come even partially true, the ecological action groups will become a force of the first order in domestic politics and one that can no longer be ignored. On the one hand, they express powerful and legitimate needs of those who engage in these activities; on the other hand, they set their sights on immediate targets, which are not understood politically, and incline to a kind of indulgence in social illusion. This makes them ideal fodder for demagogues and interested third parties. But the limited nature of their initiatives should not conceal the fact that there lies within them the seed of a possible mass movement.

Finally, there is that part of the ecological movement which considers itself to be its hard core but which, in fact, plays a rather marginal role. These are the "eco-freaks." These groups, which have mostly split off from the American protest movement, are engaged in a kind of systematic flight from the cities and from civilization. They live in rural communes, grow their own food, and seek a "natural way of life," which may be regarded as the simulation of pre- or post-industrial conditions. They look for salvation in detailed, precisely stipulated dietary habits—eating "earth food"—and agricultural methods. Their class background corresponds to that of the hippies of the 1960s—of reduced middle class origin, enriched by elements from peripheral groups. Ideologically they incline towards obscurantism and sectarianism.

On the whole one can say that in the ecological movement —or perhaps one should say movements—the scientific aspects, which derive predominantly from biology, have merged in an extremely confused alliance with a whole series of political motivations and interests, which are partly manifest, partly concealed. At a deeper level one can identify a great number of socio-psychological needs, which are usually aroused without those concerned being able to see through them. These include: hopes of conversion and redemption, delight in the collapse of things, feelings of guilt and resignation, escapism and hostility to civilization.

In these circumstances it is not surprising that the European Left holds aloof from the ecological movement. It is true that it has incorporated certain topics from the environmental debate in the repertory of its anti-capitalist agitation; but it maintains a skeptical attitude to the basic hypothesis underlying ecology and avoids entering into alliances with groups which are entirely oriented towards ecological questions. The Left has instead seen its task to be to face the problem in terms of an ideological critique. It therefore functions chiefly as an instrument of clarification, as a tribunal which attempts to dispel the innumerable mystifications which dominate ecological thinking and have encouraged it. The most important elements in this process of clarification, which is absolutely necessary, are listed and discussed below.

3. THE CLASS CHARACTER OF THE CURRENT ECOLOGICAL DEBATE

The social neutrality to which the ecological debate lays claim, having recourse as it does so to strategies derived from the evidence of the natural sciences, is a fiction. A simple piece of historical reflection shows just how far this class neutrality goes. Industrialization made whole towns and areas of the countryside uninhabitable as long as a hundred and fifty years ago. The environmental conditions at places of work, that is to say in the English factories and pits, were—as innumerable documents demonstrate—dangerous to life. There was an infernal noise; the air people breathed was polluted with explosive and poisonous gases as well as with carcinogenous matter and particles which were highly contaminated with bacteria. The smell was unimaginable. In the labor process contagious poisons of all kinds were used. The diet was bad. Food was adulterated. Safety measures were non-existent or were ignored. The overcrowding in the working-class quarters was notorious. The situation over drinking water and drainage was terrifying. There was in general no organized method for disposing of refuse. ". . . . when cholera prevailed in that district [Tranent, in Scotland] some of the patients suffered very much indeed from want of water, and so great was the privation, that on that calamitous occasion people went into the ploughed fields and gathered rain water which collected in depressions in the ground, and actually in the prints made by horses' feet. Tranent was formerly well-supplied with water of excellent quality by a spring above the village, which flows through a sand-bed. The water flows into Tranent at its head

. . . and is received into about ten wells, distributed throughout the village. The people supply themselves at these wells when they contain water. When the supply is small, the water pours in a very small stream only. . . . I have seen women fighting for water. The wells are sometimes frequented throughout the whole night. It was generally believed by the population that this stoppage of the water was owing to its stream being diverted into a coal-pit which was sunk in the sand-bed above Tranent."[2]

These conditions, which are substantiated by innumerable other sources from the 19th century, would undoubtedly have presented a 'neutral observer' with food for ecological reflection. But there were no such observers. It occurred to no one to draw pessimistic conclusions about the future of industrialization from these facts. The ecological movement has only come into being since the districts which the bourgeoise inhabit and their living conditions have been exposed to those environmental burdens that industrialization brings with it. What fills their prophets with terror is not so much ecological decline, which has been present since time immemorial, as its universalization. To isolate oneself from this process becomes increasingly difficult. It deploys a dialectic which in the last resort turns against its own beneficiaries. Pleasure trips and expensive packaging, for example, are by no means phenomena which have emerged only in the last decades; they are part of the traditional consumption of the ruling classes. They have become problematic, however, in the shape of tourism and the litter of consumerism; that is, only since the labouring masses have shared them. Quantitative increase tips over into a new quality—that of destruction. What was previously privilege now appears as nightmare and capitalist industry proceeds to take tardy, if still comparatively mild, revenge on those who up to now had only derived benefit from it. The real capitalist class, which is decreasing in numbers, can admittedly still avoid these consequences. It can buy its own private beaches and employ lackeys of all kinds. But for both the old and the new petty bourgeoisie such expenditure is unthinkable. The cost of a private 'environment' which makes it possible to escape to some extent from the consequences of industrialization is already astronomical and will rise more sharply in future.

It is after all easy to understand that the working class cares little about general environmental problems and is only prepared to take part in campaigns where it is a question of directly improving their working and living conditions. In so far as it can be considered a source of ideology, ecology is a matter that concerns the middle class. If avowed representatives of monopoly capitalism have recently become its spokesmen—as in the Club of Rome—that is because of reasons which have little to do with the living conditions of the ruling class. These reasons require analysis.

4. THE INTERESTS OF THE ECO-INDUSTRIAL COMPLEX

That the capitalist mode of production has catastrophic consequences is a commonplace of Marxism, which also not infrequently crops up in the arguments of the ecological movement. Certainly the fight for a "clean" environment always contains anti-capitalist elements. Neverthelesss Fascism in Germany and Italy have demonstrated how easily such elements can be turned round and become tools in the service of the interests of capital.[3] It is therefore not surprising that ecological protest, at least in Western Europe, almost always ends up with an appeal to the state. Under present political conditions this means that it appeals to reformism and to technocratic rationality. This appeal is then answered by government programmes which promise an "improvement in the quality of life," without of course indicating whose life is going to be made more beautiful, in what way and at whose expense. The state only "goes into action when the earning powers of the entrepreneur are threatened. Today the environmental crisis presents a massive threat to these interests. On the one hand it threatens the material basis of production—air, earth and water—while on the other hand it threatens man, the productive factor, whose usefulness is being reduced by frequent physical and mental illnesses."[4] To these have to be added the danger of uncontrollable riots over ecological questions as the conditions in the environment progressively deteriorate.

On the question of state intervention and "environmental protection from above," the Left's ideological critique displays a remarkable lack of historical reflection. Here too it is certainly not a question of new phenomena. The negative effects of environmental damage on the earning power of industry, the struggle over the off-loading of liability, over laws relating to the environment and over the range of state control can be traced back without much difficulty to the early period of English industrialization; a remarkable lack of variation in the attitude of the interests involved emerges from such a study. The previously quoted report on the water supply and the drainage problems in a Scottish mining village is taken from an official report of the year 1842—one which incidentally was also quoted by Engels in his book on *The Condition of the English Working Class*. The chairman of the commission of inquiry was a certain Sir Edwin Chadwick, a typical predecessor of the modern ecological technocrats. Chadwick was a follower of the utilitarian political philosopher and lawyer, Jeremy Bentham, of whom Marx said: "If I had the courage of my friend H. Heine, I would call Mr. Jeremiah a genius at bourgeois stupidity."[5] James Ridgeway, one of the few American ecologists capable of intervening in the present environmental discussion with political arguments, has dealt thoroughly with Chadwick's role.[6] Then as now the rhetoric of the ecological reformers served to cloak quite concrete connections between a variety of interests. The technological means with which this "reform from above" operates have also altered less than one might think.[7]

But an historical perspective fails in its object if it is used to reduce modern problems to the level of past ones. Ridgeway does not always avoid this danger: he tends to restrict himself to traditional ecological questions like water pollution and the supply of energy. Without meaning to do so he thereby reduces the extent of the threatened catastrophe. It is true that there were environmental crises before this and that the mechanisms of reformist managements set up to deal with the crises can look back on a long history. What has to be kept in mind, however, is that the ecological risks have not only increased quantitatively but have taken on a new quality.

In line with the changes which have taken place in the economic basis, this also holds true for environmental pollution and state intervention. In its present form monopoly capitalism is inclined, as is well known, to solve its demand problems by extravagant expenditure at the cost of the public exchequer. The most obvious examples of this are unproductive investment in armaments and in space exploration. Industrial protection of the environment emerges as a new growth area the costs of which can either be off-loaded on to prices, or are directly made a social charge through the budget in the form of subsidies, tax concessions, and direct measures by the public authorities, while the profits accrue to the monopolies. "According to the calculations of the American Council of Environmental Quality at least a million dollars is pocketed in the course of the elimination of three million dollars worth of damage to the environment."[8]

Thus the recognition of the problems attendant on industrial growth serves to promote a new growth industry. The rapidly expanding eco-industrial complex makes profits in two ways: on the straightforward market, where consumer goods for private consumption are produced with increasing pollution, and in another where that same pollution has to be contained by control techniques financed by the public. This process at the same time increases the concentration of capital in the hands of a few international concerns, since the smaller industrial plants are not in the position to provide their own finance for the development of systems designed to protect the environment.

For these reasons the monopolies attempt to acquire influence over the ecological movement. The MIT study commissioned by the Club of Rome is by no means the only initiative of this kind. The monopolies are also represented in all state and private commissions on the protection of the environment. Their influence on legislation is decisive, and there are numerous indications that even apparently spontaneous ecological campaigns have been promoted by large firms and government departments. There emerges a policy of "alliances from above," whose demagogic motives are obvious.[9]

By no means all ecological movements based on private initiative put themselves at the service of the interests of capital with such servility. That is demonstrated by the fact that their emergence has often led to confrontations with the police. The danger of being used is, however, always present. It must also be remembered that the interests of capital contain their own contradictions. Ecological controversies often mirror the clash of interests of different groups of entrepreneurs without their initiators always being clear as to the stakes involved in the campaigns. A long process of clarification will be necessary before the ecological movement has reached that minimum degree of political consciousness which it would require finally to understand who its enemy is and whose interests it has to defend.[10]

5. DEMOGRAPHY AND IMPERIALISM

Warnings about the consequences of uncontrolled population growth—the so-called population explosion—also contain ideological motives and behind the demands to contain it are concealed political interests which do not reveal themselves openly. The neo-Malthusian arguments which authors like Ehrlich and Taylor have been at pains to popularize found expression at a particular moment in time and in a quite particular political context. They originate almost exclusively from North American sources and can be dated to the late 1950s and early 1960s—a time, that is to say, when the Liberation movements in the Third World began to become a central problem for the leading imperialist power. (On the other hand the rate of increase in population had begun to rise much earlier, in the 1930s and 1940s.)

That this is no mere coincidence was first recognized and expressed by the Cubans. "At that time (1962) the Population Council in New York, supported by the Population Reference Bureau Inc. in Washington, launched an extensive publicity campaign for neo-Malthusianism with massive financial help from the Ford and Rockefeller Foundations, which contributed millions of dollars. The campaign pursued a double goal, which may even be attained: the ruling classes of Latin America were to be persuaded by means of skilful propaganda based on the findings of the FAO and work done by numerous, even progressive scientists, that a demographic increase of 2.5 per cent in Latin America would lead to a catastrophe of incalculable dimensions. The following excerpts from the report of the Rockefeller Foundation for 1965 are typical of this literature *made in the USA*: 'The pessimistic prediction that humanity is soon likely to be stifled by its own growth increasingly confronts all attempts to bring about an improvement in living standards. . . . It is clear that mankind will double in numbers in the lifetime of two generations unless the present growth tendency is brought under control. The results will be catastrophic for innumerable millions of individuals.' The Population Reference Bureau expresses itself even more unequivocally: 'The future of the world will be decided in the Latin American continent, in Asia and Africa, because in these developing territories the highest demographic rates of growth have been registered. Either the birth rates must be lowered or the death rate must rise again if the growth is to be brought under control. . . . The biologists, sociologists and economists of the Bureau have forecast the moment when Malthus' theory will return like a ghost and haunt the nations of the earth.' (P.R.B. press statement of October 1966)." The

Cuban report also quotes Lyndon B. Johnson's remark to the effect that "five dollars put into birth control is more useful in Latin America than a hundred dollars invested in economic growth."[11] It adds: "A comment on this cynical statement seems to us to be superfluous."

Indeed not much intelligence is needed to discover behind the benevolent pose of the Americans both strong political motivation and the irrational fears which are responsible for the massive attempt by official and private groups in the USA to export birth control to the countries of the Third World. The imperialist nations see the time coming when they will be only a small minority when compared to the rest of the world and their governments fear that population pressures will become a source of political and, in the last analysis, military power. Admittedly fears of another kind can be detected underneath the rational calculations: symptoms of a certain panic, the precursors of which are easily recognizable in history. One has only to think of the hysterical slogans of the heyday of imperialism—"The Yellow Peril"—and of the period of German Fascism—"the Red Hordes." The "politics" of population have never been free of irrational and racist traits; they always contain demagogic elements and are always prone to arouse atavistic feelings. This is admittedly true not only for the imperialist side. Even the Cuban source does not stop at the extremely enlightening comment that has been quoted but continues as follows: "Fidel Castro has spoken on the question many times. We recall his words now: 'In certain countries they are saying that only birth control provides a solution to the problem. Only capitalists, the exploiters, can speak like that; for no one who is conscious of what man can achieve with the help of technology and science will wish to set a limit to the number of human beings who can live on the earth . . . That is the deep conviction of all revolutionaries. What characterized Malthus in his time and the neo-Malthusians in our time is their pessimism, their lack of trust in the future destiny of man. That alone is the reason why revolutionaries can never be Malthusians. *We shall never be too numerous* however many of us there are, if only we all together place our efforts and our intelligence at the service of mankind, a mankind which will be freed from the exploitation of man by man.' "[12] In such phrases not only does the well-known tendency of the Cuban revolution to voluntarism find expression together with a rhetoric of affirmation; but there is also the tendency to answer the irrational fears of the imperialist oppressor with equally irrational hopes. A materialist analysis of concrete needs, possibilities and limits, cannot be replaced by figures of speech. The Chinese leadership recognized that long ago and has therefore repeatedly modified its earlier population policy, which was very similar to the Cuban one in its premises. As far as the neo-Malthusians in the USA are concerned, a violent conflict has been raging for several years over their theses and their motivation.

6. THE PROBLEM OF GLOBAL PROJECTION

A central ideological theme of the ecological debate as it is at present conducted—it is perhaps at its very heart—is the metaphor of "spaceship earth." This concept belongs above all to the repertory of the American ecological movement. Scientific debates tend to sound more sober, but their content comes to the same thing: they consider the planet as a closed and global eco-system.

The degree of "false consciousness" contained in these concepts is obvious. It links up with platitudes, which are considered to be "idealistic" but to which even that word is misapplied: "The good of the community takes precedence over the good of the individual," "We are all in the same boat," and so on. The ideological purpose of such hasty global projections is clear. The aim is to deny once and for all that little difference between first class and steerage, between the bridge and the engine room. One of the oldest ways of giving legitimacy to class domination and exploitation is resurrected in the new garb of ecology. Forrester and Meadows, the authors of the MIT report, for instance, by planning their lines of development from the start on a world scale, and always referring to the space-ship earth—and who would not be taken in by such global brotherliness?—avoid the need to analyze the distribution of costs and profits, to define their structural limitations and with them the wide variation between the chances of bringing human misery to an end. For while some can afford to plan for growth and still draw profits from the elimination and prevention of the damage they do, others certainly cannot. Thus, under accelerated state capitalism, the industrial countries of the northern territories of the world can maintain capital accumulation by diverting it to anti-pollution measures, to the recycling of basic raw materials, to processes involving intensive instead of extensive growth. This is denied to the developing countries which are compelled to exploit to the utmost their sources of raw materials and, because of their structural dependence, are urged to continue intensive exploitation of their own resources. (It is worth quoting in this connection the remark of a Brazilian Minister of Economics to the effect that his country could not have enough pollution of the environment if that was the cost of giving its population sufficient work and bread.)[13]

The contradictions which the ecological ideologies attempt to suppress in their global rhetoric emerge all the more sharply the more one takes their prognoses and demands at their face value. What would be the concrete effect, for instance, of a limitation of the consumption of energy over the whole of "space-ship earth" such as is demanded in almost all ecological programmes? "Stabilization of the use of energy—certainly, but at what level? If the average per capita consumption of a United States citizen is to serve as a measure, then a future world society stabilized at this level would make an annual demand on the available reserves of energy of roughly 350×10^{12} kilowatt hours. The world production of energy would then be almost seven times as great as at present and the thermal, atmospheric and radioactive pollution would increase to such a degree that the consequences would be unforeseeable; at the same time the available reserves of fossil fuel would disappear. If one chooses the present world average instead of the energy standard of the United States today as a measure of a future 'stable' control of energy, then the exploitation of the available source of energy and the thermal, chemical and radioactive effects in the environment would settle at a level only slightly higher than at present and one which would be tolerable in the long run. The real question would then be, however, how the available energy should be distributed globally. In arithmetical terms the solution would look something like this. The developing countries would have to have three times as much energy at their disposal as they do today; the socialist countries could by and large maintain their present level of consumption; but the highly industrialized countries of Europe and the USA would have to reduce their consumption enormously and enter upon a period of *contraction*."[14]

It must be clear that redistributions of such magnitude could be put through only by force: this is bound to hold good not only in international but also in national terms. Admittedly the captains of industry, gathered together in the Club of Rome, appear to have another view of conditions on board the ship in which we are supposed to be sitting. They are clearly not plagued by doubts as to their own competence and qualities of leadership. On the contrary they assert that "Very few people are thinking about the future from a global point of view."[15] This minority leaves no doubt that they are determined to adjust their view of the world to suit their own interests. The scarcer the resources the more one has to take this view in distributing them; but the more one adopts this view of the world the fewer people can be considered for this high office.

An ecologist who finds himself confronted by objections of this kind will generally attempt to counter them by changing the terms of the argument. He will explain that his immediate task is to deal with a condition that exists in fact; this is a task that takes precedence over future distribution problems which it is not his task to solve. On a factual level, however, it is impossible not to treat the problem on a global scale; indeed it is inevitable. The pollution of the oceans or of the atmosphere, the spread of radioactive isotopes, the consequences of man-made changes in climate—all these are *actually*, and not merely in a ideological sense, world-wide and global phenomena and can be understood only as such.

While that is true, it does not help much. So long as ecology considered itself to be a branch of biology it was always conscious of the dialectical connection between the whole and the part; far from wishing "merely" to investigate life on earth it saw itself as a science of interdependence and attempted to investigate the relations between individual species, the ecological sub-system in which they live and the larger systems. With the expansion of its research aims, its claims to hegemony and the consequent methodological syncretism, human ecology has forfeited that ability to differentiate which characterized its founders. Its tendency to hasty global projection is in the last analysis a surrender in the face of the size and complexity of the problem which it has thrown up. The reason for this failure is not difficult to determine. An ecologist researching the conditions of life in a lake has solid methodological ground to stand on; ecological arguments begin to become shaky only when the ecologist involves his own species in them. Escape into global projection is then the simplest way out. For in the case of man, the mediation between the whole and the part, between subsystem and global system, cannot be explained by the tools of biology. This mediation is social, and its explication requires an elaborated social theory and at the very least some basic assumptions about the historical process. Neither the one nor the other is available to present-day ecologists. That is why their hypotheses, in spite of their factual core, so easily fall victim to ideology.

274

7. ENVIRONMENTAL APOCALYPSE AS AN IDEOLOGICAL PAWN

The concept of a critique of ideology is not clearly defined—nor is the object it studies. It is not only that "false consciousness" proliferates in extraordinary and exotic luxuriance given the present conditions under which opinions are manufactured, but it is also as consistent as a jelly-fish and capable of protean feats of adaptability. So far we have examined the most widely diffused components of environmental ideology chiefly with regard to the interests which they at once conceal and promote. This would have to be distinguished from an evaluation in terms of an ideological critique which sees the ecological debate as a symptom that yields conclusions about the state of the society which produces it. So that nothing may be omitted, interpretations of this kind will now be briefly surveyed, although it is doubtful whether that will bring to light any new perspectives.

From this point of view, the preoccupation with ecological crisis appears as a phenomenon belonging entirely to the superstructure—namely an expression of the decadence of bourgeois society. The bourgeoisie can conceive of its own imminent collapse only as the end of the world. In so far as it sees any salvation at all, it sees it only in the past. Anything of that past that still exists must be preserved, must be conserved. In earlier phases of bourgeois society this longing for earlier cultural conditions was concentrated on "values" which either did obtain previously or were believed to have done so. With the progressive liquidation of this "inheritance," e.g. religion, the search for the roots of things, which is now thought to reside in what is left of "nature," becomes radicalized. In its period of decadence the bourgeoisie therefore proclaims itself to be the protector of something which it itself destroyed. It flees from the world which, so long as it was a revolutionary class, it created in its own image, and wishes to conserve something that no longer exists. Like the apprentice sorcerer it would like to get rid of the industrialization to which it owes its own power. But since the journey into the past is not possible, it is projected into the future: a return to barbarism, which is depicted as a pre-industrial idyll. The imminent catastrophe is conjured up with a mixture of trembling and pleasure and awaited with both terror and longing. Just as, in German society between the Wars, Klages and Spengler sounded the apocalyptic note, so in the Anglo-Saxon lands today the ecological Cassandras find a role as preachers calling a class which no longer believes in its own future to repentance. Only the scale of the prophecies has changed. While Klages and Spengler contemplated the decline of Europe, today the whole planet must pay for our *hubris*. Whereas in those days a barbarian civilization was to win terrible victories over a precious culture, today civilization is both victim and executioner. What will remain, according to the prophecies, is not an inner but a physical desert. And so on. However illuminating such excesses may occasionally sound, they cannot advance beyond a point of view that is little more than that of the history of ideas. Besides they do not carry much conviction in view of the fact that the dominant monopolies of the capitalist world show no signs of becoming aware of their presumed decadence. Just as German industry in the 1920s did not allow itself to be diverted from its expansion, so IBM and General Motors show little inclination to take the MIT Report seriously. Theories of decline are a poor substitute for materialist analyses. If one explores their historical roots it usually emerges—as in the case of Lukács, that they are nourished by that very idealism which they claim to criticize.

8. THE CRITIQUE OF IDEOLOGY AS AN IDEOLOGY

The attempt to summarize the left's arguments has shown that the main intervention in the environmental controversy has been through the critique of ideology. This kind of approach is not completely pointless, and there is no position other than Marxism from which such a critical examination of the material would be possible. But an ideological critique is only useful when it remains conscious of its own limitations: it is in no position to handle the object of its researches by itself. As such it remains merely the interpretation of an interpretation of real conditions, and is therefore unable to reach the heart of the problem. Its characteristic gesture of "unmasking" can turn into a smug ritual, if attention remains fixed on the mask instead of on what is revealed beneath it. The fact that we name the interests which lie behind current demographic theories will not conjure the needs of a rapidly growing population out of existence. An examination of the advertising campaigns of the enterprises involved does not increase the energy reserves of the earth by a single ton. And the amount of foreign matter in the air is not in any way reduced if we draw attention to the earlier history of pollution in the working-class quarters of Victorian England. A critique of ideology which is tempted to go beyond its effective limits itself becomes an ideology.

The left in West Germany has so far been scarcely conscious of this danger, or at least has not thought about it adequately, although it is by no means new in historical terms. Even Marxist thinking is not immune to ideological deformations, and Marxist theory too can become a false consciousness if, instead of being used for the methodical investigation of reality through theory and practice, it is misused as a defence against that very reality. Marxism as a defensive mechanism, as a talisman against the demands of reality, as collection of exorcisms—these are tendencies which we all have reason to take note of and to combat. The issue of ecology offers but one example. Those who wish to deprive Marxism of its critical, subversive power and turn it into an affirmative doctrine, generally dig in behind a series of stereotyped statements which, in their abstraction, are as irrefutable as they are devoid of results. One example is the claim which is proclaimed in the pages of every other picture magazine, irrespective of whether it is discussing syphilis, an earthquake or a plague of locusts, that "Capitalism is to blame!"

It is naturally splendid that anticapitalist sentiments are so widespread, that even glossy magazines cannot avoid them altogether. But it is quite another question how far an analysis deserves to be called Marxist, which a priori attributes every conceivable problem to capitalism, and what the political effect of this is. Its commonplace nature renders it harmless. Capitalism, so frequently denounced, becomes a kind of social ether, omnipresent and intangible, a quasi-natural cause of ruin and destruction, the exorcising of which can have a positively neutralizing effect. Since the concrete problem in hand —psychosis, lack of nursery schools, dying rivers, air crashes— can, without precise analysis of the exact causes, be referred to the total situation, the impression is given that any specific intervention here and now is pointless. In the same way, reference to the need for revolution become an empty formula, the ideological husk of passivity.

The same holds true for the thesis that ecological catastrophe is unavoidable within the capitalist system. The prerequisite for all solutions to the environmental crisis is then the introduction of socialism. No particular skill is involved in deducing this answer from the premises of Marxist theory. The question, however, is whether it adds up to more than an abstract statement which has nothing to do with political praxis and which allows whoever utters it to neglect the examination of his concrete situation.

The ideological packaging of such statements is dispelled at once however, if one asks what exactly they mean. The mere question of what is meant by "capitalism" brings to light the most crass contradictions. The comfortable structure of the commonplace falls apart. What is left is a heap of unresolved problems. If one understands by capitalism a system characterized by private ownership of the means of production, then it follows that the ecological problem, like all the other evils of which "capitalism" is guilty, will be solved by nationalization of the means of production. It follows that in the Soviet Union there can be no environmental problems. Anyone who asserts the contrary must be prepared to be insulted if he produces a bundle of quotations from *Pravda* and *Izvestia* about the polluted air of the Don Basin or the filthy Volga as evidence. Such a comparison of systems is forbidden—at least by Marxists like Gerhard Kade: "For all those who are embarrassed by the question of the relationship between bourgeois capitalist methods of production and the destruction of the environment, a well-proven argument can be produced from that box of tricks where diversionary social and political tactics are kept. Scientists talk of comparing the two systems: standard common-place minds immediately think of the filthy Volga, the polluted air of the Don Basin or of that around Leuna. A whole tradition lies behind this. There is no social or political issue, from party conferences to reports on the state of the nation, where the diversionary effectiveness of such comparisons between systems has not already proved its worth. Whatever emerges from the increasing number of inquiries into environmental pollution in the socialist countries is dressed up scientifically and becomes a useful weapon in a situation where demands for replacement of the system begin to threaten those who have an interest in upholding present conditions. 'Go to East Germany if you don't like it here' or 'Throw Dutschke over the Wall' are the socially aggressive forms adopted by that diversionary maneuver."[16]

Critique of ideology as ideology: the position which lays the blame on "capitalism" is defended here at the cost of its credibility. Moreover the fact that, in the socialist countries destruction of the environment has also reached perilous proportions is not even disputed, merely ignored. Anyone who is not prepared to go along with this type of scientific thinking is guilty of drawing analogies between the systems and is denounced as an anticommunist, a sort of ecological Springer. The danger that such a denatured form of Marxism will establish a hold on the masses is admittedly slight. The relationship of the German working class to its own reality is not so remote as to exclude the possibility of a comparative examination. In the face of such narrowness, one must "bear in mind that capitalism as an historical form and as a system of production cannot be identified with the existence of a class of owners. It is an all-embracing social mode of production arising from a particular type of accumulation and reproduction which has produced a network of relationships between human beings more complicated than any in the history of man. This system of production cannot simply be done away with by dispossessing private capitalists, even when this expropriation makes it possible in practice to render that part of surplus value available for other purposes which is not used for accumulation. The socialist revolution cannot be understood merely as a transfer of ownership leading to a more just distribution of wealth while other relationships remain alienated and reified. On the contrary, it must lead to totally revolutionized relationships between men and between men and things—that is to say, it must revolutionize the whole social production of their lives. It will either aim to transcend the proletariat's situation, of alienation, of the division between work and its profit, the end of commodity fetishism or it will not be the socialist revolution."[17]

Only such a view of capitalism, i.e. as a mode of production and not as a mere property relationship, allows the ecological problem to be dealt with in Marxist terms. In this connection the categories of use value and exchange value are of decisive importance. The disturbance of the material interchange between man and nature is then revealed as the strict consequence of capitalist commodity production.[18] This is a conclusion which makes the ideological ban on thought unnecessary and explains why ecological problems survive in the socialist countries too. After all, the contradiction between use value and exchange value is not superseded any more than wage labor and commodity production. "Socialist society has remained a transitional society in a very precise meaning of the word—a social form in which the capitalist mode of production, compounded with new elements, continues to exist and exercises a decisive pressure on the political sphere, on relations between human beings and on the relationship between rulers and ruled."[19] No less decisive is the pressure which the persistence of the capitalist mode of production exercises on the relationship between man and nature—a pressure which, on very similar lines to industrial production in the west, also leads to the destruction of the environment in the countries where the capitalist class has been expropriated.

The consequences of this position are extremely grave. It is true that it is possible in this manner to derive the catastrophic ecological situation from the capitalist mode of production; but the more fundamental the categories, the more universal the result. The argument is irrefutable in an abstract sense but it remains politically impotent. The statement that "capitalism is to blame" is correct in principle, but threatens to dwindle into an abstract negation of the existing order of things. Marxism is not a theory that exists in order to produce eternal verities; it is no good Marxists being right "in principle," when that means the end of the world.

Perhaps one has to remember that Marx represented *historical* materialism. From that it follows that the time factor cannot be eliminated from his theories. The delay in the coming of revolution in the overdeveloped capitalist lands is therefore not a matter of theoretical indifference. But that it was delayed does not in any way falsify the theory; for Marx certainly regarded the proletarian revolution as a necessary but not an automatic and inevitable consequence of capitalist development. He always maintained that there are alternatives in history and that the alternative facing the highly industrialized societies were long ago expressed in the formula: socialism or barbarism. In the face of the emerging ecological catastrophe this statement takes on a new meaning. The fight against the capitalist mode of production has become a race with time which mankind is in danger of losing. The tenacity with which that mode of production still asserts itself fifty years after the expropriation of the capitalist class in the Soviet Union indicates the kind of time dimensions we are discussing. It is an open question how far the destruction which it has wrought here on earth and continues to wreak is still reversible.

In this situation one must be relentless in critically examining certain elements in the Marxist tradition. First of all, one must examine to what extent one is dealing with original elements of Marxist thought or with later deformations of theory. Compared with the range of such questions the "preservation of the classics" seems a trifling matter. Catastrophes cannot be combated by quotations.

To begin with one must examine critically the concept of material progress which plays a decisive part in the Marxist tradition. It appears in any case to be redundant in that it is linked to the technical optimism of the 19th century. The revolutions of the 20th century have throughout led to victory in industrially under-developed countries and thereby falsified the idea that the socialist revolution was tied to a certain degree of "ripeness" and to "the development of the productive forces," or was actually the outcome of a kind of natural necessity. On the contrary it has been demonstrated that "the development of the productive forces" is not a linear process to which political hopes can be attached.

"Until a few years ago most Marxists accepted the traditional view that the development of the productive forces was by its nature positive. They were persuaded that capitalism, in the course of its development, would provide a material base which would be taken over by a socialist society—one on which socialism could be constructed. The view was widely diffused that socialism would be more easily developed the higher the development of the productive forces. Productive forces like technology, science, human capabilities and knowledge, and a surplus of reified labor would considerably facilitate the transition to socialism.

"These ideas were somewhat mechanistically based on the Marxist thesis of the sharpening of the contradictions between the productive forces on the one hand and the relationships of production on the other. But one can no longer assume that the productive forces are largely independent of the relationship of production and spontaneously clash with them. On the contrary, the developments of the last two decades lead one to the conclusion that the productive forces were formed by the capitalist productive relationships .and so deeply stamped by them that any attempt to alter the productive relationships must fail if the nature of the productive forces—and not merely the way they are used—is not changed."[20]

Beyond a certain point therefore, these productive forces reveal another aspect which till now was always concealed, and reveal themselves to be destructive forces, not only in the particular sense of arms manufacture and in-built obsolescence, but in a far wider sense. The industrial process, in so far as it depends on these deformed productive forces, threatens its very existence and the existence of human society. This development is damaging not only to the present but the future as well and with it, at least as far as our "Western" societies are concerned, to the utopian side of communism. If nature has been damaged to a certain, admittedly not easily determinable, degree and that damage is irreversible, then the idea of a free Society begins to lose its meaning. It seems completely absurd to speak in a short-term perspective, as Marcuse has done, of a "society of super abundance" or of the abolition of want. The "wealth" of the over-developed consumer societies of the west, in so far as it is not a mere mirage for the bulk of the population, is the result of a wave of plunder and pillage unparalleled in history; its victims are, on the one hand, the peoples of the Third World and, on the other, the men and women of the future. It is therefore a kind of wealth which produces unimaginable want.

The social and political thinking of the ecologists is marred by blindness and naïveté. If such a statement needs to be proven, the review of their thinking that follows will do so. Yet they have one advantage over the utopian thinking of the left in the west, namely the realization that any possible future belongs to the realm of necessity not that of freedom and that every political theory and practice—including that of socialists—is confronted not with the problem of abundance, but with that of survival.

9. WHAT ECOLOGY PROPOSES

Most scientists who handle environmental problems are not visible to the general public. They are highly specialized experts, exclusively concerned with their carefully defined research fields. Their influence is usually that of advisers. When doing basic research they tend to be paid from public funds; those who have a closer relationship with industry are predominantly experts whose results have immediate application. Most non-specialists, however, aim to achieve direct influence on the public. It is they who write alarmist articles which are published in magazines such as *Scientific American* or *Science*. They appear on television, organize congresses, and write the bestsellers that form the picture of ecological destruction which most of us have. Their ideas as to what should be done are reflected in the reforms promised by parties and governments. They are in this sense representative of something. What they say in public cannot decide how valid their utterances are as scientific statements; yet it is worth while analyzing their proposals, for they indicate where the lines of scientific extrapolation and dominant "bourgeois" ideology intersect.

The Americans Paul and Anne Ehrlich are among the founders of human ecology, and are still among its most influential spokesmen. In their handbook on ecology they summarize their proposals under the heading "A Positive Program," excerpts from which are extremely revealing.

'2. Political pressure must be applied immediately to induce the United States government to assume its responsibility to halt the growth of the American population. Once growth is halted, the government should undertake to regulate the birthrate so that the population is reduced to an optimum size and maintained there. It is essential that a grass-roots political movement be generated to convince our legislators and the executive branch of the government that they must act rapidly. The programme should be based on what politicians understand best—votes. Presidents, Congressmen, Senators, and other elected officials who do not deal effectively with the crisis must be defeated at the polls and more intelligent and responsible candidates elected.

'3. A massive campaign must be launched to restore a quality environment in North America and to *de-develop the United States*. De-development means bringing our economic system (especially patterns of consumption) into line with the realities of ecology and the world resource situation. . . . Marxists claim that capitalism is intrinsically expansionist and wasteful, and that it automatically produces a monied ruling class. Can our economists prove them wrong? . . .

'5. It is unfortunate that at the time of the greatest crisis the United States and the world has ever faced, many Americans, especially the young, have given up hope that the government can be modernized and changed in direction through the functioning of the elective process. Their despair may have some foundation, but a partial attempt to institute a "new politics" very nearly succeeded in 1968. In addition many members of Congress and other government leaders, both Democrats and Republicans, are very much aware of the problems outlined in this book and are determined to do something about them. Others are joining their ranks as the dangers before us daily become more apparent. These people need public support in order to be effective. The world cannot, in its present critical state, be saved by merely tearing down old institutions, even if rational plans existed for constructing better ones from the ruins. We simply do not have the time. Either we will succeed by bending old institutions or we will succumb to disaster. Considering the potential rewards and consequences we see no choice but to make an effort to modernize the system. It may be necessary to organize a new political party with an ecological outlook and national and international orientation to provide an alternative to the present parties with their local and parochial interests. The environmental issue may well provide the basis for this.

'6. Perhaps the major necessary ingredient that has been missing from a solution to the problems of both the United States and the rest of the world is a goal, a vision of the kind of Spaceship Earth that ought to be and the kind of crew that should man her. . . .21

This is not the only case of a serious scientist presenting the public with a program of this kind. On the contrary. Page upon page could be used to document similar ideas. They can be seen as a consensus of what modern ecology has to offer in the way of suggestions for social action. A collection of similar statements would only repeat itself; and we will therefore confine ourselves to one further piece of evidence. The following quotation is from a book by the Swede Gösta Ehrensvärd, a leading biochemist, in which he attempts a comprehensive diagnosis of the ecological situation. His therapeutic ideas are summarized as follows.

"We are not *compelled* to pursue population growth, the consumption of energy, and unlimited exploitation of resources, to the point where famine and world-wide suffering will be the results. We are not *compelled* to watch developments and do nothing and to pursue our activities shortsightedly without developing a long-term view." The catastrophe can be avoided, he says, "if we take certain measures *now* on a global scale. These measures could stabilize the situation for the next few centuries and allow us to bring about, with as little friction as possible, the transition from today's hectically growing industrialized economy to the agricultural economy of the future. The following components of a crash programme are intended to gain time for the necessary global restructuring of society on this earth.

1. Immediate introduction of world-wide rationing of all fossil fuels, above all of fluid resources of energy. Limitation of energy production to the 1970 level. Drastic restrictions on all traffic, in so far as it is propelled by fluid fuels, and is not needed for farming, forestry and the long-distance transport of raw materials.

2. Immediate total rationing of electricity.

3. Immediate cessation of the production of purely luxury goods and other products not essential for survival, including every kind of armament.

4. Immediate food rationing in all industrial countries. Limitation of all food imports from the developing countries to a minimum. The main effort in terms of development policies throughout the world to be directed towards agriculture and forestry.

5. Immediate imposition of the duty to collect and re-cycle all discarded metal objects, and in particular to collect all scrap.

6. Top priority to be given to research on the development of energy from atomic fusion as well as to biological research in the fields, of genetics, applied ecology and wood chemistry.

7. Creation of an international Centre to supervise and carry through action around the six points listed above. This Centre to have the duty to keep the inhabitants of this earth constantly informed through the mass media of the level of energy and mineral reserves, the progress of research, and the demographic situation."[22]

10. A CRITIQUE OF THE ECOLOGICAL CRASH PROGRAM

In their appeals to a world whose imminent decline they prophesy, the spokesmen of human ecology have developed a missionary style. They often employ the most dramatic strokes to paint a future so black that after reading their works one wonders how people can persist in giving birth to children, or in drawing up pension schemes. Yet at the conclusion of their sermons, in which the inevitability of the End—of industrialization, of civilization, of man, of life on this planet—is convincingly described if not proved, another way forward is presented. The ecologists end up by appealing to the rationality of their readers; if everyone would grasp what is at stake, then—apparently—everything would not be lost. These sudden about-turns smack of conversion rhetoric. The horror of the predicted catastrophe contrasts sharply with the mildness of the admonition with which we are allowed to escape. This contrast is so obvious and so central, that both sides of the argument undermine each other. At least one of them fails to convince. Either the final exhortation, which addresses us in mild terms, or the analysis which is intended to alarm us. It is impossible not to feel that those warnings and threats, which present us with the consequences of our actions, are intended precisely to soften us up for the conversion which the anxious preacher wishes to obtain from us in the end; conversely the confident final resolution should prevent us from taking too literally the dark picture they have painted, and from sinking into resignation. Every parish priest is aware of this noble form of verbal excess; and everyone listening can easily see through it. The result is (at best) a pleasurable *frisson*. Herein may lie the total inefficacy of widely distributed publications maintaining that the hour will soon come not only for man himself, but for his whole species. They are as ineffective as a Sunday sermon.

In its closest details, both the form and content of the Ehrlichs' argument are marked by the consciousness (or rather the unconsciousness) of the WASP, the white Protestant middle-class North American. This is especially obvious in the authors' social and political ideas: they are just as *unwilling* to consider any radical interference with the political system of the United States as they are *willing* to contemplate the other immense changes which they spell out. The US system is introduced into their calculations as a constant factor: it is introduced not as it is, but as it appears to the white member of the middle class, that is to say in a form which has been transformed out of recognition by ideology. Class contradictions and class interests are completely denied: the parliamentary mechanism of the vote is unquestionably considered to be an effective method, by means of which all conceivable conflicts can be resolved. It is merely a question of finding the right candidate and conducting the right campaigns, of writing letters and launching a few modest citizens' activities. At the most extreme, a new parliament will have to be set up. Imperialism does not exist. World peace will be reached through disarmament. The political process is posed in highly personalized terms: politics is the business of the politicians who are expected to carry the "responsibility." Similarly, economics is the business of the economists, whose task is to "draw up" a suitable economic system—this, at least, one has the right to ask of them. "Marxism" appears only once, as a scarecrow to drive recalcitrant readers into the authors' arms. All that this crude picture of political idiocy lacks are lofty ideas: the authors are not averse to make good the lack. What is needed is a "vision," since only relatively "idealistic programs" still offer the possibility of salvation. Since the need is so great, there will be no lack of offers, and the academic advertising agency promptly comes up with the concept of "Spaceship Earth," in which the armaments industry and public relations join hands. The depoliticization of the ecological question is now complete. Its social components and consequences have been entirely eliminated.

Concrete demands can now cheerfully be made. There is no danger that they may be implemented with disagreeable consequences. A brake on population increase, de-development of the economy, draconian rationing, can now be presented as measures which, since they are offered in a spirit of enlightened, moral commonsense, and are carried out in a peaceful, liberal manner, harm no interests or privileges, and demand no changes in the social and economic system. Ehrensvärd presents the same demands in more trenchant, apparently radical terms—those of the coolly calculating scientist. Like the Ehrlichs, his arguments are so unpolitical as to be grotesque. Yet his sense of reality is strong enough for him to demand privileges for himself and his work—that is to say, the highest priority for the undisturbed continuation of his research. One particular social interest, if a very restricted one, thereby finds expression: his own.

"Many of the suggestions," say the Ehrlichs, "will seem 'unrealistic,' and indeed this is how we view them."[23] The fact that not even the authors take their own "crash program" seriously at least makes it clear that we are not dealing with madmen. They reason why they seek refuge in absurdity is that their competence as scientists is limited precisely to the theoretical radius of the old ecology, that is to say, to a subordinate discipline of biology. They have extended their researches to human society, but they have not increased their knowledge in any way. It has escaped them that human existence remains incomprehensible if one totally disregards its social determinants; that this lack is damaging to all scientific utterances on our present and future; and that the range of these utterances is reduced whenever these scientists abandon the methodology of their particular discipline. It is restricted to the narrow horizons of their own class. The latter, which they erroneously regard as the silent majority is, in fact, a privileged and very vocal minority.

11. CONCLUSIONS: HYPOTHESES CONCERNING A HYPOTHESIS

There is a great temptation to leave matters there and to interpret the forecast of a great ecological crisis as a maneuvre intended to divert people from acute political controversy. There are even said to be parts of the left which consider it a luxury to trouble themselves with problems of the future. To do that would be a declaration of bankruptcy; socialist thinking has from the beginning been oriented not toward the past but towards the future. Herein lay one of its real chances of success. For while the bourgeoisie is intent on the short-term interests of the accumulation of capital, there is no reason for the left to exclude long-term aims and perspectives. As far as the competence of the ecologists is concerned, it would be a mistake to conclude that, because of their boundless ignorance on social matters, their statements are absolutely unfounded. Their methodological ineptitude certainly decreases the validity of their overall prognoses; but individual lines of argument, which they found predominantly on the causality of the natural sciences, are still useable. To demonstrate that they have not been thought through in the area of social causes and effects is not to refute them.

> The ideologies of the ruling class do not reproduce mere falsifications. Even in their instrumental form they still contain experiences which are real in so far as they are never optimistic. They promise the twilight of the gods, global catastrophe and a last judgment; but these announcements are not seen to be connected with the identification and short-term satisfactions which form part of their content.[24]

All this applies admirably to the central "ecological hypothesis" according to which if the present process of industrialization continues naturally it will in the foreseeable future have catastrophic results. The central core of this hypothesis can neither be proved nor refuted by political discussion. What it says is of such importance, however, that what one is faced with is a calculation like Pascal's wager. So long as the hypothesis is not unequivocally refuted, it will be heuristically necessary to base any thinking about the future on what it has to say. Only if one behaves "as if" the ecological hypothesis was valid, can one test its social validity—a task which has scarcely been attempted up to now and of which ecology itself is clearly incapable. The following reflections are merely some first steps along this path. They are, in other words, hypotheses based on other hypotheses.

A general social definition of the ecological problem would have to start from the mode of production. Everywhere where the capitalistic mode of production obtains totally or predominantly—that is to say, where the products of human labor take the form of commodities—increasing social want is created alongside increasing social wealth. This want assumes different forms in the course of historical development. In the phase of primitive accumulation it expresses itself in direct impoverishment caused by extensive exploitation, extension of working hours, lowering of real wages. In the cyclical crises, the wealth that has been produced by labor is simply destroyed—grain is thrown into the sea and so on. With the growth of the productive powers the destructive energies of the system also increase. Further want is generated by world wars and armaments production. In a later phase of capitalistic development this destructive potential acquires a new quality. It threatens all the natural bases of human life. This has the result that want appears to be a socially produced natural force. This return of general shortages forms the core of the "ecological crisis." It is not, however, a relapse into conditions and circumstances from the historical past, because the want does not in any sense abolish the prevailing wealth. Both are present at one and the same time; the contradiction between them becomes ever sharper and takes on increasingly insane forms.

So long as the capitalist mode of production obtains—that is to say not merely the capitalist property relationships—the trend can at best be reversed in detail but not in its totality. The crisis will naturally set in motion many processes of adaptation and learning. Technological attempts to level out its symptoms in the sense of achieving a homeostasis have already gone beyond the experimental stage. The more critical the situation becomes the more desperate will be the attempts undertaken in this direction. They will include: abolition of the car, construction of means of mass transport, erection of plants for the filtration and desalination of sea-water, the opening up of new sources of energy, synthetic production of raw materials, the development of more intensive agricultural techniques and so on. But each of these steps will cause new critical problems; these are stop-gap techniques, which do not touch the roots of the problem. The political consequences are clear enough. The costs of living accommodation and space for recreation, of clean air and water, of energy and raw materials will increase explosively as will the cost of recycling scarce resources. The "invisible" social costs of capitalist commodity production are rising immeasurably and are being passed on in prices and taxes to the dependent masses to such a degree that any equalization through controlling wages is no longer possible. There is no question, needless to say, of a "just" distribution of shortages within the framework of western class society: the rationing of want is carried out through prices, if necessary through grey or black markets, by means of corruption and the sale of privileges. The subjective value of privileged class positions increases enormously. The physiological and psychic consequences of the environmental crisis, the lowered expectation of life, the direct threat from local catastrophes can lead to a situation where class can determine the life or death of an individual by deciding such factors as the availability of means of escape, second houses, or advanced medical treatment.

The speed with which these possibilities will enter the consciousness of the masses cannot be predicted. It will depend on the point in time at which the creeping nature of the ecological crisis becomes apparent in spectacular individual cases. Even dramatic phenomena such as have principally appeared in Japan—the radioactive poisoning of fishermen, illnesses caused by mercury and cadmium—have not yet led to a more powerful mobilization of the masses because the consequences of the contamination have become apparent only months or years later. But once, at any point in the chain of events, many people are killed, the indifference with which the prognoses of the ecologists are met today will turn into panic reaction and even into ecological rebellions.

There will of course be organizational initiatives and political consequences at an even earlier stage. The ecological movement in the United States, with its tendency to flee from the towns and industry, is an indication of what will come, as are the citizen's campaigns which are spreading apace. The limitations which beset most of these groups are not fortuitous; their activity is usually aimed at removing a particular problem. There is no other alternative, for they can only crystallize round particular interests. A typical campaign will, for example, attempt to prevent the siting of an oil-refinery in a particular district. That does not lead, if the agitation is successful, to the project being cancelled or to a revision of the policy on energy; the refinery is merely built where the resistance of those affected is less strongly expressed. In no case does the campaign lead to a reduction of energy consumption. An appeal on these grounds would have no sense. It would fall back on the abstract, empty formulae which make up the "crash programmes" of the ecologists.

The knot of the ecological crisis cannot be cut with a paper-knife. The crisis is inseparable from the conditions of existence systematically determined by the mode of production. That is why moral appeals to the people of the "rich" lands to lower their standard of living are totally absurd. They are not only useless but cynical. To ask the individual wage-earner to differentiate between his "real" and his "artificial" needs is to mistake his real situation. Both are so closely connected that they constitute a relationship which is subjectively and objectively indivisible. Hunger for commodities, in all its blindness, is a product of the production of commodities, which could only be suppressed by force. We must reckon with the likelihood that bourgeois policy will systematically exploit the resulting mystifications—increasingly so, as the ecological crisis takes on more threatening forms. To achieve this, it only needs demagogically to take up the proposals of the ecologists and give them political circulation. The appeal to the common good, which demands sacrifice and obedience, will be taken up by these movements together with a reactionary populism, determined to defend capitalism with anticapitalist phrases.

In reality, capitalism's policy on the environment, raw materials, energy, and population, will put an end to the last liberal illusions. That policy cannot even be conceived without increasing repression and regimentation. Fascism has already demonstrated its capabilities as a savior in extreme crisis situations and as the administrator of poverty. In an atmosphere of panic and uncontrollable emotions—that is to say, in the event of an ecological catastrophe which is directly perceptible on a mass scale—the ruling class will not hesitate to have recourse to such solutions. The ability of the masses to see the connection between the mode of production and the crisis in such a situation and to react offensively cannot be assumed. It depends on the degree of politicization and organization achieved by then. But it would be facile to count on such a development. It is more probable that what has been called "internal imperialism" will increase. What Negt and Kluge have observed in another connection is also relevant to the contradiction between social wealth and social poverty, which is apparent in the ecological crisis: "Colonialization of the consciousness or civil war are the extreme forms in which these contradictions find public expression. What precedes this collision, or is a consequence of it, is the division of individuals or of social groups into qualities which are organized against each other."[25]

In this situation, external imperialism will also regress to historically earlier forms—but with an enormously increased destructive potential. If the "peaceful" methods of modern exploitation fail, and the formula for coexistence under pressure of scarcity snaps, then presumably there will be new predations, competitive wars, wars over raw materials. The strategic importance of the Third World, above all of those lands which export oil and non-ferrous metals, will increase and with it their consciousness that the metropolitan lands depend on them. The "siege" of the metropolises by the village—a concept which appeared premature in the 1950s—will acquire quite new topicality. It has already been unmistakably heralded by the policy of a number of oil-producing countries. Imperialism will do everything to incite the population of the industrialized countries against such apparent external enemies whose policy will be presented as a direct threat to their standard of living, and to their very survival, in order to win their assent to military operations.

Talk in global terms about "Spaceship Earth" tells us almost nothing about real perspectives and the chances of survival. There are certainly ecological factors whose effect is global; among these are macro-climatic changes, pollution by radio-active elements and poisons in the atmosphere and oceans. As the example of China shows, it is not these overall factors which are decisive, but the social variables. The destruction of mankind cannot be considered a purely natural process. But it will not be averted by the preachings of scientists, who only reveal their own helplessness and blindness the moment they overstep the narrow limits of their own special areas of competence. "The *human* essence of nature first exists only for *social* man; for only here does nature exist as the *foundation* of his own *human* existence. Only here has what is to him his *natural* existence become his *human* existence, and nature become man for him. Thus *society* is the unity of being of man with nature—the true resurrection of nature—the naturalism of man and the humanism of nature both brought to fulfilment."[26]

If ecology's hypotheses are valid, then capitalist societies have probably thrown away the chance of realizing Marx's project for the reconciliation of man and nature. The productive forces which bourgeois society has unleashed have been caught up with and overtaken by the destructive powers released at the same time. The highly industrialized countries of the west will not be alone in paying the price for the revolution that never happened. The fight against want is an inheritance they leave to all mankind, even in those areas where mankind survives the catastrophe. Socialism, which was once a promise of liberation, has become a question of survival. If the ecological equilibrium is broken, then the rule of freedom will be further off than ever.

Translated by Stuart Hood

Notes

THE INDUSTRIALIZATION OF THE MIND

1. This delusion became painfully apparent during the Nazi régime in Germany, when many intellectuals thought it sufficient to retreat into 'inner emigration', a posture which turned out to mean giving in to the Nazis. There have been similar tendencies in Communist countries during the reign of Stalinism. See Czeslaw Milosz's excellent study, *The Captive Mind* (London, 1953).

2. Karl Marx, *Die deutsche Ideologie*, (I Teil, 1845–46).

3. A good example is the current wave of McLuhanism. No matter how ingenious, no matter how shrewd and fresh some of this author's observations may seem, his understanding of media hardly deserves the name of a theory. His cheerful disregard of their social and political implications is pathetic. It is all too easy to see why the slogan 'The medium is the message' has met with unbounded enthusiasm on the part of the media, since it does away, by a quick fix worthy of a cardsharp, with the question of truth. Whether the message is a lie or not has become irrelevant, since in the light of McLuhanism truth itself resides in the very existence of the medium, no matter what it may convey: the proof of the network is in the network. It is a pity that Goebbels has not lived to see this redemption of his *oeuvre*.

4. The importance of the transistor radio in the Algerian revolution has been emphasized by Frantz Fanon, and the role of television in the political life of Castro's Cuba is a matter of common knowledge.

5. A good example of this instinctive sense of insecurity shared by the most entrenched political powers is offered by Senator Joseph McCarthy's lunatic crusade against Hollywood producers, actors, and writers. Most of them had shown an abject loyalty to the demands of the industry throughout their career, and yet no abnegation of their talents could free them from suspicion. Much in the same way, Stalin never trusted even his most subservient lackeys of the intellectual establishment.

6. Among those who blithely disregard this fact, I would mention some European philosophers, for example Romano Guardini, Max Picard, and Ortega y Gasset. In America, this essentially conservative stance has been assumed by Henry Miller and a number of Beat Generation writers.

CONSTITUENTS OF A THEORY OF THE MEDIA

1. Bertolt Brecht: *Theory of Radio* (1932), *Gesammelte Werke*, Band VIII, pp. 129 seq., 134.

2. *Der Spiegel*, 20/10/1969.

3. El Lissitsky, 'The Future of the Book', *New Left Review*, No. 41, p. 42.

4. *Kommunismus, Zeitschrift der Kommunistischen Internationale für die Länder Südosteuropas*, 1920, pp. 1538–49.

5. Walter Benjamin: *Kleine Geschichte der Photographie* in *Das Kunstwerk im Zeitalter seiner technischen Reproduzierbarkeit* (Frankfurt: 1963), p. 69.

6. Walter Benjamin: 'The Work of Art in the Age of Mechanical Reproduction', *Illuminations* (New York: 1969), pp. 223–7.

7. Ibid., p. 229.

8. Op. cit., p. 40.

9. Benjamin, op. cit., p. 42.

THEORY OF TREASON

1. Quoted from Günther Weisenborn, *Der Lautlose Aufstand. Bericht über die Widerstandsbewegung des deutschen Volkes 1933 bis 1945*, p. 250 ff. (Reinbek: 1962).

2. Margaret Boveri, *Der Verrat im 20 Jahrhundert. I: Für und gegen die Nation* (Hamburg: 1956), p. 12.

3. With respect to the following, compare Sigmund Freud, *Totem und Tabu. Gesammelte Schriften Band IX.* (London: 1940).

4. J. G. Frazer, *The Golden Bough,* Part II. *Taboo and the Perils of the Soul.* Third Edition (London: 1911), p. 132.

5. Montesquieu, *L'Esprit des Lois*, XII, 7.

6. Hannah Arendt provides a very trenchant analysis of the concept of the "objective opponent" in her book *Origins of Totalitarianism* (New York: 1951).

7. Ibn Batuta, *Die Reise des Arabers Ibn Batuta durch Indien und China.* Bearbeited von H. von Mzik. (Hamburg: 1911). Quoted from Elias Canetti, *Masse und Macht*, Hamburg, 1960, p. 497. (English transl., *Crowds and Power*, New York: Viking Press, 1962). Canetti's work is indispensable for the study of the connection between sovereignty and paranoia.

8. The figure 150,000 is based on data of the Dieter Posser, a lawyer from Essen, who has made a name for himself as a defense attorney in political trials. Compare the *Süddeutsche Zeitung* of April 30, 1964.

REFLECTIONS BEFORE A GLASS CAGE

1. Eleventh edition, Vol. VII, p. 447.

2. *Leviathan*, XXVII chapter.

3. Chapter 5. In: *Totem and Taboo* (Vienna: 1913). Freud's argument is not necessarily dependent on the teachings of psychoanalysis. It makes sense even if one deletes motivation through the Oedipus complex and the question of incest.

4. Malinowski's investigation of *Sex and Repression in Savage Society* is a good characteristic example of the scientific criticism of Freud's hypotheses. Malinowski attempts an empirical reconstruction of fratricide and its consequences, an undertaking which has led to hypotheses *ad absurdum*. His critique shows the limits of Freud's presentation; Freud, however, who expressedly called it a "scientific myth" was fully aware of these limitations himself. A refutation in this manner is just as impossible as is a proof. The question of the priority of crime and social organization leads to philosophical and semantic conundrums into which anthropology can enter but which it cannot solve.

5. Canetti, *Masse und Macht*, cf. pp. 259–282.

6. "The Taboo and Emotional Ambivalence" in *Totem und Tabu* (Vienna: 1913).

7. Canetti, *op. cit.* 542.

8. *Fischer Lexikon*, Volume 12: Recht. (Frankfurt am Main: 1959), p. 137 f.

9. *Politik* (Leipzig: 1897).

10. *"Zeitgemässes uber Krieg und Tod"* (1915), in *Das Unbewusste. Schriften zur Psychoanalyse* (Frankfurt am Main: 1960). p. 191 f.

11. Gerhard Schoenberner, *Der gelbe Stern. Die Judenverfolgung in Europa 1933 bis 1945* (Hamburg: 1960), p. 12.

12. *Es gibt keinen jüdischen Wohnbezirk in Warschau mehr* (Facsimile edition of the Stoop Report) Neuwied: 1960.

13. Felix Kersten, *Totenkopf und Treue,* p. 144. Quoted from Joachim C. Fest, *Das Gesicht des Dritten Reiches* (München: 1963), p. 169 f.

14. Internationales Militärtribunal, *Der Prozess gegen die Hauptkriegsverbrecher* (Nürnberg: 1947) Volume XXIX, p. 145, ff.

15. *On Thermoneuclear War,* p. 21.

16. Op. cit. p. 133 and passim.

17. *Der Spiegel,* Nr. 47/1963, quoting the *Journal of Abnormal and Social Psychology,* Boston, October 1963.

18. In reference to this compare Eric J. Hobsbawm, *Primitive Rebels: Studies in Archaic Forms of Social Movements in the 19th and 20th Century* (New York: 1963).

19. Quoted from Donald Kaplan and Armand Schwerner, *The Doomsday Dictionary* (London: 1964), p. 157.

RAFAEL TRUJILLO

NOTES

A radio version of this chapter was put out by the Hessian broadcasting corporation. I owe a special debt of gratitude to the Iberian-American Institute in Berlin and its director, Dr Bock, for getting hold of not easily available material.

Bibliography:

Jesus de Galindez, *L'ere de Trujillo. Anatomie d'une dictature latino-americaine*: Paris, 1962

Juan Jiminez Grullon, *Una Gestapoen America*: Havana, 1946

Albert C. Hicks, *Blood in the Streets. The Life and Rule of Trujillo*: New York, 1946

Felix Mejia, *Via crucis de un pueblo. Relato sinoptico de la tragedia dominicana*: Veracruz, Mexico, 1951

German E. Ornes, *Trujillo. Little Caesar of the Caribbean*: New York, 1958

Rafael L. Trujillo, *Discursos, mensajes y proclamas*: Madrid, 1957

1. Over and above these particular difficulties there is another peculiarly local one. I am thinking of the unfortunate predilection of Latin-American authors for statistics. Bewitched by the great God precision, they like to operate with hard figures. Unfortunately this does not lead to any kind of consensus. Surveys, censuses, estimates. Such propaganda figures are indiscriminately quoted. Sources are seldom named and for the most part dubious. I am not in a position to rectify this state of affairs. All figures quoted in the article should be seen as a rough guide. I accept them and pass them on in the same way as the big European banks accept Dominican National Debt Bonds, that is to say: with the usual reservations, etc.

2. Trujillo, p. 135 and following pages.

3. Quoted by Ornes, p. 36.

4. Quoted by Hicks, p. 29.

5. Quoted by Galindez, p. 40.

6. Quoted by Galindez, p. 46.

7. Quoted by Ornes, p. 55.

8. Quoted by Ornes, p. 59.

9. Hicks, p. 29.

10. Trujillo, p. 180 and following pages.

11. Ornes, p. 27.

12. Trujillo, 'Dictator tropical y folklorico', in his *Combate*, Publicacion del Instituto Internacional de Estudios Politico-Sociales, San Jose, Costa Rica, 1962. No 25, pp. 27–31.

13. Trujillo, p. 190 and following pages.

14. These figures come from Juan Bosch, elected president in 1962 after the death of the Benefactor. He is one of the few Dominican politicians who is quite incorruptible. Quoted by Harry Kantor, 'Ascenso y caida de Rafael Trujillo', in *Cuadernos 72*, Paris 1963, p. 53.

15. Compiled from information in Galindez, Ornes and Kantor.

16. A complete version of the *Citizen's Primer* can be found in Lawrence de Besault's *President Trujillo. His work and the Dominican Republic*, third edition, Santiago de Los Caballeros, 1941, pp. 399–410. This amusing book is one of the numerous biographies commissioned by Trujillo himself from the literary hacks of American journalism. These works were sent free to

foreign libraries at government expense. In his book De Besault actually suggests Trujillo as a candidate for the Nobel Peace Prize.

17. This figure is to be found in an essay by Ramon Grullon, 'Antecedentes y perspectivas del movimiento politico dominicano', in *Cuadernos americanos* XXI/1., Mexico, DF, 1962, pp. 221–252.

18. Quoted by Ornes, p. 287.

19. Excerpt from a speech of 4 June 1961 printed in the newspaper *Revolucion*, Havana, 5 June 1961, quoted in *Cuardernos del Condreso por la libertad de la Cultura* 54, Paris, 1961, p. 74. (Comments in brackets are editor's additions.)

20. All pre-marxist analyses of the Trujillo phenomenon are worthless; but equally worthless are those deliberations based on Lenin which desperately try and ignore his maxim that a badly executed revolution is counter-revolutionary.

DREAMERS OF THE ABSOLUTE: PART ONE

A radio version of this essay was broadcast by the Hessian Radio Network.

Literature:

Michail Bakunin, *Staatenthum und Anarchie*. Zurich, 1973. (Michail Bakunin and Sergej Netchajev) *Katechismus des Revolutionärs*. Zurich, no date.

Albert Camus, *L'Homme révolté*. Paris, 1951.

Vera Figner, *Nacht über Russland*. Berlin, 1926.

Hans Kohn, ed., *Die Welt der Slawen II: Russen, Weissrussen Ukrainer*. Frankfurt am Main, 1962.

Peter Krapotkin, *Memoiren eines Revolutionärs*. Zweite Auflage. Zwei Bände. Stuttgart, 1901.

Karl Oldenberg, *Der Russische Nihilismus von Seinen Anfängen bis zur Gegenwart*. Leipzig, 1888.

Boris Sawinkov, *Erinnerungen eines Terroristen*. Berlin, 1930.

Peter Scheibert, *Von Bakunin zu Lenin. Geschichte der Russisschen revolutionären Ideologien 1840–1895*. Volume I. Leiden, 1956.

Stepniak (S. M. Krawtshinskij), *Das unterirdische Russland*. Berne, 1884.

Alphons Thun, *Geschichte der revolutionären Bewegungen in Russland*. Leipzig, 1883.

Dmitrij Tschischewskij, *Russland zwischen Ost und West. Russische Geistesgeschichte*. Volume II. Hamburg, 1961.

Franco Venturi, *Roots of Revolution. A History of the Populist and Socialist Movements in 19th Century Russia*. London, 1960.

1. Tschischwewskij, *op. cit.*, p. 147; Sawinkov, p. XIX; Kohn, p. 91.

2. Oldenberg, *op. cit.*, p. 24.

3. Camus, *op. cit.*, p. 167.

4. and 5. Kohn, p. 92 f.

6. Under the pseudonym Jules Elysard and the title *Die Reaction in Deutschland. Ein Fragment von einem Franzosen*. Quoted after Scheibert.

7. Oldenberg, p. 66 f.

8. Oldenberg, p. 77.

9. Thun, p. 67.

10. Thun, p. 95 f.

11. & 13. Oldenberg, p. 87 f.

12. Figner, p. 52.

13. Thun, p. 149.

14. Figner, p. 89.

15. Figner, p. 88.

16. Figner, p. 89.

17. Figner, p. 96.

18. Thun, p. 273.

19. Figner, p. 116.

20. Figner, p. 138.

21. Figner, p. 125.

22. Oldenberg, p. 167 f.

23. Oldenberg, p. 173.

DREAMERS OF THE ABSOLUTE: PART TWO

This essay adheres closely to the previously mentioned *Erinnerungen* by Boris Sawinkov.

About the Ochrana: Maurice Laporte, *Histoire de l'Okhrana*. Paris, 1935.

About the Bolshevik evaluation of the terror compare: Vladimir

Iljitsch Lenin, *Die Kinderkrankheit des Kommunismus.* Berlin, 1957.

About the double role of the secret police in a somewhat different connection: Hannah Arendt, *Origins of Totalitarianism.*

A dramatization of Sawinkov's recollections is Albert Camus' *Les Justes.* Paris, 1950.

PORTRAIT OF A PARTY

1. Evidence in Robert J. Alexander, *Communism in Latin America.* New Brunswick, N.J., 1957, p. 272, and Charles E. Thompson, Foreign Policy Reports XI/21, 1935.

2. *Communist International* of February 15, 1934; quoted from Boris Goldenberg, *The Cuban Revolution and Latin America,* New York, 1965, p. 115.

3. Yves Gilbert, Castro l'infidèle, quoted from Goldenberg *op. cit.,* p. 117.

4. Segunda Asamblea Nacional del Partido Socialista Popular, *Los Socialistas y la realidad cubana.* La Habana, 1944. Quoted from Robert Scheer and Maurice Zeitlin, *Cuba. An American Tragedy,* Harmondworth, 1964, p. 123.

5. Figures from Theodore Draper, *Castroism, Theory and Practice,* New York, 1965, p. 204, as well as from Wyatt MacGaffey and Clifford R. Barnett, *Twentieth-Century Cuba: The Background of the Castro Revolution,* New York, 1965, p. 157.

6. *Daily Worker,* New York, of August 5, 1953. The declaration itself could not be published in Cuba at that time because the party's official organ was prohibited.

7. Fidel Castro, Basta ya de mentiras! In: *Bohemia,* La Habana July 15, 1956. Quoted from Draper, *op. cit.* p. 28. Blas Roca was secretary general of the party, Peña a leading Communist union man.

8. Caude Julien, *La Révolucion Cubaine,* Paris, 1961, p. 81, and in Goldenberg, *op. cit.,* p. 166.

9. Theodore Draper, *Castro's Revolution. Myths and Realities.* New York, 1962, Sheer/Zeitlin, *op. cit.,* p. 127.

10. Conversation between Maurice Zeitlin and Carlos Fernandes,

304

in R. Scheer/Zeitlin, *op. cit.*, p. 128; *Noticias de Hoy*, La Habana, January 11, 1959.

11. Proof in Goldenberg, *op. cit.*, p. 162.

12. Information from Carlos Rafael Rodríguez, given to Herbert Matthews. See the latter's biography of *Fidel Castro*, New York, 1969, p. 176.

13. *Guia del pensamiento político-económico de Fidel.* In: *Diario Libre*, La Habana, 1959, p. 48.

14. Andrés Suárez, *Cuba: Castroism and Communism, 1959–1966.* Cambridge, Mass., 1967, p. 61.

15. Ernesto Ché Guevara, Un año de lucha armada. In: *Verde olivo*, La Habana, January 5, 1964.

16. MacGaffey/Barnett, *op. cit.*, p. 309.

17. Linoel Soto in *Cuba Socialista*, La Habana, February 1963.

18. Quoted from Theodore Draper, *Castro's Revolution*, p. 84.

19. Quoted from Draper, *op. cit.*, p. 149 f. and Scheer/Zeitlin, *op. cit.*, p. 225.

20. Goldenberg, *op. cit.*, p. 264.

21. Scheer/Zeitlin, *op. cit.*, p. 227, and Goldenberg, *op. cit.*, p. 265.

22. Matthews, *op. cit.*, p. 315, and Scheer/Zeitling *op. cit.*, p. 227.

23. Jorge Dominguez, The Politics of the Institutionalization of the Cuban Revolution: The Search for the Missing Links. Unpublished manuscript. New Haven, Conn., 1968. Also compare: *Cuba Socialista*, La Habana, of June–November, 1962.

24. *Cuba Socialista*, La Habana, of January, 1965.

25. Dominguez, *op. cit.*

26. Lee Lockwood, *Castro's Cuba, Cuba's Fidel.* Second edition, New York, 1969. p. 152.

27. Matthews, *op. cit.*, p. 317.

28. *Consideraciones sobre el trabajo ideólogico*, Material de estudio. (1968) Editiones COR. La Habana.

29. Fidel Castro, Speech of October 30, 1963. Quoted from Draper, *Castroism*, p. 217.

30. Matthews, *op. cit.*, p. 187.

31. Fidel Castro, *op. cit.*

TOURISTS OF THE REVOLUTION

1. Herberto Padilla, *Ausserhalb des Spiels* (Frankfurt am Main: 1971), pp. 113–115.

2. Lev Davidovic Trockij, *Verratene Revolution* (Frankfurt am Main: 1968), pp. 5–7.

3. Victor Serge, *Beruf: Revolutionär* (Frankfurt am Main: 1967), pp. 122, 169 ff.

4. Franz Jung, *Der Weg nach unten* (Neuwied: 1961), p. 169 ff.

5. Victor Serge, *op. cit.*, pp. 265–267.

6. Arthur Loestler, *Arrow in the Blue* (New York: 1970).

7. Panait Istrati, quoted from Jürgen Rühle, *Literatur und Revolution* (München: 1960), p. 402.

8. André Gide, *Retuschen zu meinem Russlandbuch* in Reisen (Stuttgart: 1966), pp. 413–415.

9. Bertolt Brecht, *Kraft und Schwäche der Utopie*, in *Gesammelte Werke* VIII (Frankfurt am Main: 1967), pp. 434–437.

10. André Gide, *op. cit.*, p. 404. Gide is referring here to a pamphlet by M. Yvon, 'Ce qu'est devenuc la Revolution Russe.'

11. *Nouvelle Revue Française*, March, 1936.

12. André Gide, *op. cit.*, p. 8.

13. Lev Davidovic Trockij, *op. cit.*, p. 8.

14. Umberto Melotti, in *Terzo Mondo* (Milano: March, 1972), pp. 93 ff. The book by Maria Macciocchi that he criticizes appeared in Milano in 1971 under the title *Dalla Cina, dopo la rivoluzione culturale*.

15. Susan Sontag, *Trip to Hanoi* (New York: 1969).

16. Jan Myrdal, *Report from a Chinese Village* (New York: 1965).

CRITIQUE OF POLITICAL ECOLOGY

1. *Ecology and Revolutionary Thought*, by Murray Brookchin, New York 1970, p. 11. Brookchin argues that to ask an ecologist *exactly* when the ecological catastrophe will occur is like asking a psychiatrist to predict exactly when psychological pressure will so affect a neurotic that communication with him will be impossible.

2. *An Inquiry into the Sanitary Conditions of the Labouring Population of Great Britain*, Report from the Poor Law Commis-

sioners to the Home Department, London, 1842, p. 68. Quoted in *The Politics of Ecology*, by James Ridgeway, New York 1971.

3. Examples of this are not lacking in the ecology movement. In France there is an organization for environmental protection which has an extremely right-wing orientation. The president of these "Eco-fascists" is none other than General Massu, the man responsible for the French use of torture in the Algerian war.

4. *Profitschmutz und Umweltschmutz*, in *Rote Reihe*, Heidelberg 1973, vol. I, p. 5.

5. *Capital*, vol. I, Moscow 1961, p. 510 n.

6. Ridgeway, op. cit. pp. 22–5 sees Chadwick as an archetypical utilitarian bureaucrat, whose function was to secure the interests of capital by achieving peace and order among the poor. Better sanitation would produce a healthier and longer-living working force. Sanitary housing would raise workers' morale, and so on.

7. Ridgeway, op. cit., p. 15f, shows that over 150 years ago the Benthamites had evolved a theory of protecting the environment to promote production. As he also points out, the measures taken in the advanced capitalist USA in the late 1960s fail to reach the standards of water and air cleanliness proposed by the utilitarians.

8. *Der Spiegel*, 8 January 1973, p. 38.

9. Ridgeway, op. cit., pp. 207–11, analyses the "eco-industrial complex", i.e., the growing role played by business in promoting ecological campaigns, such as Earth Day, and the liaison between business, politicians, local government and "citizen campaigns".

10. For illustration of the "eco-industrial complex" in West Germany see *Profitschmutz*, p. 14 and the pamphlet *Ohne uns kein Umweltschutz*.

11. "Primera Conferencia de Solidaridad de los Pueblos de América Latina", in *América Latina: Demografía, Población indígena y Salud*, vol. 2, Havana 1968, pp. 15f.

12. Ibid. pp. 55–7.

13. Claus Koch, "Mystifikationen der 'Wachstumskrise'. Zum Bericht des Club of Rome", *Merkur*, vol. 297, January 1973, p. 82.

14. Giorgio Nebbia in his preface to *La Morte Ecologica*, Bari 1972, pp. XVf.

15. *The Limits of Growth, Report of the Club of Rome on the State of Mankind*, London 1972, p. 13.

16. *Kapitalismus und "Umweltkatastrophe"*, by Gerhard Kade, duplicated manuscript, 1973.

17. "Die sozialistischen Länder: Ein Dilemma des westeuropäischen Linken," by Rossana Rossanda, *Kursbuch* 30, 1973, p. 26.

18. Cf. "Marx und die Oekologie" in *Kursbuch* 33, 1973, pp. 175–87.

19. Rossana Rossanda op. cit., p. 30.

20. André Gorz, "Technique, Techniciens et Lutte de Classes" *Les Temps Modernes*, August–September 1971, vol. 30–12. p. 141.

21. Anne H. and Paul R. Ehrlich, *Population, Resources, Environment*, San Francisco 1970, pp. 322–4.

22. *Före-efter, En Diagnos*, by Gösta Ehrensvärd, Stockholm 1971, pp. 105–7.

23. Ehrlich, op. cit., p. 322.

24. *Öffentlichkeit und Erfahrung. Zur Organisationsanalyse von bürgerlicher und proletarischer Offentlichkeit*, Frankfurt 1972, p. 242.

25. Ibid., pp. 283f.

26. *Economic and Philosophical Manuscripts of 1844*, by Karl Marx (ed. D. Struik), London 1970, p. 137.

Index